AN INSIDER'S GUIDE TO
PUBLISHING

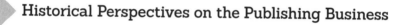

Historical Perspectives on the Publishing Business

Insights from Agents & Editors

Tips for Breaking In

New Publishing Alternatives

DAVID COMFORT

WD
WRITER'S
DIGEST
BOOKS
www.writersdigest.com
Cincinnati, Ohio

For more resources for writers, visit www.writersdigest.com.

17 16 15 14 13 5 4 3 2 1

Distributed in Canada by Fraser Direct
100 Armstrong Avenue
Georgetown, Ontario, Canada L7G 5S4
Tel: (905) 877-4411

Distributed in the U.K. and Europe by F+W Media International
Brunel House, Newton Abbot, Devon, TQ12 4PU, England
Tel: (+44) 1626-323200, Fax: (+44) 1626-323319
E-mail: postmaster@davidandcharles.co.uk

Distributed in Australia by Capricorn Link
P.O. Box 704, Windsor, NSW 2756 Australia
Tel: (02) 4577-3555

media

Edited by James Duncan
Cover designed by Bethany Rainbolt
Interior designed by Grace Ring
Production coordinated by Debbie Thomas

ABOUT THE AUTHOR

David Comfort has published three popular nonfiction trade titles from Simon & Schuster. In 2009, Citadel/ Kensington released his best-selling *The Rock and Roll Book of the Dead*. He has been a Pushcart Fiction Prize nominee, as well as a finalist for the Faulkner Award, the *Chicago Tribune* Nelson Algren Award, the America's Best contest, the *Narrative* Prize, the *Glimmer Train* Award, the Helicon Nine Award, and the Heekin/Graywolf Fiction Fellowship. The author's current short fiction appears in *The Evergreen Review, Cortland Review, Scholars & Rogues, Inkwell*, and *The Morning News*. His most recent novel, *The Reborn Bible 2.0: The 2nd Coming of the American Rapture*, is available from Amazon. His pop culture blogs appear in TheWrap, Culture Catch, and BlogCritics.

Sections from *An Insider's Guide to Publishing* have appeared in *The Stanford Arts Review, The Montreal Review, Pleiades, InDigest, Writing Disorder, Line Zero*, and *Eyeshot*.

ACKNOWLEDGMENTS

Sincere thanks to my editor, James Duncan, to Rachel Randall, and to my courageous agent, Don Fehr.

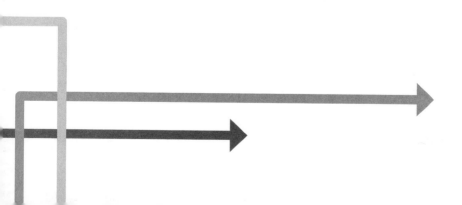

TABLE OF CONTENTS

INTRODUCTION

For today's writer, attempting publication is an assault on Everest.
Everybody with a romantic idea of high-altitude adventure is giving it
a shot. Armed with ropes, ice axes, oxygen, and the next great novel, a
million future Hemingways are lined up in five camps, from sea level
through thin air to the Death Zone to literary immortality.

1. Katmandu: Jumping off point for all "emerging writers," each with
   a PowerBar, a short resume, and a sample of his or her project.

2. Base Camp (16,000 feet): Recon and R&R point for bloggers who
   have scored a Sherpa agent and can compose a coherent query
   letter with a catchy log line.

3. Assault Camp One (20,000): Sheltered glacier for novelists with a
   Manhattan AAR Sherpa, an MFA, and/or awards they didn't invent.

4. Assault Camp Two (25,000): Pre-Death Zone bivouac for those
   with #3 qualifications, plus a blood relation to a Pulitzer recipient,
   Oprah, or a *New Yorker* security guard.

5. Final Assault Camp (28,000): Ironman scribes who are not suffering from edema, angina, or altitude psychosis.

Now, from Camp #5, weather permitting, publication is a 1,029-foot
scramble past the frozen bodies of one's predecessors who cashed in
on the way up or down this homestretch.

If the writer reaches the summit, he has a Warhol-15 minute window to behold the view, to plant his book cover banner with the others
that the gales have not torn down, and to pause for an iPhone photo op
just in case he is remaindered on the way back down, suddenly or in
reacclimation.

What are the odds of conquering the literary Everest—Mount Parnassus, home of the Muses, now with offices in the Random House and Time Warner Towers?

»»

R.R. Bowker reported 316,480 new traditional book titles published in 2010.[1] Fifteen percent (47,472) were novels. Statistically, about nine of ten novels do not sell out their first printing and are remaindered.

The 4,700 successful titles almost equal the number of times Mount Everest has been summited (5,104 since the 1953 Sir Hillary ascent). Each year nearly ten times more competitors (45,103 in 2010) finish the annual marathon in New York, the capital of publishing.

Today, just as more hardy souls are attempting dizzying peaks and grueling marathons, far more still are attempting novel publication, the most demanding of all ascents.

Ninety-nine percent are crapping out.

No thorough census has ever been taken on fiction manuscript submission numbers. Only educated estimates are possible. Eighty years ago, during the Hemingway-Fitzgerald-Faulkner golden age of American fiction, perhaps a thousand novelists were seriously competing for publication. The numbers today rival the national deficit.

The New York Times reported that, according to a recent survey, 81 percent of Americans say they have a book they'd like to write someday.[2] Thankfully, few get around to it. According to a National Endowment for the Arts survey, two million Americans published creative writing in 2002.

"There are enough people writing novels, God knows,"[3] grimly observed *The World According to Garp* author, John Irving, whose hero, Garp, was also a novelist.

---

1   "Book Production by the Numbers." *Publishers Weekly,* May 23, 2011, Vol. 258. Bowker reported that new nontraditional (print-on-demand and electronic) titles for 2010 were eight times that at 2,776,260—a 169 percent increase from 2009. www.bowker.com/en-US/aboutus/press_room/2011/pr_05182011.shtml

2   Joseph Epstein, "Think You Have a Book in You? Think Again," *The New York Times,* September 28, 2002. www.nytimes.com/2002/09/28/opinion/think-you-have-a-book-in-you-think-again.html

3   Ron Hansen, *The Paris Review* interview with John Irving. The Art of Fiction No. 93. 1986.

"Call me a pessimist, call me Ishmael, but I think that book publishing is about to slide into the sea," writes Garrison Keillor. "Eighteen million authors in America, each with an average of fourteen readers, eight of whom are blood relatives."[4]

New York Times executive editor, Bill Keller, complains that he is losing his staff because like "cliff-bound lemmings ... everyone who works for me is either writing [a book] or wants to," in spite of his strenuous effort to persuade them that the process is "agony."[5]

Literary agencies receive hundreds of submissions a week. Their stated rejection rate is 95 to 99 percent.

In 1972 there were seventy-three creative writing programs in the United States; by 2009, there were 822.[6] Twenty thousand apply annually; 95 percent are rejected.

"The profession of book writing makes horse racing seem like a solid, stable business," said John Steinbeck, even before the industry was taken over by the conglomerate oddsmakers.

Responding to the literary population explosion and the long odds of its dark horses, countless self-helpers have been released by industry bookies. In 2013, Amazon listed over two thousand titles in the fiction writing reference category (up from 668 in 2009). They included "Essential" guides on how to put your passion on paper, the one hundred ways to improve your writing, the thirty-eight most common fiction mistakes, the twenty-eight-day bestseller, the damn good novel, writing the bones, bird by bird, on both sides of the brain. Marketing manuals also proliferate: how to land a dream agent, how to write the perfect query and bulletproof proposal, and how to escape the slush pile. Making the writer's self-help genre even more irresistible are *American Idol* titles such as *Damn! Why Didn't I Write That?: How Ordinary People are Raking in $100,000.00.*

---

4 "In a World Where Everything's Free on the Web, What Will Happen to Publishing?" *Baltimore Sun,* May 25, 2010.

5 Bill Keller, "Let's Ban Books, Or at Least Stop Writing Them," *The New York Times,* July 13, 2011.

6 Louis Menand, "Show or Tell: Should Creative Writing Be Taught?" *The New Yorker,* June 8, 2009. www.newyorker.com/arts/critics/atlarge/2009/06/08/090608crat_atlarge_menand?

While some guides admit the difficulty of the profession, many are so gingerbreaded with optimism and pep talk that the SASE scribe goes postal when she still can't get published.

So the question for the 99 percenter pondering an Occupy Publishing protest boils down to this:

Do I want the truth?

Or do I want more smoke blown up my ass?

>>>

The truth is, all's fair in love, war, and publishing. The novel business is—from conception to execution through publication and marketing—ruled by Murphy's Law of the Muse. So, today's Dickens is well advised, for the sake of his own sanity, to lower great expectations about winning the Publishers Clearing House and becoming the next King, Rowling, or Larsson.

But even these talents had to overcome formidable obstacles, as did their predecessors from Dante to Dickens to Danielle Steele. The stories of climbs to the top by these masters and many others will be told here. In search of the practical truth about how to storm the literary Bastille, we will not depend on the commentary of sideline quarterbacks but on the words of historic authors and their editors who lived and died for literature.

Writers—journalists, screenwriters, speech writers, scholars, ad copy writers, owner's manual writers, catalog writers, greeting card writers— have always been, on average, the lowest paid professionals in the workforce. Novelists and poets are at the bottom of this food chain.

Said Mario Puzo: "For hundreds of years, writers have been giving it away like country girls in the big city, and it is not astonishing that their lovers (that is, the publishers) balk at giving a mink coat when a pair of nylons will do the job." He got nylons for his first three novels, then a $5,000 advance from the Putnam godfathers for *Godfather*, which paid them about $200 million (not counting movie rights) for the 12,140,000 copies they moved in six years. But from *Godfather* on, Puzo got mink coats, earning $2.55 million alone for the paper rights of his next novel, *Fools Die*.[7]

---

7   John Bear, *The Number One New York Times Best Seller* (*Ten Speed Press*, 1992).

As James Michener complained, "In America you can make a fortune as a writer, but not a living."[8]

What about editors, many of whom are writers themselves? They average about $50,000 for their day job[9]—or about $15 an hour for sixty-hour weeks. Some throw in the towel and become agents. In that case, as Jerry Maguires, they work longer hours for 15 percent of their authors' 7.5 to 12 percent.

Though, since Homer's day, scribes have been the most exploited professional group, no united protest has been made, only individual ones.

When he thought he'd been cheated on a movie deal for his novel *An American Tragedy*, Dreiser threw hot coffee in his publisher, Horace Liveright's, face at the Ritz restaurant. Upset with Alfred Knopf, Shirley Jackson—who had studied witchcraft for her famed story "The Lottery"—made a voodoo doll of him and impaled it with pins. The publishing patriarch soon suffered a serious ski accident while riding a rope tow *uphill*. When an Irish publisher cancelled his contract for *Dubliners*, Joyce complained fruitlessly to more than a hundred newspapers and then to King George himself. At last, he threatened to buy a pistol and "put some daylight into my publisher."

But Dreiser, Jackson, and Joyce never tried to rally their colleagues for a mass mutiny on the bounty. And their successors have never demanded a piece of the Occu-pie.

Why?

After all, writers love revolutions: They started the French, the Communist, and the Arab Spring. Why not one just for themselves—at Rock Center or Random House Towers?

A few theories about this anti-activism from an otherwise hyperactive group keenly sensitive to social injustice:

- Writers don't have time to get maced. They're focused 24-7 on the next great American blockbuster.

---

8 Erin Barrett, *It Takes a Certain Type to Be a Writer* (Conari Press, 2003).

9 According to the job site Glassdoor.com, the average salary for a New York book, magazine, or newspaper senior editor is $53,500. Associate book editors average from $42,000 to $45,000. ("How Much Do Book Editors Earn?" *Media Bistro/Galley Cat*, August 12, 2011.)

- They are so delighted about getting published, they think charging for it would be bad form.

- They secretly agree with nine-to-fivers that they don't have a real job, so why should they get paid for it?

Or, quite simply, they are E.L. James masochists.

But hope springs eternal. The masses are restless. The tectonic plates of publishing are groaning. As today's queen of literary agents, Binky Urban, says: "I think we are in the midst of a revolution. Bad things happen in a revolution, but revolutions always give rise to opportunities."[10]

So, writers, throw off your chains. Unite. And remember Thoreau! The penniless *Walden* author refused to pay taxes. Visiting him in the Concord jail, his friend, Emerson, asked, "Henry, what are you doing in there?"

To which the fed-up writer replied: "Waldo, what are you doing *out there*?"

»»»

An Insider's Guide to Publishing is cross-genre. It marries history, self-help, horror, and humor.

"If you want to tell people the truth, make them laugh, otherwise they'll kill you," advised the gay wit Oscar Wilde before being thrown in prison for failing to do so.

Beyond genre, this manual is the first 99-percent solution for fed-up, starving writers—debut literary novelists in particular. To this end, it is an MFA Gonzo Crash Course, revealing for the first time who's who, what's what, and what the dickens is going on in the truth-is-stranger-than-fiction world of publishing. Covering every dimension of the industry, this book provides a full revolutionary curriculum: in lit, linguistics, history, econ, psych, and sales.

"Who is behind this mad manifesto, and what are his credentials?" the reader rightfully demands.

Your humble Deep Throat—your host and moderator—has spent decades in the belly of the literary beast. Like Jonah, he has little to

---

10 "Brave New Literary World," *Haaretz* online magazine, February 24, 2009.

recommend himself but his indigestibility. He gives the floor to his superiors, his guest Che Guevaras, the maddest novelists of the last four hundred years. Having long been awaiting this open-mic forum to air their views, caveats, and grievances, Nobel and Pulitzer laureates will do the lions' share of the debriefing and deprogramming.

This manual, as promised, is the first no-smoke or -spin zone for the true professional. For those who tough out our MFA program of hard knocks and take to the street: Congratulations, you will be the proud and the brave, ready to take the Bastille, claim its cake, and eat it, too.

At commencement, you will throw your cap to the sun and repeat after Gustave Flaubert, whose first novel, *Memoirs of a Madman,* wasn't published until he was twenty years in the ground: "Writing is a dog's life, but the only one worth living."

On that note, the concluding words of another revolutionary member of our faculty, Henry Miller:

"For a hundred years or more the [literary] world, our world, has been dying. And not one man, in these last hundred years or so, has been crazy enough to put a bomb up the asshole of creation and set it off."

This book is dedicated to that challenge.

PART I

PUBLISH & PERISH

Into the Belly
of the Manuscript-Eating Beast

"In today's publishing climate,
it's eat or be eaten."
—Betsy Lerner, editor/agent/author, 2005

CHAPTER 1

THE AGE
OF INNOCENCE

"For Random House, which is Donald and Bennett, the nicest, the
sweetest, the kindest and most spoiling of publishers."

—Gertrude Stein's inscription on a photo of herself,
which Bennett Cerf kept on his office wall

In what literary agent Al Silverman called "The Golden Age of Great
American Publishers,"[1] houses were run by men of letters and breeding: Bennett Cerf and Donald Klopfer at Random House; Charles
Scribner and Max Perkins at Scribner; the Harper brothers at Harpers;
Alfred A. Knopf at Knopf; Roger Straus and Robert Giroux at Farrar,
Straus and Giroux; among a host of others.

Many were from money. Cerf was heir to a tobacco distribution company; his partner, Donald Klopfer, inherited his family's diamond-cutting
fortune. Straus's mother was a Guggenheim, and his father ran the family's American Mining and Smelting. Knopf's father was an ad executive
and financial consultant.

---

1 Al Silverman, *The Time of Their Lives: The Golden Age of Great American Publishers, Their Editors,
and Authors* (New York: St. Martin's, 2008).

These editor-owners and their colleagues decided to publish a book based first on its merit and second on its salability. They did more than print, package, and distribute. They first edited, intensively.

Sometimes they even boasted of releasing books that were over their heads. In his introduction to Gertrude Stein's 1936 *The Geographical History of America or the Relation of Human Nature to the Human Mind,* Bennett Cerf wrote: "I must admit frankly I do not know what Miss Stein is talking about. I do not even understand the title." When he asked Ms. Stein to explain, the "rose is a rose" Montparnasse matriarch told the Columbia Phi Beta Kappa, "Well, I've always told you, Bennett, you're a very nice boy but you're rather stupid."[2]

The Random House founder, who fancied the idea of publishing unique and challenging authors "at random," took the aside with his customary good humor. He liked Gertrude's playful abuse no less than her iconoclasm. A few years earlier he had accompanied her on her national publicity tour for *Portraits and Prayers.* "I was her slave," he reported. "She ordered me around like a little errand boy."

The golden age publisher/editors were satisfied with the modest receipts of their leading artists, subsisting on 3 to 4 percent net profit. In 1925 Boni & Liveright published Hemingway's *In Our Time,* Faulkner's *Soldier's Pay,* Dreiser's *An American Tragedy,* Anderson's *Dark Laughter,* among other masterpieces. Their annual profit: $8,609.12.[3] The sum would have been far less had they not also published that year's (and decade's) bestseller, Anita Loos' *Gentlemen Prefer Blondes.*

But by the time Macmillan made a killing on *Gone with the Wind* in the mid-'30s, publishers were starting to discuss among themselves an unheard-of notion: Why not just sell bestsellers? Most concluded that the idea, though appealing, was impractical because a) even the most reliable golden goose never laid a golden egg every time, b) no one had a crystal ball, and c) even if they were psychic, most felt an old-fashioned obligation to provide readers the enrichment they needed, rather than the escapist entertainment

---

2 Bennett Cerf, *At Random: The Reminiscences of Bennett Cerf* (New York: Random House, 1977).

3 Allen Churchill, *The Literary Decade: A Panorama of the Writers, Publishers, and Litterateurs of the 1920's* (New York: Prentice Hall, 1971).

many wanted. In short, as agents of culture, they felt responsible for quality control.

Frank Nelson Doubleday II thought the attitude both burdensome and patronizing. When taking over the family business in 1934, he declared: "I sell books, I don't read them." His father's literary stars were Rudyard Kipling and Joseph Conrad. Ironically, his own was Somerset Maugham, whose most popular Doubleday title was *The Razor's Edge*, the hero of which abandons materialism and seeks spiritual enlightenment while "loafing" on his inheritance. Edna Ferber, Frank II's other best-selling author, defended him against his detractors, saying that he "put books in the hands of the unbookish."[4]

Since Maugham's 1944 bestseller, Doubleday's front list—and that of many other major houses—followed a downward literary trajectory, decade to decade: Herman Wouk's *The Caine Mutiny* (1951), Arthur Hailey's *Airport* (1968), Peter Benchley's *Jaws* (1974), Stephen King's *Pet Semetary* (1983), John Grisham's *The Pelican Brief* (1992), Dan Brown's *The Celestine Prophesy* (2003), Terry Pratchett's *Snuff* (2011).

As a practical matter, the bigger the business, the more money—best-selling titles—it takes to feed it. By 1947, after mergers and acquisitions, Doubleday was the largest U.S. publisher, selling more than 30 million books annually. During World War II, Cerf wrote to his partner, Klopfer, from the front: "[There is] no possibility ... of [our] ever developing a sprawling and unmanageable menagerie like the Doubleday outfit. I share your abhorrence for impersonal 'big business.'"

But by 1960, deciding if he couldn't beat them he'd join them, Cerf got into the acquisition mode himself, buying out Knopf, Pantheon, and Singer (textbooks).

"Oh, God, it's the end of publishing!" Nan Talese, the young Random House editor (now publisher and editorial director of Talese/Doubleday), told her husband, Gay, the writer.

But publishing lived on as these corporate consumers were consumed themselves.

---

4 Al Silverman, *The Time of Their Lives: The Golden Age of Great American Publishers, Their Editors, and Authors* (New York: St. Martin's, 2008).

In 1986, the German media giant Bertelsmann gobbled up Doubleday. In '98, it swallowed Random House with hardly a belch. By that time, Cerf was long gone and his operation was hemorrhaging red ink. In '97, Random House had written off $80 million in unearned advances for front list Hindenburgs and was on 0.1 percent profit life support.[5] On taking over the venerable American house, Bertelsmann issued a press release announcing that they expected a double-digit annual profit from then on.

The German giant had started out by publishing Christian hymnals. By World War II, its father and son owners, Heinnrich and Reinhard Mohn, both SS members, printed mostly Nazi propaganda as well as the novels of Will Vesper, who gave the keynote speech at the 1933 Nazi book burning in Dresden.[6]

Today, Bertelsmann is run by Thomas Rabe, a former doctor of economics. Random House, one of its two hundred subdivisions, is headed by Lord Philip Gould's widow, Dame Gail Rebuck, whose Latvian ancestors were in the rag trade. Bertelsmann's other subsidiaries are in Internet, telephone, television, radio, and music rights management (repping everyone from The Foo Fighters to Taylor Swift and Jay-Z).

These other enterprises are less dicey than publishing. So how did the media conglomerate propose to resurrect Cerf's Random House, boosting its annual profits from .01 percent to 10 percent or more? By reviving the idea their predecessors had dismissed as impractical and philistine: by only selling bestsellers.

Even so, Jason Epstein, former Random House editorial director, predicted, "Bertelsmann will someday discover … that it's bought the wrong kind of business because you cannot run a publishing company if you think of it as a source of profit. You run it for entirely other reasons." [7]

---

5 André Schiffrin, *The Business of Books: How the International Conglomerates Took Over Publishing and Changed the Way We Read* (UK: Verso, 2000). (Schiffrin is founder of *The New Press*, New York.)

6 Four years after acquiring Random House, Bertelsmann, according to BBC News, admitted to lying about their Nazi involvement so as not to jeopardize the deal.

7 Jason Epstein interview. *Booknotes,* 2001.

CHAPTER 2

SLAUGHTERHOUSE-SIX

"To my grandfather the book business today would be unrecognizable. It belongs to the entertainment industry much more than to the literary world."

—**Charles Scribner, Jr., whose company was bought out by CBS**[1]

Today, six multibillion dollar Super Publishing Action Committees control nearly 90 percent of the bestseller real estate: Bertelsmann (Random House, Knopf, Doubleday, Ballantine), Pearson PLC (Penguin, Putnam, Author Solutions), Hachette (Little Brown, Grand Central), Holtzbrinck (Macmillan), CBS (Simon & Schuster, Scribner), and Rupert Murdoch's News Corp (HarperCollins). After the 2012 Random House/Penguin merger, *The New York Times* predicted that the Big Six might soon enough become "the Big Three, or even the Big One."[2]

---

1   Charles Scribner Jr., *In the Company of Writers: A Life in Publishing* (Easton Press, 1984).

2   Adam Davidson, "How Dead Is the Book Business?" *The New York Times*, November 13, 2012. http://www.nytimes.com/2012/11/18/magazine/penguin-random-house-merger.html

The Super PAC heads are no longer editors. They do the books, not *books*. Pearson's chairman, Glen Moreno, is an independent director at Lloyds; his CEO, Dame Marjorie Morris Scardino, was the former Economist Group head. In addition to HarperCollins, Rupert Murdoch—worth $8.3 billion in 2012, according to *Forbes*—owns the Dow Jones Company, *The Wall Street Journal, Barrons, Marketwatch,* the *Financial News,* and Fox television network. Leslie Moonves is a TV programmer (*ER, Friends,* etc.) who accomplished the impossible—rescuing CBS from the financial Marianna Trench.

Transforming publishing from a family-run 4 percent profit cottage industry to a double-digit percent communications juggernaut required a revolutionary no-holds-barred NFL type of approach.

Every editor and every published writer got a virtual helmet, knee pads, and a jersey. On the jersey was printed his or her Profit and Loss ratio—number of bestseller touchdowns divided by number of flops, fumbles, or sacks. Low P&L editors in red ink jerseys—those who cost the franchise more than they made—were benched or laid off. Authors in the red—midlist and backlisters—were euthanized. Meanwhile, accountants in green were added. Bertelsmann now has about four thousand cashiers, far outnumbering editors.

Necessity is the mother of execution. Unlike yesterday's publishers, today's conglomerates must give retail outlets credit for unsold titles, pay exorbitant warehouse inventory taxes on returned books or pulp them all, and hand out stratospheric advances to best-selling authors[3] and commensurate salaries to a handful of high-rolling editors. But, most daunting of all, they must compete with Hollywood and Silicone Valley. Luckily, they control a hefty chunk of these, too. Television, movies, and video games are conceived and written by writers, but they are paid less than anybody else and are the first to be fired.

Not surprisingly, "literary" authors have born the brunt of the

---

3 In 2009, Robert S. Miller, the HarperStudio publisher, told Motoko Rich of *The New York Times,* "The two biggest sucking sounds on profits in our business are on advances and returns." (HarperStudio caps advances at $100,000 and persuaded Borders to take its first titles on a nonreturnable basis.) Threatened with financial ruin during the Depression, Simon & Schuster was the first publisher to offer credit for returned books. In 2001, S&S editor Michael Korda told *Booknotes:* "Sometimes it seems to me that we get more books back than we printed."

conglomerate housecleaning. The actuaries couldn't be ignored any longer. Serious fiction has been in precipitous decline for fifty years. In the '20s, six of ten best-selling titles were literature. By the '60s, three of ten. In the last decade, three of one hundred. In the '70s, Pulitzer prize-winning Philip Roth estimated that 120,000 Americans read daily and that the number was dropping by half every five years.[4]

Among the top fifty best-selling authors of all time, only six are literary: #1 Shakespeare (2–4 billion copies sold), #7 George Simenon (500 million), #12 Tolstoy (413 million), #18 Pushkin (357 million), #37 C.S. Lewis and #38 Dickens (200 million). The numbers would be substantially lower if these authors weren't on school syllabi. Those who are not on syllabi but are in Walmarts are: Agatha Christie (#1 tie with Shakespeare), Barbara Cartland (#3), Danielle Steel (#4), Harold Robbins (#5), Sidney Sheldon (#7), and J.K. Rowling (#11). [5]

Bowker reported a 29 percent decline in 2010 literature titles (in contrast to a 51 percent increase in computer books). Six years earlier, the National Endowment for the Arts released its "Reading at Risk" report, which estimated that twenty million readers had been lost since the early '80s. Calling the news "tragic," Association of American Publishers president Patricia Schroeder convened the AAP "Where Have All the Readers Gone? And How Can You Find New Ones?" conference in 2006.[6] Steve Jobs himself weighed in on the dilemma, bluntly informing *The New York Times*: "It doesn't matter how good or bad the product is, the fact is that people don't read anymore."

In his "Where Have All the Mailers Gone?" exposé, provocateur Lee Siegel wrote that "for about a million reasons" fiction has become "culturally irrelevant" and "a museum-piece genre."[7]

The prognosis for the literary novel is a hotly contested issue these days—some insist that it is already posthumous, others say it's on life support, and still others believe it is rising, phoenix-like, in bold, new

---

4   Boris Kachka, "The End: Publishing Might Have to Look for its Future Outside the Corporate World," *New York Magazine*, September 14, 2008.

5   http://en.wikipedia.org/wiki/List_of_best-selling_fiction_authors

6   Diane Cole, "Publish or Panic," *U.S. News & World Report*, March 13, 2006.

7   Lee Siegel, *New York Observer*, June 22, 2010.

postmodern form.

According to Bowker, twenty-one thousand small publishers now exist—houses that release up to ten new titles annually and earn up to $5 million. The Independent Book Publishers Association reports[8] that, collectively, their earnings from 2008 to 2011 increased almost 25 percent—double the general industry rate—making them "the industry's healthiest and fastest growing segment." A small percentage publish fiction, very few of these literary fiction, and fewer still debut literary fiction. Most in the latter category[9] no longer consider an unsolicited novel. The few who do require agent submission or open their transoms only briefly, often taking six or more months to issue a boilerplate rejection. There is good reason for this.

In 1982, even before the decline in serious fiction reading, Viking editor-in-chief Elisabeth Sifton told *The Nation* that the average first novel sells two thousand to four thousand copies. Hoping to buck the tide, Robert Lasner founded Ig Publishing in 2002 and released his debut, *For Fucks Sake*. "Nostalgic for the good old days, when publishers actually tried to build an author's career, we dedicated Ig to publishing the work of overlooked or first-time authors," wrote Lasner in "The Death of First Fiction."[10] He released two other seemingly promising titles but, after 60 percent of the runs were returned, he concluded: "Literary first novels are almost impossible to introduce into the marketplace. ... If something is not done, soon, not only first fiction, but all literary fiction, will disappear as a viable part of the publishing world."

Indeed, even major conglomerate novelists are failing to earn their advances. Richard Ford left Knopf for Ecco, which fronted him $750,000 for *The Lay of the Land*, but the serial sold less than one hundred thousand copies. Mailer's Egyptian Ishtar, *Ancient Evenings*, cost Little Brown $1 million. In 1999, Holt suffered Rushdie's *Ground Beneath Her*

---

8 Kelly Gallager, "Independent Publisher Power," IDPA, February 2013. https://www.ibpa-online.org/article/independent-publisher-power/#.USe98Y5OROe

9 Among them: Algonquin, Graywolf, McSweeney's, Granta/Portabello, Coffee House, Tin House, Melville House, Black Lawrence, Red Hen, Soft Skull, New Press, Alternative Press, Dzanc.

10 Robert Laner, *Mobylives* (blogspot For Melville House Publishing, March 14, 2005).

Feet. Since then, the former *Satanic Verses* fugitive defected to Random House. Here, without the fatwa PR machine, he sold, according to Bowker, only 26,000 copies of *Shalimar the Clown.*

In 2012, Penguin tried to compensate for its own losses by suing five A-list authors for repayment of their advances, with interest. Among them was the author of blockbuster *Prozac Nation,* Elizabeth Wurtzel, who, one imagines, has renewed her prescription.

The Super PACs have recently revived hope for literature with *Wuthering Bites, Little Vampire Women, Pride and Prejudice and Zombies,* and *Android Karenina.* In 2009, National Book Award winner and Princeton lit prof Joyce Carol Oates joined the bandwagon with *Zombie.*

Meanwhile, in reaction to the string of highbrow Edsels that came off the line earlier, the conglomerates celebrated Black Wednesday on December 3, 2008. They rounded up editors with clouded crystal balls and axed them.

First on the chopping block were Irwyn Applebaum, Bantam Dell CEO, and Stephen Rubin, head of Doubleday. The year before, Doubleday had fired 10 percent of its staff after their $1.25 million baby, Andrew Davidson's *The Gargoyle,* tanked, selling only 34,000 copies. Heads also rolled at Random House, Simon & Schuster, and Macmillan.

From Black Wednesday on, surviving editors have worked under the sword of Damocles. They have traded their red pencils for calculators and their shopworn copies of *The Art of Fiction* for *Swim with the Sharks Without Being Eaten Alive.*

Where in pre-Super PAC days many senior editors had the power to "greenlight" a title, few now have the privilege. And few want it for fear of a career-killing big-advance bomb. Today no major title is purchased without approval from the sales department. Sometimes buyers at Barnes & Noble, Amazon, Walmart, or Target are also consulted.

"The bestseller lists of the nineties made for relatively depressing reading, except to accountants," wrote Simon & Schuster editor-in-chief Michael Korda. "In fiction, it became enormously difficult to break through the sheer weight of numbers generated by perhaps two dozen, or fewer, top writers who virtually dominated the list."[11] Korda edited early members of the Dirty Dozen, Jacqueline Susann and Harold Robbins,[12] while also handling high-quality but commercially viable artists such as Larry McMurtry.

Today, Susann's and Robbins' Top 10 successors, the golden geese of the conglomerates are: James Patterson (2010 earnings: $70 million), Stephenie Meyer ($40 million), Stephen King ($34 million), Danielle Steele ($32 million), Ken Follett ($20 million), Dean Koontz ($18 million), Janet Evanovich ($16 million), John Grisham ($15 million), Nicholas Sparks ($14 million), and J.K. Rowling ($10 million).[13]

The conglomerates have succeeded in turning these authors and the few dozen others Korda mentions into corporate brand names.

The matriarch of the blockbuster club is Margaret Mitchell. After selling 1,375,000 copies of *Gone with the Wind* in 1936, she made a promise to Harry Scherman, the Book of the Month Club founder. She said she would try to read Tolstoy, Dostoyevsky, Thackeray, and Jane Austen for the first time so that "when people are kind enough to mention them in the same breath with my book, I ought to be able to do more than duck my head and suck my thumb and make unintelligible sounds."[14]

Some of today's conglomerate Midases don't suffer the same insecurity. "Their sin," writes Patrick Anderson in *The Triumph of the Thriller*,[15] "is that they treat their readers like idiots. Some of them can't help it—that's how their minds work—but others deliberately dumb down their work because a lot of money is made that way."

---

11 Michael Korda, *Making the List: A Cultural History of the American Bestseller, 1900–1999* (New York: Barnes & Noble, 2001).

12 In his 1991 *New Republic* feature "Rough Trade," editor-in-chief Jacob Weisberg asserted that writing for Simon & Schuster was "often a Faustian bargain" confirming the words of its former trade division director, Dan Green, to *The Wall Street Journal* in 1984: "There is no level below which we will not go." The bottom line paid off: In 1975, S&S grossed $40 million; by 1994 it reached $2 billion.

13 "The Highest Paid Authors," *Forbes* magazine, August 19, 2010.

14 Al Silverman, *The Time of Their Lives: The Golden Age of Great American Publishers, Their Editors and Authors* (St. Martin's 2008).

15 *The Triumph of the Thriller: How Cops, Crooks, and Cannibals Captured Popular Fiction* (New York: Random House, 2007).

Anderson, a popular thriller novelist himself, reserves his greatest scorn for the Guinness World Record holder of the most best-selling hardcover novels (sixty-three)—James Patterson.

He ranks the former advertising executive who created the "Toys R Us Kid" campaign a "bloated, odoriferous 10 ... on the bullshit scale." Stephen King called Patterson "terrible."[16] When asked to respond to the criticism by his populist peers, detective Alex Cross's creator told *Time* magazine in 2010, "I am not a great prose stylist. I'm a storyteller. There are thousands of people who don't like what I do. Fortunately, there are millions who do." But he hastened to add, "My favorite books are actually very complicated—*One Hundred Years of Solitude, Ulysses.*"

The New York Times Magazine calls the one-man fiction factory—he's released seventy-one novels in thirty-three years—Hachette/Little Brown's "most prized possession." The PAC treats its golden goose accordingly. It provides him two editors, three full-time assistants, a marketing director, a "brand" manager, and a personal sales manager. Hachette's CEO, David Young, accompanies these retainers for regular meetings at Patterson's Palm Beach manse where the novelist demands sales projections and market-share charts.

Says his Little Brown editor, Michael Pietsch: "Jim is at the very least co-publisher of his own books."[17]

---

16 Harold Bloom, whom many consider the greatest living critic, called King himself "a writer of penny dreadfuls" unworthy of his National Book Foundation Lifetime Award. Bloom also dismissed J.K. Rowling as "terrible ... governed by clichés and dead metaphors."
"Dumbing Down American Readers," *Boston Globe,* September 24, 2003.

17 Jonathan Mahler, "James Patterson, Inc." *The New York Times,* January 20, 2010.

CHAPTER 3

CANARIES IN THE CONGLOMERATE COAL MINE

"My judgment doesn't count any longer. There used to be a reason to get into publishing. Whether they know it or not, [editors] all want to be Maxwell Perkins. ... They didn't flock to publishing because they want to publish Danielle Steel."

—Kent Carroll, who left Carroll & Graf, after a conglomerate buy-out

The late, great editors of the American Golden Age included Max Perkins at Scribner, T.R. Smith at Boni & Liveright, Robert Linscott at Houghton Mifflin, Cass Canfield at Henry Holt, Alfred Harcourt at Harcourt, and William Jovanovich at Harcourt Brace Jovanovich.

"Only a writer can understand how a great editor is a father, mother, teacher, personal devil and personal god," wrote John Steinbeck, whose own editor at Viking, Pat Covici, helped bring him the Pulitzer and Nobel.

H.L. Mencken was another legend who, as a writer himself, was "one of the few editors in history who genuinely liked writers," according to Allen Churchill.[1] In fact, many editors, yesterday and today, are writers themselves and understand the hardships of the literary life.

In his publishing career memoir, *Another Life*, Michael Korda confides: "It was always a common joke among publishing people that this would be a great business if it weren't for writers." Yet Korda, a popular and prolific author himself, had a soft spot for serious novelists. A few of his colleagues have had so much affection for them that they have published their work at the expense of company profits and suddenly found themselves unemployed.

Max Perkins Prize Lifetime Achievement laureate Jonathan Galassi—now president/publisher of Farrar, Straus, and Giroux—was fired by Random House in 1986, the year of the Bertelsmann buyout. He had been with Cerf's company for five years and edited titles that won critical acclaim but had sold modestly. In his own right, Galassi has published two volumes of poetry and translated the work of Nobel Prize winner Eugenio Montale.

Of his former employer, Galassi told *Poets & Writers*,[2] "In the Bennett Cerf days, Random House had been in some ways an ideal publisher because they were what I would call a 'best of breed' publisher." He had tried, quixotically, to carry on that tradition. When asked to identify the "hardest lesson" he had learned as a young editor, he replied: "... Realizing how much of a crapshoot publishing is—how you can love something and do everything you can for it, and yet fail at connecting it to an audience." His track record has improved under the Holtzbrinck umbrella, but his literary romanticism remains intact. "Being a novelist or a poet whose books aren't popular is a wonderful accomplishment," he insists.

Random House president, Ann Godoff—who launched *Midnight in the Garden of Good and Evil*, *The Alienist*, and other bestsellers—experienced her own Black Friday in 2003. Characterized by some as a "literary snob," she had bombed on Charles Frazier's *Cold Mountain* follow-up, *Thirteen Moons*, for which she paid $8 million, as

---

1 Allen Churchill, *The Literary Decade: A Panorama of the Writers, Publishers, and Litterateurs of the 1920's* (New York: Prentice Hall, 1971).

2 *Poets & Writers* Q&A with Jonathan Galassi, July 2009.

well as on McLaughlin and Kraus' *The Nanny Diaries* for which she shelled out $3 million.

Godoff's colleague, Daniel Menaker, was then promoted to editor-in-chief. The former *New Yorker* editor had nurtured both literary novelists such as Pulitzer Prize-winning Elizabeth Strout and more commercial authors such as *Primary Colors'* Joe Klein. In taking the fiction helm at Random House, he told *Publisher's Weekly* that his goal would be to "satisfy the expectations of a company that needs to see revenue while continuing a really vital part of our culture of letters." As for his new bottom-line boss, Gina Contrello, who had replaced Goldoff, he added: "I want to emphasize, and not in a publishing bullshit way, I have a wonderful relationship with Gina." Ms. Contrello fired him when his P&Ls redlined a few years later, beginning with his ill-fated gamble on Benjamin Kunkel's expensive debut novel, *Indecision.* In "It's Economics, Stupid," *PW* broke the news of Menaker's 2007 termination, reporting that insiders said it "signals Random House's loss of interest in 'literary publishing.'"

In discussing the commercial failure of *Indecision*, Menaker explained the difficulty of launching a big novel in the current marketplace: "There has to be this constellation of events. Not only a *Times Book Review* front cover, but Don Imus talking about it and Ellen Pompeo actually reading the book on camera. And Barack Obama has just bought it."

Barney Rosset—founder of Grove Press and editor of Jack Kerouac, Henry Miller, Samuel Beckett, Jorge Luis Borges, Jean Genet, William Borroughs, and Octavio Paz—was yet another canary in the coal mine. Ann Getty of Getty Oil bought out Grove in 1985 and remaindered Barney the next year. For his epitaph, the maverick publisher told agent Al Silverman, "I had a very good publishing career, but not moneywise. We got rid of the money." At least he saved on publicity expenses thanks to the *Lady Chatterley's Lover, Tropic of Cancer,* and *Naked Lunch* obscenity trials.

His confederate, Gordon Lish, aka Captain Fiction, was even more cavalier about profits and made no bones about it. In 1993, the legendary Knopf editor told *Bookworm* that he had spent his life "in the enemy camp" and that his mission had always been to "befuddle" publishers and "make off with their purse." The literary Robin Hood—himself the author of three novels and two short story collections—edited Richard Ford, Don DeLillo, Reynolds Price, T.C. Boyle, Barry Hannah, Vladimir Nabokov, among others. All were deeply indebted to him, no less than Fitzgerald, Hemingway, Wolfe, and others had been to Scribners' Max Perkins. Short story master Raymond Carver wrote to Lish: "If I have any standing or reputation or credibility in the world, I owe it to you." Knopf fired Captain Fiction in 1994.

Lish's compatriot Ted Solotaroff was the resident author lover at Harpers. Seeing the writing on the wall during the 1989 Murdoch take-over, he phased himself out after years of editing the likes of Robert Bly, Bobbie Ann Mason, Philip Roth, and E.L. Doctorow. Two years before, he published *A Few Good Voices in My Head*, which included his "What Has Happened to Publishing?" based on his 1987 "The Literary-Industrial Complex" diatribe for *The New Republic*. The essay charged that the conglomerate-controlled industry had "largely sold out its cultural purpose to its commercial one" and created in the houses "an atmosphere of fear, cynicism, rapaciousness, and ignorance."

In 1997, Murdoch pirated Knopf's star editor and vice president, Jane Friedman, to help fill Solotaroff's shoes. Enthused Murdoch's Harper head, Michael Morrison: "Jane has the best heart, mind and conscience in the business. She's part Hilary Clinton, part Mother Teresa and part Mae West. Who could ask for more?"[3] His president, Brian Murray, praised her "unbridled positive energy and enthusiasm for publishing." Harpers' Hyperion head, Bob Miller, called her "the best cheerleader in the business ... and always thinking about ways to build new audi-ences." Accomplishing this while also editing heavy hitters ranging from Michael Crichton to Nobel laureate Doris Lessing, Friedman doubled Harpers' profits in her first two years. Murdoch called her "a tremendous success." In 2006, *PW* named her Publishing Person of the Year, while *The Wall Street Journal* included her on the 50 Women to Watch list.

Two years later, Murdoch summoned Friedman to his office. She thought she might be getting a raise. Instead, "she got a two-by-four

---

3 Jim Milliot, "Jane Friedman Publishing Person of the Year," *Publishers Weekly*, December 8, 2006.

across the face," confided an "anonymous" editor friend.[4]

Days later, the papers reported her "retirement" from Harpers. Rumor had it that she was offed by O.J.'s *If I Did It.* Editor Judith Regan had scored the Simpson title for her Harpers' imprint, public outrage erupted, Murdoch begrudgingly cancelled the contract, 400,000 copies were pulped, and Friedman fired Regan not as a "disgusting opportunist" (as the Goldman family called her) but for allegedly making anti-Semitic remarks. Regan sued Friedman and Murdoch's News Corp. for wrongful termination. In an out-of-court settlement, Regan collected a good chunk of the $100 million in damages she had demanded.

Another anonymous editor—anonymity often being the precondition when editors disclose an inconvenient truth—told *New York Magazine*'s Boris Kachka, "If someone like Jane Friedman can't survive the industry, who *can*?"

Ms. Friedman threw a "nonretirement" party for herself. A who's who of publishing showed, including ex-Random House "godfather" Peter Olson who had been "whacked," as *New York Magazine* called it,[5] the week before the hostess. All wore *Phantom of the Opera*-like Jane masks as if to say, "We are all Jane tonight." Reminding them that this was not a retirement party, much less a wake, she delivered an "I'll be back!" Terminator speech.

"Books mean civilization," she said. "I am not done, and I am not done by a long shot!"

---

4 Boris Kachka, "The End," *New York Magazine,* September 14, 2008.

5 Marion Maneker, "Just Business, The Fall of Book Publishing's Last Don," *New York Magazine,* May 11, 2008.

CHAPTER 4

SURVIVORS

Other wunderkind editors-in-chief—Doubleday's Gerald Howard, Scribner's Nan Graham, Knopf's Nan Talese, etc.—know they are in their conglomerate's crosshairs and make sure they never lose their green jerseys and Kevlar underwear. Only bulletproof Goldfingers such as Sonny Mehta and Robert Gottlieb have walked the Big Apple streets without fear of suddenly finding themselves unemployed like Jane.

Their lesser counterparts just keep moving. As superagent Mort Janklow told *New York Magazine* in 2008: "You hear every day of an editor changing houses." Musical chairs is now simple survivalism in an industry where the editor can have a shorter shelf life than one of her books.

Amid the fear and trembling, though, is the hope and inspiration provided by the industry Lazarus: Jonathan Galassi. After getting shelved by Random House, his savior, Scott Turow, came along with *Presumed Innocent*. The former Marshall Scholar at Christ's College dropped his winding sheet, walked into the paradise of Farrar, Straus and Giroux, and sold 600,000 copies of Turow's thriller, plus even more of Tom Wolfe's *Bonfire of the Vanities*. Here the poet editor has become president, disproving F. Scott Fitzgerald's pronouncement that there are no second acts in American lives.

"We [FSG] are still doing it the old way," Galassi told *Harvard Magazine.* "We want to publish books that make a difference. ... We don't expect them all to sell 100,000 copies. So much of what is new and good starts out modest. You can't be driven by sales figures, or you'll miss the real action."[1]

Bob Loomis was another miraculous survivor. He retired from Random House in 2011 after a fifty-four-year run, editing the likes of William Styron, Maya Angelou, and Calvin Trillin. He prospered thanks to his roll-with-the-punches attitude. "All the books that I think are going to sell don't work, and all the books I don't think are going to work sell a lot and win awards—that's why I love this business so much," he told *The New York Times.*[2]

When asked about the pre-PAC days, he would only say, "It seems as though it was more fun," displaying the kind of diplomacy that allowed him to hang onto his head. His friend Peter Matson, the Sterling Lord Literistic director, was less circumspect. "There will be no more Bob Loomises, at least not in the big companies," he said. "The publishing business has been turned on its head. The authority that people like Bob Loomis had has been captured by the marketing side of publishing."

Loomis' colleague Robert Gottlieb, former editor-in-chief at Knopf as well as *The New Yorker,* shared his professional longevity by being equally adaptable and pragmatic. Having discovered and published Joseph Heller, "the *enfant terrible,* boy genius of Simon & Schuster," as Michael Korda called Gottlieb, managed to regard his profession's catch-22s with bemused good humor. Another popular author of his, John Le Carre, identified the key to his editorial prosperity. Though Gottlieb "is a very fastidious man," he observed, "he can live with bad books if they're *good* bad books."

Pat Strachan is yet another survivor thanks to her optimism and team spirit. "That's my professional job—not to lose money," the Little Brown

---

1   "High Type Culture, Editor Extraordinaire Jonathan Galassi on the Risky Art of Publishing Books." *Harvard Magazine,* 1997. http://harvardmagazine.com/1997/11/books.html

2   Julie Bosman, "Nurturer of Authors Is Closing the Book," *New York Times,* May 8, 2011

senior editor told *Poets & Writers* in 2008, "and I try very hard not to lose money. And having a great big book to offset some of the books that sell less well would be wonderful." An example of the former would be Tom Wolfe's latest LB offering, *Back to Blood*, that might offset Strachan-edited poetry collections from Donald Hall and Galway Kinnell. Grove Atlantic editor Jofie Ferrari-Adler calls Ms. Strachan "a gentle and unassuming presence—an echo of Max Perkins in the era of Judith Regan." Much the same, however, was said of Strachan's LB predecessor, Sarah Crichton, daughter of novelist Robert Crichton, who was fired in 2001 due to what some colleagues called "creeping commercialism" and "bad blood" with her bottom-line boss, Maureen Egen.[3]

Ms. Egen earned her stripes with two of the biggest bestsellers of the last century. She bought *Scarlett*, Alexandra Ripley's 1991 sequel to *Gone with the Wind*, at auction for $4.94 million; though critically panned, the novel sold 2.5 million copies in four years. In 1992 she released Robert James Waller's *The Bridges of Madison County* for which she had laid out a mere $32,000. When chains showed no interest in stocking the novel, Ms. Egen sent out 4,000 advance copies to independent sellers, along with a personal letter urging each to "hand sell" the title as a must-read, and offering "co-opt money" to those who did so. Due to her tireless marketing, Barnes & Noble and Waldenbooks offered Valentine's specials for the romance, *Cosmopolitan* and *Ladies Home Journal* ran excerpts, and sales went stratospheric after Oprah called *Bridges* her "favorite book of the year," "a gift to the country," and confessed that it had made her cry.[4] (Erich Segal's Valentine's Day release, *Love Story*, enjoyed the same good fortune after Barbara Walters announced to her viewers that the novel had made her cry.) When *Bridges* won the 1993 American Booksellers Book of the Year Award as well as the New York Library's Literary Lion Award, a lively debate arose as to whether it was "literature," as Egen insisted, or "an insipid, fatuous, mealy-mouthed third-rate soap opera," as the *Chicago Tribune's* reviewer Jon Margolis asserted. But

---

3 Marion Maneker, "House Cleaning," *New York Magazine*, February 9, 2001.

4 Jack Doyle, "Of Bridges & Lovers, 1992–1995," *PopHistoryDig.com*, June 25, 2008.
http://www.pophistorydig.com/?tag=amblin-entertainment

to the industry bookies the argument was moot since the dark horse romance went on to sell 50 million copies. And Maureen Egen went on to become "the heart and soul of this company," as her boss, David Young, Hachette Book CEO, called her. What was the visionary editor's secret? How did she spot such great books? She confided to *USA Today* that she'd always been guided by "a little motto in my mind: 'Would my Aunt Marie Louise like it?'"[5]

Though he has no Aunt Marie Louise, Knopf vice-president and editor at large Gary Fisketjon won the 2006 Max Perkins Lifetime Achievement Award. He has edited titles from Raymond Carver, Cormac McCarthy, Richard Ford, Donna Tartt, and Jay McInerny. Like his colleagues, he has persevered by being very selective. Asked by *Slushpile* in 2005 how many agent pitches he has agreed to pursue and publish, he replied: "One in a million, more or less." But he added that he considers more authors than "the fools ... who go to Yankee Stadium and demand a tryout." As if to imply that publishing, like pro sports, is a purely objective enterprise—that luck or subjective judgment had no part in his Casey Stengel decision to pick his former Williams' friend and *On the Road* sidekick, Jay McInerny, as Mickey Mantle before his *Bright Lights Big City* got to the batter's box.

How will he pick the next literary A-Rod for Knopf, and what will be his platform?

"Well, I'd like to be able to fly," said Fisketjon. "Tell me how I'd go about doing such a thing."

In spite of being the greatest author lover among those left on the island, Morgan Entrekin has been spared the Scarlet Letter. In 2004, *The Christian Science Monitor* profiled him in "The Publisher as Protagonist." He confessed that a conglomerate executive had once warned him: "'You shouldn't allow yourself to become such good friends with your authors, Morgan,' And I said, 'But that's one of the joys of this business.' And he said, 'Yeah, but you'll get hurt and disappointed by them.' ... [But] one of the great pleasures of this business is the friendships that you have with authors." They include Bret Easton Ellis, Sherman Alexie, Mark Bowden, Jim Harrison, and P.J. O'Rourke.

---

5 "Publisher of Best Sellers Steps Down," *USA Today,* December 12, 2006.

Entrekin started his career as a junior editor at Delacorte, where he edited Vonnegut's *Jailbird.* He bought Atlantic Monthly Press in 1991 and now owns and directs Grove/Atlantic, which earns $20 million annually. His biggest hit was Charles Frazier's three million-copy *Cold Mountain.* Comparing himself to a rock climber, he says, "You can get just enough of a grip to drag yourself up to the next level." But it hasn't been quite so simple. Entrekin attributes his success, in no small part, to having no personal life. "I've never married," he points out. "I don't have children, obviously. I eat, drink, live, sleep, dream this."

With men and women such as these, who said literature was dead?

CHAPTER 5

SUPER PACs

The Conglomerate Caste System

Since the dawn of the blockbuster, publishers have developed an eight-rung Jacob's tennis ladder for living novelists. From the top down:

1. FRANCHISES (approx. .000001% of writer population)

Authors whose books have sold more than 100 million copies.

Members: The aforementioned Top 10 genre masters Patterson through Rowling, plus others like Jeffrey Archer, Mary Higgins Clark, Nora Roberts, Anne Rice, Janet Dailey.

Comments: The Franchise can sell a million units of anything, even in a recession.

2. BREAD-AND-BUTTERS (.000009%)

10–100 million-sales authors.

Members: John Grisham, Tom Clancy, Sue Grafton, Dan Brown, Tami Hoag, Patricia Cornwell, E.L. James, etc.

Comments: Like a Franchise, a BB enjoys an evangelical following. But, unlike the Franchise, a BB may not survive serial bombs.

3. ONE-HIT WONDERS (.00009%)

Those who have homered but have yet to do so again.

Members: Robert James Waller (*Bridges of Madison County*), James Redfield (*Celestine Prophesy*), Charles Frazier (*Cold Mountain*), Xaviera Hollander (*The Happy Hooker*), etc.

Comments: OHW novelists pray, and OHW editors take Prilosec while trying to divine the Kelley Blue Book value of their next title.

4. PRESTIGES (.00001%)

Award-winning literary writers who have provided a fresh perspective on the human condition and/or get half-page ads in the *NYT Review of Books* and/or get reviewed by Maslin, Yardley, or Kakutani.

Members: Philip Roth, Tom Wolfe, Richard Ford, Toni Morrison, Alice Walker, Anne Tyler, E.L. Doctorow, Michael Chabon, Jonathan Franzen, Denis Johnson, etc.

Comments: These writers' Pulitzers defer honor on their house, making the enterprise seem more interested in masterpieces than mammon. Some conglomerates still advance a platinum-club member seven figures and take a bath. So most Prestiges don't have to sell plasma or worse, teach. They have the luxury of keeping their public epiphanies down to an MFA worship service or a Meet-and-Greet-the-Genius conference mixer.

5. MIDLISTERS (.002%)

Those who have not been serial remaindered and sent to the Gulag. Each of their titles has sold at least 10,000 copies and maybe a few thousand per year afterwards.

Members: Anybody who still appears on her publisher's webpage roster and/or who still has the audacity to identify herself at a cocktail party as an author.

Comments: With luck, suck, or pluck, MLs teach an adult ed night class. If not, they can apply for grants or Section 8 housing.

6. DEBUTS (.00015%)

Those who have published their first novel with a conglomerate house or reputable indie.

Members: Anybody listed in *Publishers Weekly*, *Publishers Marketplace*, or in their alumni or Lions Club newsletter.

Comments: Like the Inca, the industry loves a virgin. But losing your virginity doesn't always live up to expectations. Said Amy Tan, "The very first time I was published [*The Joy Luck Club*], I went into severe depression and could not stop crying."

7. BLACK-LISTED BACKLISTERS (1%)

According to industry expert, John B. Thompson, conglomerate accountants call these writers "Subperforming Marginal People."[1]

Members: The living dead.

Comments: The SUMP is often not responsible for a loss. The editors may have embalmed his title; the PR department may have ignored it; sales may have failed to supply stores at the right time; a similar title may have been released just before; media spots or endorsements may have fallen through. But the king kills the messenger for the Waterloo.

Thompson quotes an anonymous Brooklyn author who, after releasing fourteen books from major publishers, was unable to sell another: "I wear the sales figures I forged in life," he said, echoing Marley's ghost in *A Christmas Carol*. "I've become no better than my last sales figures ... I feel trapped. ... That's what most of my writing friends feel as well."

Another Thompson SUMP, with ten titles and many awards, changed his name because "you're better off in this industry being a completely unknown person. It's better to have no history than a mixed history. It's insane. It makes no sense. But that's publishing."

Noted novelist and New School professor Dale Peck scolded albatross authors for "mourning the death of an industry that's done so little for them for so long," expecting them to tolerate "decreased advances, sales, and opportunities to publish work that doesn't fit into

---

1   John B. Thompson, *Merchants of Culture: The Publishing Business in the Twenty-First Century* (UK: Polity, 2010).

an increasingly homogenized marketplace."[2]

Author sour grapes, or reality?

In 2008, *Poets and Writers* asked agent Molly Friedrich, "What about a literary writer ... who has published a couple of books that haven't sold too well?"

"They are in trouble. I'm not going to soft-pedal that. It's very, very, very painful," replied Friedrich, who has been in the business for forty years and represents a broad spectrum of authors from Sue Grafton to Frank McCourt.

Her colleague, Donald Maass—agent, author of The Breakout Novel series and seventeen novels—agrees: "Unless an author today finds a sizable audience very quickly, they will be washed out."[3]

8. THE UNTOUCHABLES (98.9876%)

The terminally unpublished.

Members: Lepers.

Comments: Many resort to vanity, print-on-demand, or e-publishing. A few become e-Cinderellas. Others succeed in selling to their mother and a handful of friends who also donate to the ASPCA.[4]

---

2 "Dale Peck Criticizes Publishing Industry: Says Writers Must Stand Up," *Newsweek/Daily Beast,* May 19, 2011. http://www.thedailybeast.com/articles/2011/05/19/dale-peck-says-writers-and-readers-must-fight-against-publishing-industry.html

3 Michael Neff, 2003 *Algonkian* interview with Donald Maass. http://webdelsol.com/Algonkian/interview-dmaass.htm

4 American Society for Prevention of Cruelty to Authors

CHAPTER 6

SHIT MY EDITOR SAYS

"The sad, awful truth was that there was hardly any evidence at all of talent in the slush pile and plenty of proof ... that the country was full of crazy people armed with typewriters."
—Michael Korda, *Another Life* (2000)

In the old days, direct contact with a publisher was known as an over-the-transom submission. The manuscript (ms.) fell directly from the door vent into a "slush pile." If, eventually, it worked its way out, a Michael Korda might take a look, hoping to find a diamond in the rough. In 1975 a Viking editor did this with Judith Guest's unagented novel, *Ordinary People*, the first over-the-transom manuscript the house had published in twenty-six years.

After weathering six hundred OT rejections, Jack London triumphed with *The Call of the Wild*. "The chief qualification of ninety percent of all editors is failure," he wrote. "They have failed as writers, and right there is the cursed paradox. Every portal to literature is guarded by those watchdogs."

Michael Korda calls manuscript rejection "soul-destroying work." "Learning to say no is the first, hardest, and most important lesson for a fledgling editor," he writes.

Editors and agents generally agree that nine out of ten fiction sub-missions are unpublishable. This was said to be true in the old days as well. In his memoir, *At Random*, Bennett Cerf wrote that, after lectures, he was beset by aspiring Hemingways who told him, "'Well, I'm a young writer and I have a work of genius,'" only to discover on review that it was "unbelievable junk."

In a word: shit.

In the industry of the carefully chosen word, the most-used noun is *shit*. Writers themselves find it as universally applicable as do publishers, editors, agents, and critics.

In his introduction to *On Writing*, the usually long-winded Stephen King began, "This is a short book because most books about writing are filled with bullshit."

In a 1993 speech to the country's leading magazine publishers and editors, Ray Bradbury got a standing ovation when he declared, "Can you keep downgrading people's intelligence and insult them with the shit you're publishing?"[1]

Hemingway believed that the novelist's most indispensable tool was a "built-in, shock-proof shit detector."

Voltaire called Shakespeare's plays "a vast dunghill." D.H. Lawrence called Joyce's last novel "Punnigan's Wake" and "Olla Putrida." Turgenev deemed Dostoyevsky's *Crime and Punishment* "an interminable stomach ache." Louisa May Alcott called Twain's *Huckleberry Finn* "trash suitable only for the slums." Twain called Ambrose Bierce's *Nuggets and Dust* "ten shudders and a vomit." Other greats were ruthless with themselves. "Oh, with what trash I began!" said Chekhov. Vonnegut warned *Playboy* at the beginning of his interview, "You understand, of course, that every-thing I say is horseshit."

The shitstorm became perfect with the dawn of the bestseller. "The world is prepared to praise only shit," declared America Book Award winner William Gass. Some best-selling authors agreed. "I'm a lousy writer; a helluva lot of people have got lousy taste," said Grace Metalious, whose *Peyton Place* outsold all the works of Hemingway,

---

1 *Playboy* interview with Ray Bradbury, 1996.

Fitzgerald, Melville, Dreiser, and Joyce combined. "Seventy percent of the fiction and nonfiction bestseller lists is dreck, and that *The Da Vinci Code*, by Dan Brown, stands as a prime example," Stephen King told *Entertainment Weekly*.[2] Other populist novelists disagree, insisting that work like Gass's is elitist crap.

Poet John Dolan called James Frey's *A Million Little Pieces* "A Million Little Pieces of Shit." *Liar's Club* author Mary Karr considered it "horse dookie," while *Gawker* dismissed it as "a pile of shit," and *The New York Daily News* branded Frey himself as "a lying sack of dung."

The screenwriter turned novelist begged to disagree. "Let the haters hate, let the doubters doubt," he wrote on his website. "I won't dignify this bullshit with any sort of further response." By 2011, realizing that the best defense is an offense, he told *Esquire* magazine that he, "for sure," thinks he'll be a pillar of the future literary "canon" for his shit. But like so many ahead-of-their-time geniuses, he complained, post-Oprah inquisition and crucifixion: "I've been through so much shit. ... I've been stabbed over and over and over again. All I want to do is make shit that I think is cool."

Which, of course, is what every writer has done, from Homer to Shakespeare to Proust to Patterson. Only their definitions of cool shit have differed.

»»»

Today's publishers divide shit into four categories.

1. **VERY BAD SHIT (30 percent):** Writing that is ungrammatical, incoherent, and/or nonsense.

2. **BAD SHIT (67 percent):** Writing that is confusing, clumsy, clichéd, and/or boring.

3. **GOOD SHIT (2 percent):** Writing that seems like it might sell to elitists (good) or to escapists (better).

4. **VERY GOOD SHIT, aka Hot or Cool Shit (1 percent):** Writing such as *Fifty Shades of Grey* that has already proved itself

---

2 Michael Slezak, "Stephen King: Celebrating Seven Years with 'Uncle Stevie,'" *EW Popwatch*, July 26, 2010

irresistible or that which has been recommended by Oprah.

In an industry where disagreements far outweigh agreements, everybody seems to agree on this: To get to a little Good Shit (3 and 4), agents and editors have to wade through a lot of Bad Shit (1 and 2). Especially agents, the first screeners at the treatment plant.

The real problem in traditional publishing proctology is in Case 3: The Good Shit. Even for rookie agents or editors, The Bad and the Very Bad, the 2s and 1s, are easy to ID, as is the 4, the Cool or Hot. Good Shit, can be a subjective call and is sometimes determined by the process of elimination—the manuscript is not a 1, 2, or 4, so it must be a 3. And though 3s are in the second percentile, there are still too many to be published by the Super PACs or independents.

Agents and editors concede that some good writers, like good shit, "fall through the cracks." But, to borrow the phrase of J.D. Salinger's hero, Holden Caulfield, they "fall off a crazy cliff." Editors try their best to be catchers in the rye by rescuing good new authors from being buried in the slush, but they can't save everybody.

Only a small percentage of 3s get published. And, as we will discuss in Chapter 4, those authors come out of the Luck, Suck, and Pluck pile, not the Slush.

Why?

Because there are not enough traditional publishers because there are not enough readers because there's so much shit out there.

Where promising writers used to fall, now many just fade away or jump because they buy the party line that publishing is a game that must be played by the rules. That's what the Catcher's English lit teacher told him after he flunked out of prep school and almost did a Thelma and Louise but wound up in an asylum instead.

"Game, my ass," Holden wrote. "Some game. If you get on the side where all the hot-shots are, then it's a game, all right— I'll admit that. But if you get on the other side, where there aren't any hot-shots, then what's a game about it? Nothing. No game."

In the old days when an author didn't make the cut, he or she often received an apologetic note from the editor. Now such notes are rare. There are too many manuscripts, too few editors, and not enough hours in their day. In our digital age, the ms. DOC or JPEG goes out and usually goes MIA in e-space with no trace of its submission other than its listing in the author's Sent folder. The process would be less dispiriting if publishers would bring back the old form rejection—like this one from the Max Perkins of Chinese editors.[3]

Illustrious Brother of the Sun and Moon—

Thy honored manuscript has deigned to cast the light of its august countenance upon me. With raptures I have perused it. By the bones of my ancestry, never have I encountered such wit, such pathos, such lofty thoughts. With fear and trembling I return the writing. Were I to publish the treasure you sent me, the Emperor would order that it should be made the standard, and that none be published except such as equaled it.

Your servant's servant.

---

3 Robert Hendrickson, *The Literary Life and Other Curiosities* (New York: Viking, 1981).

CHAPTER 7

THE PUBLISHER'S FICTION LIST

The "Bulls" of Pamplona

Myths about the publishing industry are many. Let's run the seven biggest bulls...

1. EDITORS EDIT

As a practical matter, most don't have time. Max Perkins had a few manuscripts to deal with in a day and took a four-martini Algonquin lunch break. Today's editor can have a hundred manuscripts to juggle between marketing meetings, focus meetings, jacket meetings, meetings about meetings. So she doesn't read. She skims.

Seven years ago, agent Noah Lukeman wrote that you get just *The First Five Pages* before the skimming starts. "God help the publishing professional who needs 50 pages to evaluate every manuscript, he'd never survive," he told the *Algonkian*. "He wouldn't be able to get to the 10,000 manuscripts behind it."[1]

---

1   Michael Neff, *Algonkian* interview with Noah Lukeman. http://webdelsol.com/Algonkian/inter-view-lukeman.htm

Today's editor is an industrial wine taster. She uses a spit bucket. By mid-afternoon her palette is OD'ed. She can't tell shit from chardonnay.

As longtime agent Susan Rabiner writes, "Today you are fortunate if your materials get into the hands of an editorial assistant, many of whom are just months out of college and may know less about what makes a manuscript publishable than you do."[2]

Still, assistant editors carry the heaviest screening workload. They get pauper wages and they live in New York. Meaning they can't afford a Monster or Cocaine Energy Drink, much less the original recipe.

2. EDITORS ARE PSYCHIC

Like economists, weathermen, and Vegas bookies, editors soon learn that the more clouded the crystal ball, the more important it is to make it look crystal (at least to civilians, no less than to Super PAC CFOs).

Writer/editor Andre Gide at Gallimard broke the rule long ago. He called his rejection of Proust's *Remembrance of Things Past* the most "bitter regret" of his life. "Would I have been able to recognize right away the obvious value of Baudelaire, of Rimbaud? Wouldn't I have dismissed Lautreamont at first as a madman?"

No such second-guessing has been heard from the twelve who dismissed Harry Potter, the fifteen who rejected *A Time to Kill,* the sixty who opposed *The Help*, the two hundred who spurned *Roots.*

On the other hand, many auction bidding-war titles have tanked.

As the ever-candid editor Michael Korda noted: "At least half the books on any given week's bestseller list are there to the immense surprise and puzzlement of their publishers."[3]

3. THE CREAM ALWAYS RISES TO THE TOP

Shit floats, too. But cream—*always*?

---

2 Susan Rabiner and Alfred Fortunato, *Thinking Like Your Editor: How to Write Great Serious Nonfiction—and Get It Published* (New York: W.W. Norton, 2002).

3 Laura Miller, "Recipe for a Bestselling Book," *Salon,* May 1, 2012. www.salon.com/2012/05/01/recipe_for_a_bestselling_book/singleton/

From Guttenberg on, this has been the publisher party line plagiarized from Van Gogh's headstone.

Historically, dying is the best accelerant for slow cream. The richest artistic cream—whether it finally surfaces in words, symphonies, or wildflower canvases—is always recognized on a corpse.

Outside the DOA statute: Could it be that there was or is another Dante, Dickens, Brontë, Pynchon—whose cream *still* hasn't risen to the top? Whose manuscripts are now in ashes, out to sea, or under the rubble of a lonely garret?

Impossible, say industry stalwarts and seminar gurus: There are no unrecognized writers, otherwise we'd *know* about them.

This fiction is based on another publishing Confucianism: Birds of a feather flock together. In other words, if another Dickens existed or exists, his MFA or writer's group friends or lovers or somebody else in his network would have reported him to FSG or Knopf.

4. CONTROVERSY SELLS

...for Hunter Thompson, and maybe a few other dead licensed shock-and-awe jocks. But most everybody else is slushed. PC publishers will not chance the blowback on a nonprime-time loose cannon, even if he's the next Swift or she's the next Dorothy Parker.

5. PASSION SELLS

Editors and agents are often asked what they look for in a manuscript. What excites them. What makes them miss their subway stop. The number one reason for most?

Passion.

Gurus agree: Don't follow fashion, write with passion.

"The true writer always plays to an audience of one," wrote E.B. White in *The Elements of Style.* "Let him start sniffing the air, or glancing at the Trend Machine, and he is as good as dead."

But the Literary Law of Equal and Opposite Reaction applies: "Anything that is written to please the author is worthless," countered Pascal.

Practically, who is right in today's market?

Another hypothetical: Before sitting down to work, Novelist 1 Googles her story idea, discovers somebody has already published something like it, and drops it. Novelist 2, without research, passionately finishes his story and fires it off. The editor replies, "Compelling [powerful, deeply felt, whatever]. But derivative."

"But I wrote it with passion!" the writer protests.

"Try the French," suggests the editor.

6. WRITERS PROVIDE THE PROSE, PUBLISHERS EVERYTHING ELSE

This used to be more or less the case in the Golden Age. So a publisher's 92 percent cut of the action didn't seem extortionate. A few small differences between yesterday and today, vis-a-vis who brings what to the potluck:

- Yesterday: The publisher brought its audience to you.
- Today: You bring your audience to the publisher.

- Yesterday: The publisher helped build your platform or personality cult.
- Today: You build your own platform or personality cult.

- Yesterday: The publisher did all the marketing and PR.
- Today: You do all the marketing and PR.

- Yesterday: The publisher did most of the line editing and fact-checking.
- Today: You do most of the line editing and fact-checking.

- Yesterday: The publisher paid the price for a Hindenberg.
- Today: You pay the price for a Hindenberg.

Even so, for the 92 percent bite, today's author still gets the publisher's historic seal of excellence on his spine and royalty statement: the bounding greyhound, the rooster, the fish, the flame, the sowing farmer.

7. LITERATURE IS THRIVING LIKE NEVER BEFORE!

James Frey and E.L. James—yes. Henry James and James Joyce—no.

Industry lobbyists might argue this. As today's tea party politicians, trickle-down executives, and anti-global warming experts prove, statistics are countless: There's one for every pocketbook and POV.

While many editors concede that literature is a "tough sell" today, most nevertheless insist the cup is half full. But how much longer can Jonathan Galassi, Morgan Entrekin, Pat Strachan, and the few other champions of quality fiction keep their heads off the chopping block? Meanwhile, corporate goldfish will refuse to admit that the bowl is losing water until they're high and dry. And the editors who see the level going down can only say, "It might be a little shallower in here—but, hey, shallow is good. Shallow sells."

Then they reach for their snorkels and Patterson's next *Ulysses*.

PART II

WRITER 911!

Burned, Blocked, and Blitzed

"One day, I shall explode like an artillery shell
and all my bits will be found on the writing table."
—Gustave Flaubert

CHAPTER 8

THE MOST DANGEROUS GAME

"The artist is extremely lucky who is presented with the worst possible ordeal which will not actually kill him. At that point, he is in business."
—**John Berryman, 1970 interview**

Other masters agreed with the Pulitzer Prize-winning poet. Even before being racked by hemorrhoids, epilepsy, and the German croupiers, Dostoyevsky declared: "In order to write well one must suffer much!"

God seemed happy to bring great artists to their full potential. Before the twentieth century, most surrendered to consumption, the clap, cirrhosis, and/or lunacy. Many also seemed accident prone, even those who enjoyed career luck. Survivors published their misadventures eventually, but most would have preferred their health.

Cervantes had his arm shot off, an insane nephew gunned down Jules Verne, Tolstoy's face got rearranged by a rogue bear. Samuel Pepys was sterilized during a gallstone operation. Marlowe was shanked in a bar brawl, Dashiell Hammett got stabbed in the leg, Lowry almost got castrated. Kerouac was twice nearly beaten to death in bar brawls. Beckett took a shiv to the chest from a Paris pimp, Monsieur Prudent. When later asked by the existentialist why, Prudent replied: "I do not know, sir. I'm sorry." Then there was Sherwood Anderson who, just before his liver shut down, swallowed a martini toothpick and died of peritonitis.

Historically, drunk or sober, novelists in or around cars have been accidents waiting to happen. After declaring, "I know nothing more stupid than to die in an automobile accident," the absurdist Nobel prize winner Camus took a lift in his publisher's Facel-Vega. An unused train ticket was later found next to his body.

Returning to L.A. to grieve the death of his friend F. Scott Fitzgerald, Nathanael West ran a stop sign and, with his wife of two days, was killed in a collision. By that time, F. Scott's wife, Zelda, was a longtime asylum resident who, before being committed, had lain down in front of her husband's town car and said, "Drive over me, Scott."

Another southern belle, Margaret Mitchell, stepped off a curb on Peachtree and 13th and was delivered to the hereafter by an off-duty cabbie. Otherwise one of the luckiest novelists in history, she'd started Gone with the Wind while laid up with a broken ankle from a less serious mishap. She'd never written a query to a publisher, but Macmillan's Harold Latham had begged her for a story while she squired him around Atlanta in search of homegrown talent.

Edna St. Vincent Millay suffered a fatal staircase fall after one too many. Virginia Woolf toppled from a hotel balcony into a Venice canal. Steinbeck crashed through a balcony railing, shattering a kneecap. When F. Scott Fitzgerald threatened to jump out a window at the Yale Club, nobody tried to stop him.

During an after-work stroll in 1999, Stephen King was struck and nearly killed by a minivan. At the time, he was busy with his On Writing memoir as well as another thriller, From a Buick 8, about a man-eating car from another dimension.

King's fear that the accident might kill his muse proved unfounded, but he complained that his subsequent output was seriously reduced. By contrast, near-fatal ordeals stimulated other authors, bearing out Berryman's argument. Flannery O'Connor considered her debilitating lupus a creative blessing. Katherine Ann Porter caught the writing bug after her obituary was written and funeral arrangements made while she was in a flu-induced coma. Anthony Burgess finished five novels after he was diagnosed with inoperable brain cancer in 1959 and given a year to live; he pressed on until 1993 to finish twenty-five more. In the introduction to his first novel, *Queer*, William Burroughs confessed to coming to the "appalling conclusion" that he never would have become a writer had he not accidentally shot and killed his common law wife in 1951 during a drunken William Tell game which caused "a lifelong struggle ... to write my way out."

>>>

Historic authors seem to have suffered more from the fates, or from the Almighty himself, than from publishers or critics.

The disaster-prone Hemingway declared through his hero, Nick Adams, "Other people get killed, but not me." His fisherman, Santiago, echoed, "To hell with luck, I'll bring the luck with me." Papa had had a thing about luck ever since taking shrapnel on the Italian Front during a chocolate run, then being struck by a falling apartment skylight while he wrote *A Farewell to Arms*. Even so, he found it amusing that his Catholic colleagues, Fitzgerald and Joyce—who sustained most of their injuries in and around bars—were terrified of thunder and lightning.

After the skylight mishap, Hemingway drove his former EMT colleague, John Dos Passos, to hunt in Montana and—to the relief of the local wildlife—missed a cliff-side turn. He broke an arm. Later, when the two fished off Key West, Papa winged himself while shooting a gaffed shark. Dos again escaped unscathed. Then, in 1947, Dos drove into a parked truck, losing an eye and his wife, Kitty, who was decapitated.

Hemingway went on to suffer many other automotive misadventures. His luck wasn't any better in airplanes. In his final bush crash in the Belgian Congo, 1954, he was rescued by a riverboat, which took him to another plane that also crashed, prompting the newspapers to print his obituary.

By the end of his career, fearing that he was being tailed by assassins, Papa was diagnosed as a paranoid psychotic and sent to the Meninger Clinic for shock treatments. En route, he tried to walk into the propellers of a Cessna at the Rapid City airport.

When hauling his shark-ravaged trophy marlin ashore, Santiago explained his creator's misfortunes not as random, nor as Job-like purgatory, but as a kind of divine blowback such as Icarus suffered. "You violated your luck when you went too far outside," the old fisherman told himself.

The literary masters might have fared better had they used Kafka's hard hat. A Workers Accident Institute personal injury specialist, the surrealist (according to industrial expert Peter Zucker) is said to have made the invention while composing *The Metamorphosis*, about his alter ego's "hard, as it were, armor-plated, back." Though the sedentary safety specialist never got run over by a minivan like King or crowned by a skylight like Hemingway, he never enjoyed their professional good luck either. He published only a few of his stories and ordered the rest to be burned, saying, "There will be no proof that I ever was a writer."

CHAPTER 9

MS.CARRIAGES & HYSTERICAL PREGNANCIES

Books change thinking. Because of this, many novelists, essayists, historians, poets, and pamphleteers have tended to be enemies of the status quo. As James Joyce noted, "Civilization may be said indeed to be the creation of its outlaws."

Since the Good Book, authors have been exiled, racked, crucified, burnt, and beheaded. Today, for lack of tyrants, inquisitors, and revolutionaries, the literary herd is no longer culled. Rather than distributing literary birth control to manage the growing population, writer's conferences and MFA programs give hormones. And every seven-figure advance alert from *Publishers Marketplace* drives hopeful writers to another breeding frenzy. These factors have led to the publishing population explosion.

But sometimes even a best-selling author will ms.carry, or come close—intentionally or otherwise. Harper Lee threw an early draft of *To Kill a Mockingbird* into the snow. Luckily, her agent persuaded her to rescue it. After the novel's completion—though her Lippincott editor, Tay Hohoff, warned her that it would sell only a few thousand copies—it went on to sell more than 30 million and win the Pulitzer Prize. Lee then set to work on *The Long Goodbye*, but abandoned the novel in the first trimester. "I've found I can't write," she complained. "I have about three hundred personal friends who keep dropping in for a cup of coffee." Her lawyer friend and research assistant, Tom Radney, said it wasn't the coffee. "She's fighting a battle between the book and a bottle of Scotch. And the Scotch is winning." Most of all, she wasn't sure she could deliver another golden child. "When you're at the top there's only one way to go," she told her cousin.[1]

Fellow Pulitzer Prize winner Michael Chabon aborted the follow-up to his own celebrated debut, *The Mysteries of Pittsburgh*. Laboring on *Fountain City* for five years, he felt it "erasing me, breaking me down, burying me alive." At last, succumbing to what he called "the Hand of Dread," he pulled the plug on the title.

After two years trying to hatch *Agnew Belittlehead*, Chang-rae Lee, the director of Princeton's creative writing program, decided that it was an "unfunny, oddly New Agey version of a David Foster Wallace toss-off."[2] Letting it die on the vine, he debuted with *Native Speaker*, which won the PEN/Hemingway Award.

Sometimes, love's labor is not lost. Jennifer Egan ms.carried her "monstrous" 600-page *Inland Souls* after all the family and friends she sent it to "became unreachable—and that includes my mother." Ten years later she managed to revive the novel as *The Invisible Circus*, which helped her win a Guggenheim Fellowship.

Stephen King resurrected *The Cannibals*, also written thirty years ago, as his 2009 *Under the Dome*. The same happened with his e-serialized novel-in-progress, *The Plant*, about a man-eating vine sent to a publisher by a rejected horror novelist.

Before receiving the AAAL Award in Literature, Richard Price ms.carried *Home Fires* at the beginning of his career in the early 1970s. The reason for its failure was much the same as that of his colleagues: "The driving force behind the novel was panic about not having a novel," he says.

---

1 Charles J. Shields, *Mockingbird: A Portrait of Harper Lee*, (New York: Henry Holt and Co., 2006).

2 Dan Kois, "Why Do Writers Abandon Novels?" *New York Times*, March 4, 2011.

CHAPTER 10

BLOCKED

Why Shitty Things Happen to Irregular Writers

A writer stops writing for any one of many reasons. The worst of them come down to two.

First, he fears or is fed up with rejection. He's exhausted. Disillusioned. Or just plain bummed. "I would prefer not to," he says, like Melville's Bartleby the scrivener.

Or, he feels creatively dead. Burned out. "I'm a worked-over claim," he says, like Steinbeck after *The Winter of Our Discontent.*

The first writer is a failophobic; the second a fatalist. In either case he is in the state dreaded by all: He's blocked.

"Writing is easy," observed Gene Fowler. "All you have to do is stare at a blank sheet of paper until drops of blood form on your forehead."

Hoping to avoid this problem, one writer, before sitting down to the manuscript itself, researches then creates a character and plot blueprint. Another does little or no research and dives right in. The first writer is like the traveler who packs her bags with a checklist, pre-books all her flights, hotels, and sight-seeing tours, and sticks to a daily itinerary. The second writer is like the traveler who tosses a tent, toiletries, and a change of underwear into a knapsack and just starts hitching around unexplored lands, come what may.

The trip of the compulsive pre-planner hits a roadblock when she realizes her travelogue is not well-structured and realized, as she had hoped, but predictable and lifeless. The impulsive adventurer may become blocked when he realizes that he's lost in the outback of her imagination.

To avoid a block, the compulsive writer should try to become a little more impulsive; and the impulsive more compulsive.

Here are seven writer's block antidotes for both types.

1. KILL THE PERFECTIONIST

Dumas, Dickens, and the Brontës may have crafted perfect, flowing first drafts. The modern writer, however, must content himself, as Anne Lamott points out in *Bird by Bird*, with a "shitty first draft" by silencing the self-sabotaging critic inside his head—the perfectionist. In short, let your gut write the first draft; let the head handle the others. In the first round, fill the basket with all low-hanging fruit in your orchard; don't waste your time on a ladder reaching for perfection, much less what Flaubert called *le mot juste*—the right word.

2. KILL THE ROYAL SHAKESPEAREAN ACADEMY

If your first draft is opening night in front of the Academy, or even a dress rehearsal – stage fright is inevitable. You'll be bleeding from the forehead even before your first line, if only you could remember it. Forget the audience! Since this is all but impossible for even mature writers, try to imagine everybody in your front row naked, lobotomized, or on mushrooms. Or put your biggest fans there: your best friend, your mother, your dog.

3. BE A JOURNALIST, NOT AN ARTISTE

In the first draft, focus on the concrete—the Who, When, What, Where, and How—not the style. Compelling content creates its own style.

4. FRAME THE HOUSE

A book is a house. Start with the foundation and framing. Trying to craft

Doric columns or Rosette moldings at the same time invites a block, if not disaster. More important: Build your own house, not somebody else's. Play the home game. Some stuck writers try to kickstart the morning's work by reading passages from their favorite author. Bad idea. "It is better to fail at originality, than succeed at imitation," as Melville said.

5. CONTROL AMBITION

Some novelists get stuck trying to build a palace when they only have the chops for a bungalow. Know your limitations as you learn your craft. Moreover, a publisher is more likely to greenlight a fully realized bungalow than a bungled Versailles.

6. FIND YOUR VOICE

The best literary fiction is driven not by character or plot, but by mood, attitude, and point of view. In a word: voice. At the heart of a block is a writer's struggle to find a voice. Voice is not found by thinking or analyzing, but by feeling. As Natalie Goldberg suggests in *Wild Mind*, tap into and cultivate your spontaneous, subconscious, instinctual self—and just start singing.

7. WRITE REGULARLY

Real pros in most professions—sports, business, the arts, whatever—punch the clock every day whether or not they *feel* like it. Whether this is self-discipline, obsessive compulsion, or masochism, the nose-to-the-grindstone MO is the way most things get done, from the Sistine Chapel to *Ulysses*. The regular writer has the wind at his back: momentum. The irregular writer is always starting from his last stop, waiting on the fickle lover he calls "inspiration."

CHAPTER 11

LITERARY DOPING

"When I have one martini, I feel bigger, wiser, taller. When I have a second I feel superlative. When I have more, there's no stopping me."

—**William Faulkner**

Civilization has firewater—the writer's Eucharist—to thank for many masterpieces, though, as Gorky once observed, "Many drink more than they write." Luckily urine tests have never been given in Stockholm. Otherwise Pearl Buck and Nelly Sachs would have been the only laureates.[1]

London loved his martinis. Kerouac, his margaritas. O'Neill, his Gibsons. Carver his Bloodies, Bukowski his boilermakers. Burgess his Hangman's Blood, Carson McCullers her Sunny Boys.

---

1 According to Tom Dardis (*The Thirsty Muse: Alcohol and the American Writer*), five American Nobel laureates in Literature were alcoholics: Sinclair Lewis, Eugene O'Neill, William Faulkner, Ernest Hemingway, and John Steinbeck. Other alcoholics Dardis studied include Jack London, Edna St. Vincent Millay, F. Scott Fitzgerald, Hart Crane, Conrad Aiken, Thomas Wolfe, Dashiell Hammett, Dorothy Parker, Ring Lardner, Djuna Barnes, John O'Hara, Tennessee Williams, John Berryman, Carson McCullers, James Jones, John Cheever, Truman Capote, Raymond Carver, Robert Lowell, and James Agee.

Few women writers have been drunks. They don't seem to have the natural aptitude. Dorothy Parker, Mary McCarthy, and Edna St. Vincent Millay threw a few back, but didn't find themselves under the table or as an alley ornament with any regularity.

Fitzgerald once challenged a friend, "Can you name a single American artist except James and Whistler who didn't die of drink?"

The *This Side of Paradise* author once warned another colleague, Robert Benchley: "Drinking is a slow death." To which the Algonquin Round Table regular replied over his Manhattan, "Who's in a hurry?"

According to his father-in-law, a judge, Fitzgerald was never sober. His daughter, Scottie, corrected the record: She said her dad was drunk only "75% of the time." Making light of it, Scott got into the habit of introducing himself, "I'm very glad to meet you, sir—you know I'm an alcoholic."

At first it was all flapper fun with his wife and friends. Once, he and Ring Lardner did the Charleston on Frank Doubleday's lawn, hoping to be joined by the publisher's houseguest, Joseph Conrad. Another time, he and Zelda barked like dogs outside Sam Goldwyn's party until the movie mogul let them in. Years later, taking a play from Scott's book, Dylan Thomas barked at, chased, and bit Chelsea Hotel guests, then pounded eighteen more whiskeys and slipped the mortal coil.

"Parties are a form of suicide," said Fitzgerald. "I love them."

After another one, he got to waving a gun around. It went off and nearly hit Thornton Wilder. The next morning, as often happened, he had no recollection of the incident.

By the mid-'30s, Fitzgerald was drinking a beer for breakfast and consuming up to thirty-six bottles more before bedtime. The fun was over. "He was a vicious drunk, one of the worst I've ever seen," said his last mistress, Sheilah Graham, with the bruises to prove it. She further recalled, "In 1935 he saw beetles and pink mice scurrying all over him and elephants dancing on the ceiling."

Before the DTs set in, Scott, like his colleagues, drank for professional reasons. "Any stories I have wrote when I was sober were stupid," he said. He explained that drink "heightens my emotions and I put them in a story."

His friend Hemingway, who carried him out of the Dingo Bar regularly, was on the same page: "Write drunk, edit sober," was his motto.

Otherwise Papa said he drank "to make people more interesting."
So, as people became less and less interesting to him, his habit grew.
His own fiction required more and more courage until, in the end, he
couldn't drink his way into a short story.

Faulkner loved his chicken soup, too. As with Fitzgerald and
Hemingway, friends and doctors tried to cut his supply. "Pouring out
liquor is like burning books," he complained. He, too, blacked out
regularly. Once, he did so on a steam pipe in a New York hotel room,
burning himself to the bone. The ER doctor asked him why he did this.
"Because I like to," replied the novelist.

In 1936, Faulkner checked into Mississippi's Wright's Sanatorium
where he underwent electro-shock therapy and anti-alcohol injections.
He became a regular patient and died at the dry-out facility twenty-six
years later.

When the author of *The Sound and the Fury* wasn't on a gurney taking voltage or at home writing under the influence, he was flying under
the influence in his airplane or fox-hunting on horseback in the Oxford
backcountry, flying headlong into fences and hedgerows. Once, after
being thrown again, his riding companion asked if he "liked" horses.

"I'm scared to death of horses," replied the Nobel laureate. "That's
why I can't leave them alone."

The American trinity's successors—Mailer, Styron, Bukowski,
Thompson, Cheever, and Carver, all the way through King, Wallace and
beyond—continued to take communion, with hapless editors and agents
trying to keep pace. When former Random House editorial director
Jason Epstein met Edmund Wilson for lunch at the Princeton Club, the
critic ordered six martinis and asked his colleague, "Would you like
a half dozen, too?"[2] Dick Snyder told the *Times'* Roger Rosenblatt that
during his heyday as Simon and Schuster CEO in the '80s and '90s: "All
you had to know to succeed was alcohol. ... The three-martini lunch was
normal. If you didn't get real business done before noon, the rest of the
day was lost in an alcoholic haze."[3]

---

2   Jason Epstein, *Book Business: Publishing Past Present And Future* (New York: W.W. Norton, 2001).

3   Roger Rosenblatt, "See Dick Run, Again," *New York Times*, October 22, 1995.

Teetotalers are hard to find in the history of literature, but not those in denial. "My sole drink is water," insisted Poe. Some wanted to be regarded as disciplined. "I never write when I'm drunk," said W.H. Auden. Others were pragmatic. "One of the disadvantages of wine is that it makes a man mistake words for thoughts," declared Samuel Johnson, who spent nine years on his *Dictionary of the English Language* and avoided any controlled substance that might aggravate his Tourettes.

Then there was Ray Bradbury who, going to the root of the matter, advised: "You must stay drunk on writing so reality cannot destroy you."

THE OLD MAN AND THE SEAGRAMS

"Always be drunk. ... You want to stop Time crushing your shoulders, bending you double. So get drunk—militantly."
—**Charles Baudelaire**

"After a few glasses, I get ideas that would never have occurred to me dead sober."
—**Irwin Shaw**

"Man seeks to escape himself in myth, and does so by any means at his disposal. Drugs, alcohol, or lies."
—**Jean Cocteau**

"No other human being, no woman, no poem or music, book or painting can replace alcohol in its power to give man the illusion of real creation."
—**Marguerite Duras**

PART III

THE DUES
TO PAY THE MUSE

"I discovered that rejections are not
altogether a bad thing. They teach a writer
to rely on his own judgment and to say
in his heart of hearts, 'To hell with you.'"
— Saul Bellow

CHAPTER 12

THE LIONS

"The book does not go from writer to reader. It goes first to the lions—editors, publishers, critics, copy readers, sales department. It is kicked and slashed and gouged. And its bloodied father stands attorney."

—John Steinbeck

In the 1920s, literature reached its zenith with the publication of *The Great Gatsby, The Sun Also Rises, Remembrance of Things Past, and To the Lighthouse.* Some masterpieces were easy to get into print, others not.

In 1925, Sherwood Anderson's wife wrote the as-yet-unpublished William Faulkner, then in '28: "Sherwood says that he will make a trade with you. If he doesn't have to read your manuscript, he will tell his publisher to accept it." The Oxford postman replied, "Done!" and later confessed: "That's how I became a writer."[1]

Anderson, the author of *Dark Laughter,* did the same for other future Nobel recipients Hemingway and Steinbeck. In 1926 Faulkner's debut novel, *Soldiers' Pay*, was released to critical acclaim.

---

1 Philip Weinstein, *Becoming Faulkner: The Art and Life of William Faulkner* (Oxford University Press, 2009).

Like his colleagues, Faulkner was attracted to literature from an early age. "I want to be a writer like my great-grandaddy," he told his third grade teacher. Colonel W.C. Faulkner, the author of *The White Rose of Memphis,* had begun his own career as a man of action, not words. A Mexican-American war hero, W.C. had had three fingers blown off by a cannonball. A hard-drinking railroad tycoon turned Mississippi states-man, he'd knifed a rival who had blocked his membership in the Knights of Temperance. In the end, he was gunned down by his railroad partner.

His 5'5", 125-pound grandson, William, was more sedentary. After being rejected by the Army for his size but accepted by Anderson's publisher, Boni & Liveright, for *Soldiers' Pay,* he finished *Flags in the Dust* in 1927. "At last and certainly, I have written THE book," he wrote his editor. "I believe it is the damdest best book you'll look at this year."[2]

"The story really doesn't get anywhere and has a thousand loose ends," the editor replied, ordering the penniless author to return his $200 advance. "You don't seem to have any story to tell."

Faulkner tried to shrug off the rejection. But "Count No Count," as he was called in Oxford, felt "like a parent who is told that its child is a thief or an idiot or a leper," he wrote a friend. "I hid my own eyes in the fury of denial." His mother, Maude, knew the feeling. So she wrote Boni & Liveright and begged them to reconsider. They wouldn't. Faulkner was furious. Thus began his consumptive affair with Southern Comfort and Wild Turkey.

The future Nobel laureate then tried stories. Anderson, F. Scott Fitzgerald, and Hemingway were now making more from their short fiction than from their novels—up to $4,000 apiece from *Harper's, Collier's, American Mercury,* or *The Saturday Evening Post.* All Faulkner's submissions were rejected.

His poetry met with the same fate. At last—urged on by his friend Phil Stone, who had introduced him to Anderson—Faulkner signed his name to John Clare's "Lines from a Northhampton Asylum" and sub-mitted it to *The Republic.* The famous poem was rejected. Upping the ante, he copied "Kublai Khan" and submitted it under the correct name,

---

2 Joseph Leo Blotner, *Faulkner: A Biography* (New York: Random House, 1974).

Samuel T. Coleridge.

"We like your poem, Mr. Coleridge, but we don't think it gets anywhere much," *The Republic* wrote back.

Recently, in a déjà vu exercise, aspiring novelist G.D. McFetridge sent an excerpt from Faulkner's *The Hamlet* to leading literary magazines. Every submission went unrecognized and was rejected. *The Chariton Review* found the Nobel Prize winner's story "under-dramatized"; the *Arkansas Review* thought it "insufficiently embellished"; others complained that characters were undeveloped and the plot slow. Pressing on, McFetridge copied and retitled a short story from a noted best-of-the-year collection, as well as one from the *Atlantic Monthly*. These were rejected for lacking "substance" and "going nowhere."[3]

Other literary desperados have tried the same MO with similar results. In 2007, rejected novelist David Lassman, director of the Jane Austen Festival in Bath, submitted to UK publishers a sample from *Pride and Prejudice* and two of her other works. All were turned away.[4] A year earlier, the *London Sunday Times* submitted pseudonymous copies of two Booker prize-winning novels—V.S. Naipaul's *In a Free State* and Stanley Middleton's *Holiday*—to twenty British publishers and agents. Only one rep expressed interest in Middleton. Nobody wanted the Nobel winner, Naipaul.[5]

"I'm astounded," said 2007 Nobel Prize winner Doris Lessing, although earlier she had been rejected by her own publisher when submitting a new novel under a pseudonym.

One of the original SASE Scarlet Pimpernels was the diehard Chuck Ross. In 1975, the struggling scribe typed the first twenty-one pages of Jerzy Kosinski's National Book Award winning novel, *Steps*, and submitted it to four publishers. All rejected it. Ross typed the entire ms. and submitted it more widely. This time, *Steps* was turned down by thirteen agents and fourteen publishers, including its original, Random

---

3 G. D. Mcfetridge, "Show Us, Mr. Faulkner," *Mobius, The Journal of Social Change*, Volume 22, Number 4; Winter 2011. http://mobiusmagazine.com/comment/essay22.4.html

4 C. Alan Joyce and Sarah Janssen, *I Used to Know That: Inside Stories of Famous Authors* (Reader's Digest, Inc. 2012).

5 Ariel Gore, *How to Become a Famous Writer Before You Are Dead* (3 Rivers Press, 2007).

House, which, like the others, didn't recognize the novel and used a form rejection.[6]

»»

Herman Melville had been celebrated for his first novel, *Typee*. But, five years later, his magnum opus, *Moby-Dick*, became his Titanic. One editor called it a "tragic-comic bubble and squeak." Another apologized: "We regret to say that … we do not think it would be at all suitable for the Juvenile Market. It is very long, rather old-fashioned."

At last Melville's mentor, Nathaniel Hawthorne, to whom the whaling saga was dedicated, got it published. In Melville's lifetime, the novel failed to sell its run of 3,000 copies. His total American edition earnings were $556.37. The Typee cannibals with whom the marooned young author had lived turned out to be more civil than his publishers who blacklisted him. Melville was devastated. "He'd pretty much made up his mind to be annihilated," said Hawthorne.[7]

The novelist's next three titles proved this. Finally, he penned *Bartleby, the Scrivener*, about a copyist who refuses to write anymore because "I would prefer not to."

The master tried to find humor in his fate. His penultimate novel, *The Confidence-Man*, belonged, according to his brother-in-law, "to that horribly uninteresting class of nonsensical books he is given to writing … [filled] with strained & ineffectual attempts to be humorous." The story, about an April Fools' Day grifter on a Mississippi steamboat, showed "all that happens to a man in this life is only by way of joke, especially his misfortunes," Melville wrote a friend.

His unfinished final masterpiece, *Billy Budd*, was not published until thirty years after he died destitute.

Jack London, a fourteen-year-old oyster pirate when his predecessor died in 1891, began writing short stories, but all were turned down. (His nearly six hundred rejections are displayed on "The House of Happy Walls" at his historic California estate.) In his novel about a

---

6   Chuck Ross, "The *Steps* Experiment." http://www.museumofhoaxes.com/hoax/archive/permalink/the_steps_experiment/

7   Newton Arvin, *Herman Melville: A Critical Biography* (New York: Viking, 1966).

struggling writer, *Martin Eden*, his alter ego complains "there was no human editor at the other end, but a mere cunning arrangement of cogs that changed the manuscript from one envelope to another"—his SASE. Later, Eden hit it big, as did London, but took his life (as some suspect that London also did).[8]

When the adventure novelist died, F. Scott Fitzgerald was working on *The Romantic Egoist*. Charles Scribner, his Princeton classmate, rejected the title. Meanwhile, living with his parents, Fitzgerald wallpapered his room with 122 pink slips for his short stories, later recalling this period in "One Hundred False Starts." His other Princeton pal, Edmund Wilson, the future dean of American criticism, consoled him: "I believe you might become a very popular trashy novelist without much difficulty."

Fitzgerald turned his DOA novel into *This Side of Paradise*. Scribner's Maxwell Perkins published it in 1920. A drunken Scott shouted out a hotel window, "I am Voltaire! I am Rousseau!"

That year he earned $18,000, ten times more than the average American. By the mid-'20s, his income had doubled. But to support his Gatsby-esque lifestyle, he still borrowed large sums from Perkins and from his agent, Harold Ober. During his nine-year hiatus—*Gatsby* in 1925, *Tender Is the Night* in 1934—he teetered on the edge of bankruptcy and alcohol-fueled insanity, which he recalled in "The Crack-Up."

His friend Ernest Hemingway wrote Perkins, "He seems to almost take pride in his shamelessness of defeat. ... He had a marvelous talent and the thing is to use it—not whine in public."

In his final year, Fitzgerald earned $33 in royalties. His former lover Dorothy Parker, one of the handful who attended his wake, quoting *Gatsby,* muttering, "Poor son of a bitch."

At age twenty-four, Charles Bukowski broke into *Story* magazine with his "Aftermath of a Lengthy Rejection Slip." A dry period ensued, and he threw in the towel for ten years, became a postman, and nearly drank himself to death. Finally he told himself: "I have one of two choices—stay in the post office and go crazy ... or play at writer and starve. I have decided to starve."[9]

---

8 James L. Haley, *Wolf: The Lives of Jack London,* (New York: Basic Books/ Perseus 2011).

9 Howard Sounes, *Charles Bukowski: Locked in the Arms of a Crazy Life* (New York: Grove Press, 1999).

On a diet of one Payday candy bar a day, he cranked out reams
of poetry, went viral with SASEs, launched "Notes of a Dirty Old Man"
column for L.A.'s *Open City* as well as his own mimeographed vanity
mags, *Laugh Literary* and *Man the Humping Guns*. At last, Black Sparrow
publisher John Martin rescued Bukowski, age 49, with a $100 per month
stipend for life. In 1986, *Time* magazine heralded him the "laureate of
American lowlife." The next year Mickey Rourke played him in *Barfly*.

John Kennedy Toole tried his luck with *A Confederacy of Dunces* but
was turned down by all. Simon & Schuster said, "It isn't really about
anything." Later the alcoholic college lit professor, then thirty-two, took
a pilgrimage to Flannery O'Connor's hometown in Georgia. He asphyxiated himself in his car, leaving his last prose on the dash: a suicide
note to his mother.

The grieving Thelma Toole, a music tutor, hand-delivered her boy's
shopworn *Confederacy* ms. to Walker Percy at Loyola State University.
Both Percy's parents had committed suicide. The novelist had also won
the 1962 National Book Award for *The Moviegoer*, about a privileged
Southern misfit much like himself—and much like John Kennedy Toole.
He loved *Confederacy* and got it published by LSU Press in 1980.

Declaring, "I walk the world for my son," Thelma Toole read her
boy's book on television and radio, singing "Sometimes I'm Happy,"
between passages.[10] The following year, the novel won the Pulitzer.
To date it has sold more than 1.5 million copies, thus fulfilling—posthumously—the prophecy of Toole's protagonist: "I suppose you want
to become a success or something equally vile."[11]

》》

American novelists aren't alone in paying dues to the muse.

Complained an editor to Gustave Flaubert about *Madame Bovary:*
"You have buried your novel underneath a heap of details which are
well done but utterly superfluous." In a 2007 writer's poll, it was voted
the second greatest novel of all time, behind *Anna Karenina*. The

---

10 Mark Seinfelt, *Final Drafts: Suicides of World-Famous Authors* (Prometheus Books, 1999).

11 Joel L. Fletcher, *Ken and Thelma: The Story of a Confederacy of Dunces* (Louisiana: Pelican
Publishing, 2005).

adulterous romance both scandalized and thrilled France, becoming a bestseller after Flaubert was acquitted of obscenity charges. He had toiled many years on the title, spending days in search of what he called "*le mot juste*"—the right word.

The same perfectionism had dominated the composition of *The Temptation of St. Anthony*. His own friends found it so superfluous they had urged Flaubert to burn it. But like his ascetic hero, the French realist conquered his demons to declare, "You can calculate the worth of a man by the number of his enemies, and the importance of a work of art by the harm that is spoken of it."[12]

Meanwhile, in Russia, Dostoyevsky enjoyed success with his Siberia memoir *House of the Dead*, but his surreal follow-up, *The Double*, tanked. In his next novel, *Notes from Underground*, he explained, "If I write as if I were addressing an audience, it is only for show. ... It is a form, nothing else; I shall never have any readers." He called himself "a mouse, not even an insect."

Meanwhile, Dostoyevsky's colleague Nikolai Gogol was working on *Dead Souls II*. The first installment had earned him kudos. But now, having found religion, he worried that a sequel might earn him a place in Hell. So he burnt the manuscript, explaining to horrified colleagues that the sacrifice was a joke played on him by the Devil. Then he took to bed and stopped eating. Vodka was poured over his head and leeches applied to his nose. Even so, nine days later, he stopped breathing, though rumors persist that he was buried alive.[13]

Most other burners were dowsed. Emperor Augustus ignored Virgil's instructions that his *Aeneid* be torched. Petrarch persuaded Boccaccio not to commit *The Decameron* to a bonfire of the vanities. Max Brod violated Kafka's dying wish that his work be destroyed. Lavinia Dickinson did the same after her sister, Emily, passed.

Evelyn Waugh followed tradition. His father was a publisher and his older brother, Alec, already a novelist of note. Before sending them his own maiden effort, *The Temple at Thatch*, he consulted his poet friend Harold Acton. "It was an airy Firbankian trifle, totally unworthy

---

12 Geoffrey Wall, *Flaubert, A life* (New York: Farrar, Straus, and Giroux, 2002).

13 James B. Woodward, *Gogol's Dead Souls* (Princeton University Press, 1978).

of Evelyn, and I brutally told him so," the critic recalled. Waugh burned the manuscript, then tried to drown himself in the sea. Luckily, he had "a sharp return to good sense" after being stung by jellyfish. He clambered to shore to write *Brideshead Revisited*.[14]

>>>

Waugh later told the BBC, "A poor dotty Irishman called James Joyce ... thought to be a great influence in my youth ... wrote absolute rot."

Many editors agreed with this assessment of this author, now acknowledged as one of the greatest fiction innovators in history.

In his 1913 application to the Royal Literary Fund for a small stipend, Joyce summed up his efforts: "My literary work in the last eleven years has produced nothing." After *Dubliners* was rejected by forty publishers, he wrote a friend from the Rome bank where he was working, "My mouth is full of decayed teeth and my soul of decayed ambitions."[15]

Five hundred copies of the story collection were finally printed. By 1915, only 379 had sold, 120 to Joyce himself. He called the venture "disastrous." He then destroyed his first novel, *Stephen Hero*, after a fight with his wife, Nora, who pestered him to write something "people can understand." He resurrected the project as *A Portrait of the Artist as a Young Man*. This title was rejected by twenty houses, finally to be published by The Egoist Press, but with scarcely more sales than *Dubliners*.

The dotty Irishman's masterpiece, *Ulysses*, was serialized in a French lit mag edited by his friend Ezra Pound. The run was killed on obscenity charges. The ms. was picked up by a hole-in-the-wall Parisian printer, Shakespeare & Co., only to be banned again, then burned at the New York post office.

While the expatriated novelist toiled seventeen years on his swan song, *Finnegans Wake*, his secretary, Samuel Beckett, was taking a beating on his own first novel, *The Dream of Fair-to-Middling Women*.

"I wouldn't touch this with a barge pole," said one editor.

Joyce refused to help because Beckett had recently spurned the advances of his schizophrenic daughter, Lucia. The two legends

---

14 Selena Hastings, *Evelyn Waugh: A Biography* (New York: Houghton Mifflin, 1995).

15 Richard Ellmann, *James Joyce* (Oxford University Press, 1983).

reconciled when the young existentialist was almost fatally stabbed in Paris, and Joyce secured him a hospital bed. But Beckett's *Women* didn't see the light of day until 1993, four years after he died and twenty-four years after he received the Nobel Prize, which he called a "catastrophe."

In spite of such difficulties, many masters in the end agreed with William Saroyan. After accumulating a pile of rejections thirty inches high (approximately 7,000 in all) the Pulitzer Prize–winning novelist declared, "We get very little wisdom from success, you know."[16]

But what of women writers?

For years they had been struggling to break the literary glass ceiling. Speaking for her sisters, Charlotte Brontë wrote, "We had a vague impression that authoresses are liable to be looked on with prejudice."[17] So she, Emily, and Anne became Currer, Ellis, and Acton Bell; Mary Anne Evans became George Eliot; the Baroness Dudevant became George Sand; and Louisa May Alcott became A.M. Barnard. But pseudonyms weren't enough to dampen the chauvinism of their male colleagues.

"She is stupid, heavy, and garrulous," said Baudelaire of Sand. "Her ideas on morals have the same depth of judgment and delicacy of feeling as those of janitresses and kept women. ... The fact that there are men who could become enamored of this slut is indeed a proof of the abasement of the men of this generation."[18]

Many attribute the dearth of pre-twentieth-century women writers to the hard-wired bias of otherwise permissive men such as Baudelaire. But any study of literary history, and of art history generally, shows that true artists compulsively create in spite of any and all obstacles and social barriers. So one can only conclude that women did indeed write, but few tried to get published knowing the futility of this in a male-dominated society and industry.

The Atlantic fiction editor James T. Fields wrote Louisa May Alcott's father, Bronson, the scholar and women's suffrage champion: "Tell

16 http://thinkexist.com/quotation

17 "Biographical Notice of Ellis And Acton Bell," from the preface to the 1910 edition of *Wuthering Heights.*

18 Charles Baudelaire, *My Heart Laid Bare* (UK: Weidenfeld & Nicolson Ltd., 1950).

Louisa to stick to her teaching; she can never succeed as a writer." The
budding novelist, then using the pen name A.M. Bernard, retorted:
"Tell him I will succeed as a writer, and some day I shall write for *The
Atlantic*!" A few years later, so she did. Soon afterwards, in 1868, she
published the best-selling *Little Women*.

In 1912, London publisher Arthur Fifield rejected Gertrude Stein's
first novel, *Three Lives*, about the struggles of three women. "Having
only one life, I cannot read your ms. three or four times," he wrote. "Not
even one time. Only one look, only one look is enough. Hardly one copy
would sell here. Hardly one. Hardly one. Many thanks. I am returning
... only one ms. by one post." Stein pressed on with closet printings
and emerged from obscurity two decades later, at age 60, with *The
Autobiography of Alice B. Toklas*. Meanwhile, her poetry was spurned
by everybody.

Three years after the release of *Toklas*, Djuna Barnes' *Nightwood*
at last saw the light of day. Following its rejection by every other publisher, Faber and Faber editor T.S. Eliot took a chance on the novel,
later described by Dylan Thomas as "one of the three great prose
books ever written by a woman." Barnes, then forty-four, received
no advance and a first-year royalty of £43. The reclusive, alcoholic
novelist, who called herself "the unknown legend of American literature," was supported by Peggy Guggenheim for the rest of her life.
When her ardent admirer Anaïs Nin later begged her to contribute
to an anthology of women's writing, she refused to even respond.
When Carson McCullers camped at her door, Barnes cried from
behind it, "Whoever is ringing this bell, please go the hell away!" Her
Greenwich Village neighbor E.E. Cummings regularly shouted out
his window, "Are you still alive, Djuna?"

Sylvia Plath's *The Bell Jar* was at last published by the UK-based
Heinemann in 1963 under the pseudonym Victoria Lucas. The autobiographical novel had been rejected by Harper & Row as "juvenile and
overwrought." While acknowledging her "female brashness," Knopf
had concluded that "there certainly isn't enough genuine talent for us
to take notice." When the novel finally came out, *The New Yorker*'s
Howard Moss dismissed it as "amateur" and "girlish." By this time, in
spite of her hypersensitivity, Plath had developed scar tissue of sorts. "I

love my rejection slips," she said. "They show me I try." Early on, she had collected forty-five from *Seventeen* magazine alone.

Today, Janet Fitch, the author of the best-selling *White Oleander*, an Oprah Book Club selection, tells all her students that rejection is a professional necessity: "Until you have a hundred rejections, you're really not a writer." Her own novel had grown from a short story published in the *Black Warrior Review* after being rejected by many other lit mag editors, including Joyce Carol Oates at *The Ontario Review*.

The late, great editor Ted Solotaroff agreed: "How well a writer copes with rejection determines whether he has a genuine literary vocation or just a literary flair."[19]

---

19 Ted Solotaroff, "Writing in the Cold," from essay collection *A Few Good Voices in My Head: Occasional Pieces on Writing, Editing, and Reading My Contemporaries* (New York: HarperCollins, 1987).

CHAPTER 13

THE WONDER

"Look, writing a novel is like paddling from Boston to London in a bathtub. Sometimes the damn tub sinks. It's a wonder that most of them don't."

—**Stephen King,** *The Paris Review* **interview**

Serious literature does not have a monopoly on rejection.

"Publishing is a brutal business," writes Patrick Anderson in *The Triumph of the Thriller: How Cops, Crooks, and Cannibals Captured Popular Fiction*. "For every writer who makes it big there are a thousand who don't."

After reviewing Jacqueline Susann's original *The Valley of the Dolls* manuscript, Don Preston reported to his boss, Bernard Geis: "She is a painfully dull, inept, clumsy, undisciplined, rambling and thoroughly amateurish writer whose every sentence, paragraph and scene cries out for the hands of a pro."[1] So the populist publisher ordered his editor to sign her anyway and go pro himself. Preston put

---

1 "One Hundred Famous Rejections," May 22, 2012.

his nose to the editorial grindstone, vetted *Dolls* from T to A, and the "porn-lite" ms. went on to sell 30 million copies.[2]

Noted New York agent Aaron Priest told singer/songwriter/business school dean Robert James Waller that his 42,000-word ms., *The Bridges of Madison County*, was "pretty odd" and "not the kind of stuff that sells." He sent it out anyway as a favor to his Pulitzer client Jane Smiley, the ex-wife of Waller's friend and essay editor Bill Silag, who ran the Iowa State University Press. Time Warner snapped the novel up for a song and unloaded 50 million copies.[3]

The professional prognosis for another industry record breaker, *Harry Potter and the Philosopher's Stone*, had seemed even gloomier. J.K. Rowling weathered twelve rejections. The magical adventure may never have seen the light of day had Alice Newton, the eight-year-old daughter of Bloomsbury's CEO, not given the ms. a thumbs-up and her father not hesitantly advanced £1,500 for the title. Topping any sorcery in the series, *Potter* turned the welfare mother into history's first billionaire author, leaving her YA colleagues in the dust. "I think it is probably fair to say that most children's authors struggle along earning about £2,000 a year," said Christopher Little, Rowling's agent.[4] While the novelist was penning the fantasy in London cafes, she had battled suicidal depression, which gave her the idea for the happiness-sucking Dementors. Though she had pressed on and overcome her demons, George W. Bush, like monarchs of old, turned her down for the Presidential Medal of Freedom because of her witchcraft.

Fellow supernaturalist Stephen King also paid his literary dues before hitting the horror mother lode. He cut his teeth on *Steve King's Garbage Truck*, a University of Maine newspaper column. After graduation he hawked stories to men's magazines. Then he hit a wall with

---

2 Richard Fuller, "Jacqueline Susann's Life in Writing," *Philadelphia Inquirer*, February 26, 1988. http://articles.philly.com/1988-02-26/entertainment/26242810_1_bernard-geis-associates-irving-mansfield-life-of-jacqueline-susann

3 Jack Doyle, "Of Bridges & Lovers, 1992-1995," June 25, 2008. http://www.pophistorydig.com/?tag=amblin-entertainment

4 *Accio Quote!* (J.K. Rowling archive). www.accio-quote.org/articles/1997/spring97-telegraph-reynolds.htm

Carrie, rejected by thirty publishers. "We are not interested in science fiction which deals with negative utopias. They do not sell," said one.[5]

Drunk and disgusted, King tossed the thriller in the trash. "My considered opinion was that I had written the world's all-time loser," he recalled. His writer wife, Tabitha, fished it out and urged him to give it another shot. Doing so, the twenty-six-year-old novelist was hardly more optimistic: "I didn't expect much of *Carrie*," he went on. "I thought, who'd want to read a book about a poor little girl with menstrual problems? I couldn't believe I was writing it."[6]

While teaching high school English by day, he finished the tale by night on a portable typewriter in his trailer. Doubleday picked it up, and the title quickly sold a million copies. His dedication read: *This is for Tabby, who got me into it—and then bailed me out of it.*[7]

Finally, we come to the case of sensation Stieg Larsson, whose *Millenium* trilogy has outsold Grisham, Brown, and King combined. As a teen he founded two science fiction fanzines and published his rejected stories; in the 1990s he turned to crime fiction, which he burned due to further rejection.[8] After failing to gain admission to the Stockholm School of Journalism, nobody would hire him even as a reporter. He traveled to Africa for fresh material but returned to Sweden broke and with malaria. He worked at the post office, then as a news agency staffer. In his spare time he launched *Expo*, an anti-Nazi leaflet and received his first fan mail—skinhead death threats. Freaked, fed up, and exhausted, he told a friend: "Nobody cares, nobody gives us any money. I need a one-time solution."[9]

Which was? "I will write a couple of books and become a

---

5 www.writersservices.com/mag/m_rejection.htm

6 Robert W. Wells, "From Textbook to Checkbook," *Milwaukee Journal*, September 15, 1980.

7 Khaled Hosseini also has his wife to thank for the completion of *The Kite Runner*. The celebrated debut novel which, like *Carrie*, became a major motion picture, started out as a short story. The author abandoned it for two years, concentrating on his L.A. medical practice. He said he returned to it after "my wife dug it up," read it, and started crying. ("Success Stories: First Novelists, Debut Novelists.") http://www.bookmarket.com/debutnovels.htm

8 Michelle Paull, "Unpublished Stieg Larsson Manuscripts Discovered," June 9, 2010. http://www.guardian.co.uk/books/2010/jun/09/stieg-larsson-unpublished-manuscripts?INTCMP=SRCH

9 Nathaniel Rich, "The Mystery of the Dragon Tattoo," *Rolling Stone*, December 23, 2010.

millionaire," he told his collaborator, Mikael Ekman, over whiskeys one night in 2001. Ekman laughed, calling him crazy. Stieg stubbornly set to work. The next year he asked another writer friend, Kurdo Baksi, if he might be interested in taking a look at a nearly completed thriller. Baksi, too, thought it was a joke. "Stieg, I don't think you're so good at literature."

The first installment of the Millennium trilogy, *The Girl with the Dragon Tattoo*, was released three years later, making its author a posthumous millionaire. Larsson suffered a fatal heart attack just prior to its release by Norstedts.[10]

But some remain skeptical about the authorship, thinking his common law wife, Eva Gabrielsson, a writer and translator, might have had a hand in it. Another former journalist colleague and mentor, Anders Hellberg, described Larrson's early writing as "impossible." "Nothing was good," he told *The New York Times'* Charles McGrath, "not the syntax, the way of putting things, nothing."

Couldn't Larsson have improved since the early years? the reporter pressed the skeptic.

Hellberg admitted that he didn't know but was certain of one thing: "I believe that to write is a talent. You don't just pick up a guy from the bus station and expect him to do it."[11]

---

10 According to *The New Yorker's* Joan Acocella ("Man of Mystery," January 10, 2011), Piratförlag, the first publisher to whom Larsson submitted, returned his ms. unopened because they refused to consider debut novelists.

11 Charles McGrath, "The Afterlife of Stieg Larsson," *New York Times*, December 20, 2010.

CHAPTER 14

THE RED BADGE OF COURAGE

"It was a crushing defeat but put iron in my backbone and sulfur in my blood. I knew at least what it was to fail."

—**Henry Miller, after the rejection of his first novel,**
Clipped Wings

"Eighty percent of success is showing up," declared *Without Feathers'* Woody Allen.

For many, the idea of writing for a living is a siren call because it seems to be the one profession exempt from this rule, that authors become rich and famous by spinning fantasies at home in bed like Proust—without ever having to change out of their pajamas and dress for rehearsal. Cheating death and becoming immortal in the written word is the cherry on top, making the profession sound too good to be true.

Which, of course, it is.

Even so, the literary population explosion has sprung from this fantasy of fame, fortune, and immortality with little or no inconvenience. And without having to bone up like, say, a brain surgeon or nuclear physicist. After all, anybody who can read can write. As for the technicalities, a NewNovelist plot generator and SmartWrite cliché check cover that.

But even before computers and million-dollar advances, writers were cropping up everywhere.

In the Book of Ecclesiastes, King Solomon was the first to sound the overpopulation alarm. "...Of making many books there is no end; and much study is a weariness of the flesh."

Martin Luther, after nailing his self-published *Ninety-Five Theses* on the Wittenberg church door, agreed: "The multitude of books is a great evil. There is no limit to this fever for writing."

Even before the flood of vanity printings and e-books, Pulitzer Prize winner James Michener told wannabes, "Unless you think you can do better than Tolstoy, we don't need you." In spite of selling 75 million books, none of his historic travelogues rivaled *War and Peace* or *Anna Karenina* except in length. But with his army of researchers, the novelist cranked out forty doorstops anyway, making no effort to reduce his own literary carbon footprint.

Other greats have tried to put a condom on the literary baby boom by depressing, if not scaring off, wannabe Tolstoys. John Gardner, the luminary of New England's Breadloaf Conference, complained: "There are other writers who would persuade you not to go on, that everything is nonsense, that you should kill yourself. They, of course, go on to write another book while you have killed yourself."

Recently *Eat, Pray, Love's* Elizabeth Gilbert scolded *Portnoy's Complaint* author Philip Roth for discouraging an upstart. When Julian Tepper, Roth's waiter at a New York deli, gave the Pulitzer Prize winner his just-published novel, *Balls*, about a songwriter with testicular cancer, Roth told him, "Quit while you're ahead. Really. It's an awful field. Just torture." In her *Bookish* piece, Gilbert told her literary idol, "Take it easy on the complaining, OK?"[1] She insisted that, compared to most other professions, writing is "f---ing great." You don't have to wear a nametag, put up with sexual abuse, or risk amputation by machinery, she pointed out. She urged Roth to appreciate that he was "*phenomenally* lucky … blessed and not blighted" and so should

---

1 Elizabeth Gilbert, "Roth's Complaint," *Bookish*, February 4, 2013. www.bookish.com/articles/elizabeth-gilbert-takes-on-philip-roth

welcome newcomers "who want to follow you into this marvelously pointless and wonderfully unproductive occupation." In fact, Roth had just announced that he was throwing in the towel after more than fifty years in the trenches.

Other veteran authors are not welcoming to newcomers because they would prefer less competition. Martin Amis, who followed in his father's footsteps to become a prolific novelist himself, confided to *The Paris Review*: "I feel generally resentful of younger writers. You're not thrilled to see some blazing talent coming up on your flank." Editor/agent/author Betsy Lerner confirms this, declaring: "Dislike and resentment of younger writers is something fairly universal among writers."

More than a few "Purple Heart" authors resent younger colleagues who have made overnight fortunes with little more than a paper cut. Recent Publishers Clearing House winners, as we will see in the next chapter, "Luck, Suck, & Pluck," include *Prep's* Curtis Sittenfeld, "Lucky Girls" Nell Freudenberger, and *Girls'* Lena Dunham.

"Nothing is more humiliating than to see idiots succeed in enterprises we have failed at," Flaubert fumed. But the real object of his resentment wasn't idiot colleagues so much as the idiot readers who made them rich. "Human stupidity is limitless," he constantly complained.

Emerson was on the same page: "People do not deserve good writing, they are so pleased with the bad."

Steinbeck went further. The reader is "part moron, part genius, and part ogre. There is some doubt as to whether he can read."

Some best-selling authors agreed. "It took me fifteen years to discover I had no talent for writing," confessed *Newsweek* editor, LBJ speechwriter, and *Jaws* creator Peter Benchley. "But I couldn't give it up because by that time I was too famous."[2]

John Grisham, who by 2008 had sold 250 million copies of his legal thrillers, beginning with his self-published *A Time to Kill*, echoed: "My success was not planned, but it could only happen in America." He

---

2 Dolores Gregory, "Benchley: Seeing a Famous Forebear Whole," *Washington Post*, February 18, 2003.

added, "I'm a famous writer in a country where nobody reads."[3]

Kurt Vonnegut grew so cynical that after writing the poorly reviewed but popular *Slapstick* he shrugged, "Everybody else writes lousy books, so why shouldn't I?"[4]

In any case, rejections—whether by colleagues, critics, editors, or readers—are the dues most every writer must pay to the muse. Some more, some less. In this sense, serious professionals are not judged by how many acceptances they have enjoyed, but how many rejections they have weathered, earning them the red badge of courage.

Today, stubborn persistence is indispensable to the writer—literary or popular—even more than yesterday.

"I finished my first book seventy-six years ago," wrote George Bernard Shaw. "I offered it to every publisher on the English-speaking earth. Their refusals were unanimous: and I did not get into print until, fifty years later, publishers would publish anything that had my name on it."[5]

Fellow Nobel laureate John Steinbeck had the same experience. By 1934, he reckoned that he'd made $870 for seven years of nonstop writing. "I am so tired. I have worked for so long against opposition, first of my parents ... then of publishers. ... Rejection follows rejection." He finally scored an agent, Mavis McIntosh, but even she couldn't place his *To a God Unknown*. She told him—as reps do their clients today—that the market for unknown writers was "extremely tight and unpredictable."

Still, *The Grapes of Wrath* creator didn't lose hope. "Eventually I shall be so good that I cannot be ignored," he decided. "These years are disciplinary for me."[6]

---

3 "Grisham's Gospel." *Newsweek/Daily Beast.* February 14, 1999.

4 *The Paris Review* self-interview, No. 69, 1977.

5 www.goodreads.com/quotes/show13709

6 Jay Parini, *John Steinbeck: A Biography* (New York: Henry Holt, 1995).

PART IV

LUCK, SUCK, & PLUCK

Secrets of Literary Success

"Once all struggle is grasped,
miracles are possible."
—Mao Tse-Tung,
after selling 1 billion copies of his poems

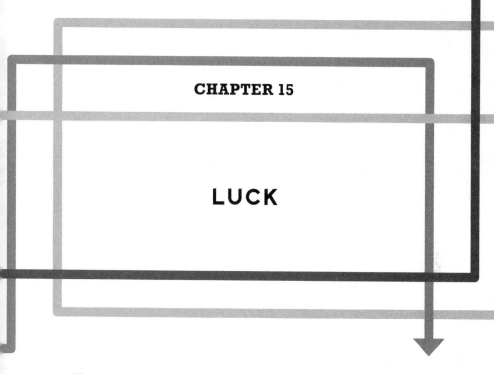

CHAPTER 15

LUCK

"Read the racing form. There you have the true art of fiction."
—Ernest Hemingway
(*The Paris Review* interview, 1958)

Authors envy athletes. When a sprinter does the one hundred in nine seconds flat—no matter what his style, training, or history—he's the best on the track. Indisputable. Same with skiing, soccer, tennis. So, too, with science and math. All are objective enterprises.

Not so with publishing. Editors and agents concede as much in their rejections. "…Not right for us at this time. But this is a very subjective business, and you may well find someone else who…" etc. Signed with the boilerplate, "Good luck."

In his "Eight Factors of Literary Success," Jack London listed "Vast good luck"[1] first, and ended with: "Because I got started twenty years before the fellows who are trying to start today." He'd decided to make a fortune from "my brain" in the casino of publishing after going bust in the Klondike Gold Rush. He won $40 from *Black Cat* magazine for

---

1 *The Silhouette* magazine, 1917.

"A Thousand Deaths." "Literally and literarily, I was saved," he wrote of
his debut story about resurrection.

Other breaks were more serendipitous. Pulitzer prize–winning
Michael Chabon thanked *Newsweek* for misidentifying him as a promising gay writer. "I feel very lucky about all of that. It really opened
up a new readership to me, and a very loyal one," the author of *The
Mysteries of Pittsburgh*, his MFA thesis, told *The New York Times*.[2]

Truman Capote, the self-proclaimed creator of the "nonfiction
novel," told *The Paris Review*, "You would have to be a glutton indeed
to ask for more good luck and fortune than I had at the beginning of my
career." His first break was when his beauty queen teen mother didn't
abort him as she had her next two children, fearing that they would be
like Truman.[3] At age ten, his first story, "Old Mr. Busybody," won the
Mobile Press children's writing contest. At seventeen, he was hired as
a gofer at *The New Yorker*,[4] but Robert Frost got him fired for walking
out of a 1944 poetry reading (due, Truman insisted, to the flu and a stiff
neck). Soon the young man's "Miriam" won *Mademoiselle's* Best First-
Published story, which he parlayed into a stint at Yaddo.

Pulitzer Prize-winner Richard Ford described himself to *The Paris
Review* as "anomalous—a rare combination of fear, an affection for
language, a reverence for literature, doggedness, and good luck." He
added, "Shit, who's going to fall heir or victim to all those things?" At
the beginning of his career he didn't have much luck at all. His first two
novels, *A Piece of My Heart* and *The Ultimate Good Luck*, sold poorly, so
he went to work for *Inside Sports* magazine. Four years later, Ford, age
forty-two, released his breakout novel, *The Sportswriter*, about a failed
novelist turned sportswriter. Celebrating his ultimate good luck with
this third at bat, and knowing that few in the profession are so blessed,
he told poet Bonnie Lyons, "My first advice to an aspiring writer is
to talk yourself out of it if you can possibly do it." Why? she asked.

---

2 Lewis Buzbee, "Michael Chabon: Comics Came First," *New York Times*, Books section,
September 24, 2000.

3 Gerald Clarke, *Capote: A Biography* (Linden Publishers, 1988) *The Winston Review.* September 9, 2001.
http://thewinstonreview.com/2011/09/09/capote-he-was-nearly-aborted/

4 Eric Hanson, "Innocence and Experience," *The Atlantic*, October 2008. www.theatlantic.com/
magazine/archive/2008/10/innocence-and-experience/6992/

"Because you'll probably fail and make yourself miserable doing it," he replied.

After Alice Sebold was raped in a Syracuse tunnel, the police told her she was lucky because she hadn't been murdered like another women recently found in the same tunnel. Her first book, *Lucky*, was a memoir about the incident written for her MFA at UC Irvine, Ford's alma mater. She followed it up with *The Lovely Bones*, her best-selling novel about another rape and murder.

Luckily, the lovely twenty-six-year-old Nell Freudenberger didn't have to suffer the same fate to write her short story "Lucky Girls," one of four debut pieces in *The New Yorker's* 2001 Fiction edition. But the Harvard grad was lucky enough to be the personal assistant to editor-in-chief David Remnick. She was soon offered a $500,000 deal from HarperCollins for a short-story collection she had not yet written. Her equally fortunate contemporary, Curtis Sittenfeld, profiled the Publishers Clearing House winner in "Too Young, Too Pretty, Too Successful" for *Salon*. Though Richard Ford himself called her "a prodigious talent," Sittenfeld wrote: "Hating Nell Freudenberger is a virtual cottage industry among ambitious literati" because she represented "all that's unfair and demoralizing about publishing."

At age seventeen, while attending the exclusive Groton School, Sittenfeld won the *Seventeen* fiction contest went on to attend Vassar, then the Stanford and Iowa writing programs. Finally, at age twenty-nine, she published her bestseller *Prep*. In her subsequent *Atlantic* magazine essay, "The Perils of Literary Success," Sittenfeld provided the backstory for her luck, which she described as, "not good but extraordinary."[5] Although a debut novel, *Prep* was assigned four Random House publicists—the kind of support which Sittenfeld's editor, Lee Boudreaux, told her only celebrity biographer Kitty Kelley rated. "Team Prep" sent to women's magazine editors pink gift baskets containing the novel, flip-flops, and Fun Flavored Lip Smackers Lip Gloss. Just after the book's release, Sittenfeld donned designer clothes and draped herself on a Groton Latin teacher's desk for a *Vanity Fair* photo

---

5 Curtis Sittenfeld, "The Perils of Literary Success," *The Atlantic,* Fiction Issue 2005. www.theatlantic. com/magazine/archive/2005/08/the-perils-of-literary-success/4132/

shoot. In her *Atlantic* memoir, she couldn't disagree with critics who characterized her as a "sell-out" and her novel as a "corporate hype job." Even so, thanks to it, when *Prep* hit the *Times* bestseller list, she confessed that she, her editors, and Team Prep "squealed profusely." She then signed a two-book deal with Random House, collecting an advance that, "to put the matter delicately," she concluded, "was more than $40,000 [her debut advance]."

At the same time, Stephenie Meyer—a thirty-two-year-old receptionist and mother of three, with no prior writing experience—scored a $750,000 advance from Little Brown for her Twilight series. By 2010, the YA vampire romance had sold 116 million copies worldwide and inspired the current blockbuster, E.L. James' *Fifty Shades of Grey* trilogy. When asked how she got published, Meyer replied, "Sheer luck or fate. I had the easiest publishing experience in the entire world."[6] Fourteen agents had rejected *Twilight.* The fifteenth—an assistant to Jodi Reamer at Writer's House—rescued the manuscript from the slush pile, and the rest was history. "It's a mystery to me," added the author, "I never intended to be a writer." She precautioned others who expected the same jackpot to "get ready for heartbreak." When asked by another interviewer how her luck might sound to still struggling peers, she said, "Ohhh, other writers are going to hate me."[7]

Publishing's current Cinderella is Lena Dunham, creator of the hit HBO series *Girls.* Based on a sixty-six-page proposal, Random House advanced the Oberlin creative writing grad $3.7 million for an essay collection, *Not That Kind of Girl: A Young Woman Tells You What She's Learned.* An "I hate Lena Dunham" Google search produces more than a million hits. According to the *Huffington Post,*[8] other scribes are even more insanely jealous of the latest lit It Girl than Salieri was of Mozart. A St. Anne's preppie and daughter of well-heeled TriBeCa artists, Dunham launched her career not with a query letter but with a

---

6 Rebecca Murray, *About.com* interview with Stephenie Meyer. http://movies.about.com/od/twilight/a/stephenie-meyer_2.htm

7 Cecilia Goodnow, "Debut Writer Shines with *Twilight,*" *Seattle Post-Intelligencer,* October 7, 2005.

8 Keli Goff, "Does Lena Dunham Prove Writers Are as Toxic as Investment Bankers?" *Huffington Post,* January 14, 2013. www.huffingtonpost.com/keli-goff/does-lena-dunham-prove-wr_b_2470162.html

six-minute YouTube clip of her outsized, tatted self soaping up in the Oberlin College fountain, followed by a $50,000 home movie (*Tiny Furniture*) bankrolled by and starring her mother. How different the history of women's literature might have been had Jane Austen and Emily Dickinson had such balls and supportive parents.

Speaking for yesterday's less fortunate, as well as the S.O.L. MFAs today who resent Freudenberger, Meyer, and Dunham, if not Ms. Sittenfeld, the surrealist poet and novelist Jean Cocteau declared: "We must believe in luck. For how else can we explain the success of those we don't like?"

》》》

Editor-speak centers around luck: "gamble," "long shot," "safe bet," "dark horse." In publishing, like at Caesars and MGM Grande, the house almost always wins, and when it loses, the losses are passed along to the customers playing the one-arm bandits—midlisters, back-listers, and untouchables. Sub-Performing Marginal People.

Many masters were compulsive gamblers: Montaigne, Poe, Twain, Dickens, Pushkin, Saroyan, and Graham Greene, to name a few.

Consider the track records of their colleagues at the tables.

At age twenty-one, Thackeray gambled away his inheritance. After going bust at cards, Conrad shot himself but missed his heart. Tolstoy covered his Chinese billiard tab by selling off the rights to his unfinished novel, *The Cossacks*. After another losing streak, the count unloaded his horses and part of his estate. Belly up again, he borrowed from Turgenev, who denounced him for "orgies, gypsy dance halls, and playing cards all night."[9]

The Russian roulette posterboy, Dostoyevsky, described his "abominable passion" as "irresistible." After losing his *Crime and Punishment* rubles at the Wiesbaden tables, he made a bet with his publisher, F.T. Stellovsky: He would deliver *The Gambler* within months or would forfeit royalties on all future novels for nine years. He won. Then he lost his *Gambler* and *Idiot* royalties to the Germans, plus his wife's wedding ring, his watch, and his trousers.

---

9 Neil Heims, *Tortured Noble: The Story of Leo Tolstoy* (Morgan Reynolds Publishing, 2007).

Dostoyevsky might have realized he had bad luck after being arrested for attending socialist meetings, thrown in front of a mock firing squad, and then sent to Siberia. But Russia's premiere novelist had the unique ability to find silver linings in his dark clouds. "Prison saved me," he wrote his brother. "I became a completely new person. ... Yes, Siberia and imprisonment became a great joy for me." His biographer, Gier Kjetsaa, found a parallel masochism in his gambling addiction, calling it "an unconscious desire to lose and punish himself by losing."[10]

Voltaire was among the few who cashed in by leaving nothing to chance. He'd seen too many of his friends fleeced, including his mistress, Mme du Chatelet, a writer herself, who lost most of her fortune at the Queen's gaming tables. "Each player," he said, "must accept the cards life deals him or her: but once they are in hand, he or she alone must decide how to play the cards in order to win the game." His words applied equally to the publishing game, then and now.

Avoiding royal "card-sharpers" as he called them, the satirist became independently wealthy by winning the French lottery with a syndicate that bought every ticket.[11] The nest egg allowed him to finish two thousand books and "blogs" with little or no royalties until, at age seventy-four, he finally hit the jackpot with *Candide*. Voltaire's hero, not unlike himself, suffers one bout of bad luck after another—he is swindled, is nearly beaten to death, and barely survives a lynching and an earthquake, and settles down on a scrub farm with a toothless wife in the end.

The Father of the French Enlightenment subtitled the novel *The Optimist*.

---

10 Gier Kjetsaa, *Fyodor Dostoyevsky: A Writer's Life* (New York: Ballantine Books, 1989).

11 Robert Hendrickson, *The Literary Life and Other Curiosities* (New York: Viking, 1981).

THE JOYLESS LUCK CLUB

"It was all pure, brute accident."

> —Wallace Stegner, of his literary success
> (*The Paris Review* interview)

"Sometimes I have good luck and write better than I can."

> —Ernest Hemingway (*The Paris Review* interview)

"Pure dumb luck ... I'm not the new Hemingway."

> —Tom Clancy, of his literary success
> (*The Triumph of the Thriller:* Patrick Anderson)

"There are writers who are much better than I am who are writing away right now who have not been as lucky as I've been."

> —Richard Ford (*Publishers Weekly* interview)

"I'm just the asshole who broke the bank at Monte Carlo."

> —Kurt Vonnegut[12]

"Pros almost always believe in luck."

> —Norman Mailer (*On Being a Writer*,
> Bill Strickland, ed.)

"Get lucky. Stay lucky."

> —Ian Rankin (his two final rules for writing)

---

12 Andrew Purcell, "Kurt Vonnegut's Last Interview," March 17, 2009. www.andrewpurcell.net/?p=50

CHAPTER 16

SUCK

"Anything they [authors] can do to help us—any contacts they may have, for example—I want to know about them. I want them to say, 'You should know that I went to school with so-and-so.' Good, get on the phone with them."

—**Algonquin Books editor-in-chief Chuck Adams**[1]

"I would go a step further ... the author [should be] so well connected that he's sleeping with a producer at ABC News or something."

—**Agent Jeff Kleinman on the "ideal" author**[2]

Most businesses are based, by necessity, on networking.

But publishing makes the Mafia look like an equal opportunity employer.

---

1 Jofie Ferrari-Adler, "A Q&A with Editor Chuck Adams," *Poets & Writers,* November/December 2008. www.pw.org/content/agents_amp_editors_qampa_chuck_adams?article_page=5

2 Jofie Ferrari-Adler, "A Q&A with Four Young Literary Agents," *Poets & Writers,* January/February 2009. www.pw.org/content/agents_amp_editors_qampa_four_young_literary_agents?article_page=2

Industry apologists insist, "The cream always rises to the top." But if the writer hopes to do so in his lifetime and without an aqualung, "suck" is indispensable. Hence the etymology of "success."

As Elaura Niles points out in Truth #16 of *Some Writers Deserve to Starve!: 31 Brutal Truths About the Publishing Industry:* "Success is 80 percent who you know. ... Slow down, Cinderella. Your pumpkin coach has been temporarily delayed until you learn to kiss ass; then you can dance the night away. ... [But] the Kissee shouldn't be aware that his ass has been kissed."

Networking, however, did not come naturally to introverts and sensitive souls like Kafka, Melville, Dickinson, and Toole. And they all suffered for it, as do their counterparts today. Dickens, Twain, Fitzgerald, Oscar Wilde, Dorothy Parker, Truman Capote, Jackie Collins, and their ilk were more fortunate in their ability to work a room.

As Algonquin's Chuck Adams mentions, some of the best luck is that which is leavened with suck—college classmate suck, especially in the Skull and Bones Ivies or MFA programs. F. Scott Fitzgerald was indebted to his Princeton brothers Max Perkins and Edmund Wilson, Bob Loomis helped launch the career of his Duke friend William Styron, Fisketjon broke the ice for his Williams' pal Jay McInerny, Bret Easton Ellis went to bat for his Bennington classmate Donna Tartt, and so on.

Today, it is imperative for even a natural talent and New York Lions Club member to enlist a suck surrogate or Sancho Panza: an agent. We will discuss these long-suffering and selfless individuals at length later on. For now let's examine the other main enablers of literary success.

FAMILY

The Ptolemies, Caesars, Medici, and Bonapartes have nothing on literary blood dynasties. First there were the Brontës, the Adams family, and James Gang; then the Sitwells, the Waughs, the Mitfords, the Tolkiens; and now *The New Yorker* clan descended, in spite of its long-standing "No Nepotism" rule, from the Whites.

Saul Bellow's son, Adam, covered today's other heirs in his *In Praise of Nepotism.*[3]

He argues that publishing has run smoothly by a DNA Darwinian imperative. Not all literary patriarchs agree: Faulkner once told his daughter, Jill, "No one remembers Shakespeare's children."

So to suggest that heirs have an edge might be unfair. But that pedigree may have helped Adam get a foot in the door could be considered a possibility, at least by the suckless.

The emerging writer does not necessarily need a pedigree to cash in on family suck, just a concerned mother: Maude Faulkner's and Thelma Toole's die-hard efforts for their sons have been mentioned.

Fitzgerald's mom, Mollie, didn't help him, per se. But he did confess to inheriting her "relentless stubborn quality," not to mention her "neurotic, half insane with pathological nervous worry." So he dedicated his *Tales of the Jazz Age* "inappropriately, to my mother." In addition to the fourteen publishers who rejected his first poetry collection, E.E. Cummings dedicated *No Thanks* to Mrs. C., who paid for the printing.

Such dedications disgusted Hemingway. Grace had pampered Ernest, outfitting him in dresses and organdy hats and calling him "Ernestine."[4] So he might have thanked his mom for his no-frills, testosterone-driven prose. Instead he told his publisher, Charles Scribner, "I hate her guts and she hates mine." She and her husband, Clarence, had ordered five copies of his *In Our Time* debut but had returned them to the publishers as "filth." Grace also found *The Sun Also Rises* "one of the filthiest books of the year." Like any good mother, wanting only what was best for her son, she'd hoped he would become a doctor like his dad.

---

3 William Buckley's, Christopher; Ann Rice's Christopher; James Dickey's Christopher; Andre Dubus II's III; Bill Styron's Alexandra; Paul Theroux's Alexander and Marcel; Kingsley Amis's Martin; Kurt Vonnegut's Mark; J.D. Salinger's Margaret; Erica Jong and Jonathan Fast's Molly; John McPhee's Martha and Jenny; John Cheever's Susan and Ben (married to NYT critic, Janet Maslin); John Updike's David; E.L. Doctorow's Cory; Joseph Heller's Ted; Norman Mailer's John Buffalo; E.B. White's Roger Angell; etc.

4 James R. Mellow, *Hemingway: A Life Without Consequence* (New York: Houghton Mifflin, 1992).

LOVERS

Hemingway dedicated his debut novel to his first wife, Hadley, eight years his senior, who some called a mother surrogate. Her $3,000-a-year trust allowed him to write and network full-time on the Montparnasse. Her praise—"Sometimes when I wake up and see his beautiful face, I think I'm sleeping with Christ"—bolstered his self-confidence. He traded in Hadley on *Vogue* editor and trust funder Pauline Pfeiffer, to whom he dedicated *A Farewell to Arms*. As a consolation, he gave Hadley his *Sun Also Rises* royalties.

Suck is a natural by-product of money, no less than royalty.

Oscar Wilde's wife, Constance, daughter of the Queen's Counsel, Horace Lloyd, provided the poet with the comforts he required as well as the connections to launch *The Happy Prince*.

The Duke of Argyll's daughter, Lady Jeanne, did the same for her husband, Norman Mailer, when his career was flagging. Heiress Peggy Guggenheim helped launch her lover Samuel Beckett's breakout novel, *Murphy*. Lit Brat Pack icon Jay McInerny has settled down with publishing heiress Anne Hearst. Jerzy Kosinski dedicated his first novel, *The Painted Bird*, to his first wife, Mary Weir, of the Pittsburgh steel fortune, then he traded up to Countess Kiki Fraunhofer, who published his collected works.

Anaïs Nin, the wife of a wealthy Boston banker, bankrolled the vanity printing of her lover Henry Miller's *Tropic of Cancer*. Calling him "a master of self-promotion … and gifted user of other people," Miller's biographer praised his "army of friends … who acted as unpaid literary agents for him." According to his friend Wambly Bald, Miller had "milked Anaïs, like he milked everyone he met."[5] Another enabler, George Orwell, helped launch the novelist's career with his 1940 "Inside the Whale" endorsement: "Here in my opinion is the only imaginative prose-writer of the slightest value … an amoral writer, a passive acceptor of evil, a sort of Whitman among the corpses."

Miller's first helpmate was his second wife, June. She married the future *Rosy Crucifixion* author though his own mother told her he was a

---

5 Robert Ferguson, *Henry Miller: A Life* (New York: WW Norton and Company, 1991).

"murderer" and would never amount to a thing. "I feel almost as if I were with a god," she said when first meeting the $17-a-week Western Union clerk who sold his poetry on the street. A sultry dancer, June spiked sales by signing her name to his pieces and hitting up drunk verse lovers in speakeasies.

Like most other businesses, a history of publication could be written based on who was shagging who, literally or metaphorically.

FRIENDS

Besides dedications to moms—Salinger's *Catcher in the Rye*, Heller's *Catch-22*, Ralph Ellison's *Invisible Man*, Ford's *Ultimate Good Luck*, McInerny's *Bright Lights*, etc.—most other tributes are to later nurturers and helpers.[6]

Tolstoy ensured Dostoyevsky's Siberian comeback when he called *The House of Dead* "the finest work in all of Russian literature." Dostoyevsky's former roommate Dmitry Grigorovich pulled strings to see that Chekhov won the Pushkin Prize for his *At Dusk* story collection. The twenty-seven-year-old doctor wrote his sponsor: "Your letter, my kind, fervently beloved bringer of good tidings, struck me like a flash of lightning. I almost burst into tears, I was overwhelmed, and now I feel it has left a deep trace in my soul."[7]

At risk of life and limb, Tolstoy expert Isaiah Berlin smuggled *Doctor Zhivago* to England. But it was Pasternak's suck with the MI6 and the CIA that brought him the Nobel in 1958 (which the author had to reject, else be exiled by Khrushchev).

As we have seen, Sherwood Anderson was among the most collegial American authors. Thanks to his introductions, the precocious networker Hemingway was soon the darling of the Montparnasse movers and shakers: Gertrude Stein, Ezra Pound, John Dos Passos, and Ford Maddox Ford.

---

6 Capote dedicated *In Cold Blood* to his secretary, Harper Lee; Melville's *Moby Dick* went to Nathaniel Hawthorne; Turgenev's *Song of Triumphant Love* to Flaubert; Tolstoy's *Woodfelling* to Turgenev. And Salinger gave *Frannie & Zooey* "to my editor, mentor and (heaven help him) closest friend, William Shawn, *genius domus* of The New Yorker, lover of the long shot."

7 Anton Chekhov, *A Life in Letters* (New York: Penguin Classics, 2004).

Ford's *TransAtlantic* accepted Hemingway's first stories, which had been rejected by *Redbook* and *The Saturday Evening Post*, but lived to regret this as well as his efforts for others. "I helped Joseph Conrad, I helped Hemingway. I helped a dozen, a score of writers, and many of them have beaten me," Ford complained. "I'm now an old man and I'll die without making a name like Hemingway. ... He disowns me now that he has become better known than I am."[8]

Papa felt Ford's meager short story runs killed his chances of getting an immediate book deal and, in the meantime, that he would be plagiarized and forgotten. "I will have to quit writing and will never have a book published," Hemingway wrote Pound. "I feel cheerful as hell. Those god damn bastards." He denounced Ford to Gertrude Stein as "a liar and a crook."

Following the *TransAtlantic* debut, Anderson persuaded his publisher, Boni & Liveright, to release *In Our Time*. "I can't tell you how grateful I am for getting myself published," Ernest wrote his sponsor. Anderson had also written a "crackerjack" review for *In Our Time*, though Hemingway had trashed Anderson's own new title, *Many Marriages*, the year before. Applying full suction, Ernest added, "Besides, all criticism is shit anyway. Nobody knows anything about it except yourself."[9]

Scott Fitzgerald lined Hemingway up with his Princeton chum Charles Scribner. But Boni held first-refusal rights for his follow-up title. So, to ensure that the rejection would free him to jump ship to the prestigious Scribner, Hemingway submitted *The Torrents of Spring*, a hatchet job on the house star, Anderson, his benefactor.

"Wrote it to destroy Sherwood and various others," he told Pound. "I don't see how he will ever be able to write again."

After the backstab, the Montparnasse bete noir was no longer welcome at Gertrude's salon.

But Ezra rode with Ernest's punches. As the Lost Generation's midwife of new literary talent, he continued to market him and other

8 George Seldes, *Witness to a Century: Encounters with the Noted, the Notorious, and the Three SOBs* (New York: Ballantine Books, 1987).

9 Carlos Baker, ed., *Ernest Hemingway: Selected Letters 1917-1961* (New York: Scribner, 2003).

expatriates. In gratitude, Hemingway taught Pound to box. Later, he donated $1,500 to his insane asylum release fund (a check Pound never cashed, but framed).

James Joyce, though not known for graciousness himself, said of Pound, "He took me out of the gutter." Indeed, he had Ezra to thank for the publications of most everything from *Dubliners* on. Also indispensable to his success, though mostly posthumous, was his publisher-bookstore owner, Sylvia Beach, and his *Egoist Press* patroness, Miss Harriet Shaw Weaver. "I hope that wretched book someday will repay you even in part for all the trouble it has caused you," he wrote her of *Ulysses*.[10]

Though Joyce struggled to the bitter end, he had the backing of an impressive network by the late '20s. His petition against American publisher Samuel Roth, who pirated *Ulysses*, bore 167 names. Among them: T.S. Eliot, E.M. Forster, D.H. Lawrence, H.G. Wells, W.B. Yeats, John Galsworthy, Andre Gide, Rebecca West, Virginia Woolf, Thornton Wilder, and Albert Einstein.

Hemingway and Fitzgerald also signed. Later, the Irish master gave audience to his young American colleagues.

The *Farewell to Arms* author, about to embark on another African Big Five carnage, promised to bring Joyce a "live" lion but never delivered. "He's a good writer," said Joyce after the summit. "He writes as he is … He's a big, powerful peasant, as strong as a buffalo." The novelist, now nearly blind, concluded, "But giants of this sort are truly modest."

F. Scott's modesty bordered on ingratiating when meeting his idol. "How does it feel to be a genius, Sir?" he asked, kissing his hand. "I am so excited at seeing you, Sir, that I could weep." He threatened to jump out the window lest Joyce's wife, Nora, say she loved him.

"I think the young man must be mad," said the master afterwards. "He'll do himself an injury some day."

Another ardent admirer of the master was Kurt Vonnegut. Like Joyce, Vonnegut toiled in obscurity for years. Thanks to friends, he finally prevailed. After collecting countless rejections from *The New Yorker, The Atlantic, Harpers*, and *American Mercury*, Knox Burger, *Collier's* fiction editor and his Cornell classmate, agreed to publish his

10 Richard Ellmann, *James Joyce* (Oxford University Press, 1983).

story "Report on the Barnhouse Effect." Then Knox got him an agent, Ken Littauer, who in turn got him a Scribners' contract for *Piano Player*. The debut novel tanked, selling only 3,600 copies of a 7,600-copy run. Knox then landed Kurt a gig at *Sports Illustrated*. Meanwhile, according to his biographer, Charles Shields, "At age 43, he was practically nowhere in the landscape of American letters."[11] Vonnegut's second title, *The Sirens of Titan*, was universally rejected. Even the University of Chicago trashed his anthropology thesis, prompting the future icon of American letters to say, "They can take a flying fuck to the mooooon." Burger managed to get *Sirens* greenlighted for a 2,500 run. "[Knox] got me started and he kept me going until he could no longer help me," said Kurt. But his second novel suffered the same fate as the first. Kurt confessed to feeling "subhuman." But then a new savior arrived: Sam Lawrence. The thirty-year-old Delacorte editor offered $75,000 for *Slaughterhouse-Five*. "That's too much money—you'll never get it back," said Kurt. The novel became a bestseller, and its predecessors rode its coattails. Knox opened his own literary agency based on Kurt's assurance that he would be his first celebrity client. But, in the eleventh hour, he reneged on the commitment. Later, he also abandoned Sam Lawrence for the deeper-pocketed Doubleday.

---

11 Charles J. Shields, *And So It Goes: Kurt Vonnegut: A Life* (New York: Henry Holt, 2011).

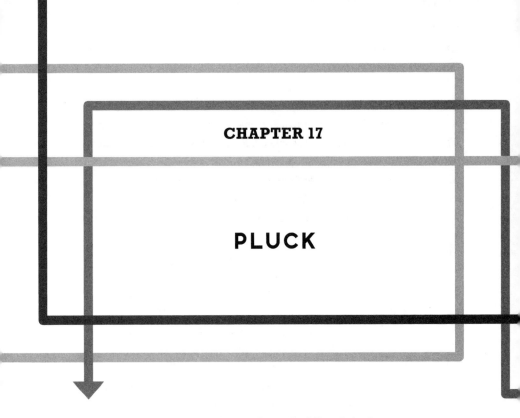

CHAPTER 17

PLUCK

"Perseverance is much more important than talent.
Because so many talented people fall by the wayside."
—James Michener

In *On Death and Dying*, Elisabeth Kübler-Ross formulated the Five Stages of Grief—DABDA—which apply to the *petit mors* of manuscript rejection:

Denial: "This can't be happening to me."

Anger: "It's not fair."

Bargaining: "Gimme another chance."

Depression: "What's the point?"

Acceptance: "It's going to be okay."

Though the last stage eludes pessimists, most writers—even manic depressives—are, deep down, optimists. Though the writer may never really accept that her labor of love is roadkill, she reaches Acceptance by rejecting rejection. And so she presses on, heroically or compulsively.

In another groundbreaking title, *Outliers*, *The New Yorker's* Malcolm Gladwell argues that success in most fields depends not so much on

Luck or Suck, but on the Ten-Thousand-Hour Pluck Law. Statistically, professionals bust ass for at least that long before collecting the fruits of their labor. Calculating at eight hours a day, that's about three year's work. Gladwell estimates that it took him ten years (thirty thousand hours) to go from journalistic "basket case" to *The New Yorker* staff writer, and four more before his first book (*Tipping Point*) came out. As we have seen, historically, most writers have worked ten to thirty years before becoming "successful," if not legendary.

Let's look at three literary Outliers now to see how they supplemented their Luck and/or Suck with even greater Pluck to survive rejection.

Norman Mailer's debut novel, *The Naked and the Dead* (1948), made him an overnight sensation. The precocious Harvard grad, though only twenty-five, had already put in his Outlier ten thousand hours. His next title—*Barbary Shore*—tanked. Fearing that he was a one-hit war story wonder, Rienhart, Knopf, Simon & Schuster, Scribner, Harpers, and Harcourt Brace rejected his third *roman à clef, The Deer Park.* "Perversely, this energized Norman," wrote his biographer.[1] "He went into overdrive promoting his manuscript." Mailer described himself as its "messenger boy, editorial consultant, Machiavelli of the luncheon table, fool of the five o'clock drinks." At last, Putnam gambled on *The Deer Park* and took a bath. Mailer didn't write another novel for ten years. Meantime, stuck in the second circle of grief, he lashed out with *Advertisements for Myself,* eviscerating all his more successful colleagues.[2] At the cost of many friends, the "Village Villain" and "The General," as he called himself, was now back in the headlines building an Outlier personality cult which would buoy his career. He became a talk show provocateur, he ran for mayor, he knifed his wife, he threw a Four Seasons bash. He wrote about Marilyn, Ali, Oswald, Gilmore. He climaxed with Jesus in the first person (*The Gospel According to the Son*). No one had more Pluck than The General.

---

1 Mary V. Dearborn, *MAILER: A Biography* (New York: Houghton Mifflin, 1999).

2 James Jones, William Styron, Truman Capote, Jack Kerouac, Saul Bellow, Nelson Algren, J.D. Salinger, Paul Bowles, Gore Vidal, Anatole Brouillard, Ralph Ellison, James Baldwin, Herbert Gold, William Burroughs, Mary McCarthy, Jean Stafford, Carson McCullers.

In *Advertisements for Myself,* Mailer charged that his Beat colleague Jack Kerouac lacked "discipline, intelligence, honesty, and a sense of the novel." Early on, many editors shared the view. Kerouac's *Visions of Neil, Dr. Sax,* and *Maggie Smith* were universally rejected. "Will I be rich or poor? Will I be famous or forgotten?" he wrote in his journal. Finally, Harcourt agreed to publish *The Town and the City.* "I'm going to sell it," declared Kerouac. "I'm ready for any battle there is!"[3] He failed to even make back his $1,000 advance on the novel. He grieved that he suffered the "curse of Melville." Unlike his more stoic predecessor, he found that only expletives could vent his disgust and rage, and he often blamed his novel's failure on "the worst shit luck" and the publishers who had "f---ed" him. But Kerouac compensated for his lack of Luck and Suck with Pluck: "Because I'm not famous they don't care," he said. "But what they don't know is that I am going to be famous, and the greatest writer of my generation, like Dostoyevsky." In five years, by his estimation, he had written "600,000 words, all in the service of art"; now he redoubled his efforts while working as a day laborer and trying to launch his own press with Allen Ginsberg. At last he entered the literary pantheon with *On the Road.*

James Joyce was one of Kerouac's greatest inspirations—not only for his work but for his diehard attitude in the face of unrelenting opposition.

At age twenty, Joyce, poems in hand, started knocking on the doors of Dublin literati. He was still in college and living at home with his parents, six sisters, and three brothers. He had written his Aunt Josephine: "I want to be famous while I'm still alive."

The young artist cold-called W.B. Yeats. "The first spectre of the new generation has appeared. His name is Joyce," the poet wrote a colleague. "I have suffered from him and I would like you to suffer." He gave the upstart a hand, though "such a colossal self-conceit with such a Lilliputian literary genius I never saw combined in one person."

Still unpublished, Joyce later started his debut autobiographical novel, *Stephen Hero* (released posthumously in 1944). Meanwhile, he was competing in opera-singing contests (he won a bronze in the 1904 *Feis Ceoil*); he was wearing a hole in the seat of his pants writing 250

---

3 Paul Maher Jr., *Kerouac: The Definitive Biography* (Taylor Trade Publishing, 2004)

letters a day in an Italian bank; and he was "blogging" about Ireland for the *Il Piccolo della Sera.* "I may not be the Jesus Christ I once fondly imagined myself," the lapsed Catholic wrote a friend, "but I think I must have a talent for journalism."

Stephen Hero was turned down by everybody. So, too, was its follow-up, *Portrait of the Artist as a Young Man.* At last, Irish publisher George Roberts agreed to take a gamble on his story collection, *Dubliners.* But in the eleventh hour he backed off. Joyce contacted seven different lawyers about suing Roberts and complained to 120 different newspapers—all to no avail. At last he wrote King George V himself. But the monarch refused to be interrupted from his stamp collecting and bird hunting. At last Joyce threatened to shoot Roberts.

Yeats, Pound, and friends petitioned the Royal Literary Fund to rescue "this man of genius." Though it agreed to pay him a small sum for nine months, he suffered a nervous breakdown. Pound sent a Get Well card. "Dear Job," it began. By this time, Joyce called himself "Melancholy Jesus" and "Crooked Jesus."

Drinking was his only relief from the cross. He left pubs doing his "spider dance." Recalled his daughter-in-law, "Liquor went to his feet, not to his head." Nora Joyce had seen one too many tarantellas. One night when her husband waltzed home, she told him she'd torn up *Ulysses.* He sobered up long enough to find she was bluffing.

Joyce drank not so much for inspiration but for pain relief. He met another chronic sufferer, Marcel Proust, for the first and last time in 1922 at the Paris ballet. Neither had condescended to read the other's work. They spoke only of their health. Joyce complained of his headaches, bad eyes, and ulcers. Proust, who spent the equivalent of $20,000 annually for narcotics and elixirs, wept about his "poor stomach" that was "killing" him. The two agreed to a shared love of truffles. With that, the penurious Ulysses took his leave of the trust-funder Swann without hitting him up for a few francs.

Months later Proust died of pneumonia in his cork-lined room, leaving behind his unrevised 3,200-page *Remembrance,* which won him immortality. The novelist had weathered his share of the storm over the years, too. But he had gone on to claim the coveted Goncourt Prize by "actively courting the judges with expensive presents and fine meals," according to a rival who called him "a talent from beyond the tomb."[4]

Joyce died two decades later from a perforated ulcer. His mad daughter, Lucia, asked her mother, "What is he doing under the ground, that idiot? When will he decide to come out? He's watching us all the time."[5]

So the master must know that his tenacity paid off posthumously, making him—like Kerouac, Mailer, and the other literary Outliers—required reading on every syllabus.

》》

Besides building a personality cult, begging already-famous writers for endorsement, threatening to shoot a publisher, or petitioning charitable organizations for support, here are a few other time-tested DIY career accelerators.

RUN A CLASSIFIED AD

In 1897, W. Somerset Maugham was learning about the razor's edge and human bondage: His first novel, *Liza of Lambeth,* was dying on the vine because his publisher refused to market it. So he took matters into his own hands. He placed a personal in several London newspapers.

"Young millionaire, lover of sports, cultivated, with good taste of music and a patient and empathetic character wishes to marry any young and beautiful girl that resembles the heroine of W.S. Maugham's new novel."

The first edition of *Liza* quickly sold out. Critical praise and serial printings followed.[6]

---

4 Edmund White: *Marcel Proust* (Fides, 2002).

5 Richard Ellman, James Joyce (Oxford University Press, 1983).

6 "Success Stories: First Novelists, Debut Novelists" www.bookmarket.com/debutnovels.htm

BECOME YOUR OWN REVIEWER

By 1869, Charles Dickens was the first international rock star of fiction. But that didn't prevent Little Nell's creator from writing a glowing anonymous review of his *The Innocents Abroad*.

Fitzgerald prevailed upon his wife, Zelda, to review his *The Beautiful and Damned* for *The New York Tribune*. She entitled her 1922 blurb "Friend Husband's Latest" and urged readers to buy the novel so she could afford a new winter coat.

EDIT YOUR OWN MAGAZINE

Masters who advanced themselves using this MO were legion.[7]

The benefits were, and still are, inestimable. The writer-editor becomes the rejector, not the rejectee. Escaping the slush, he can revive his old ms.carriages. He gains suck by running movers' and shaker's work, even if substandard, and promotes his own aesthetics.

Dostoyevsky's editorial assistants called the touchy epileptic "Spitfire" for his reaction when they tampered with his punctuation or modifiers.

Poe terrified everybody in his *Messenger* office. "Even a typographical error threw him into an ecstasy of passion," his co-editor noted. Although the perfectionist complained of being overworked—"I must do *everything!*"—he went on to found *Literati*. In it, the essayist, poet, and short story specialist pilloried every rival, including Dickens, Longfellow, Emerson, and Thoreau.

START YOUR OWN PUBLISHING COMPANY

At age fifty, dissatisfied with middlemen, the financially insatiable Twain launched his own press, Webster & Co. Its two debut titles—his own *Huck Finn* and Ulysses Grant's *Memoirs*—were hits. In the next

---

7 Balzac had his *Chronique de Paris* and Revue *Parisienne*; Twain, his *Buffalo Express*; Dickens, *Daily News*; Poe, *Messenger, Journal,* and *Stylus*; Dostoyevsky, *Citizen, Epoch,* and *Time*; Proust, *Le Banquet*; Cather, *McClure's*; Orwell, the *Tribune*; Maugham, the *Legal Observer*; Robert Penn Warren, the *Southern Review*; Mencken, the *Baltimore Herald*.

nine years Webster followed up with *Connecticut Yankee*, plus some Whitman and Tolstoy. Twain's enterprise folded after disasters such as a biography of Leo XIII, the poet pope, which sold two hundred copies.

Balzac was less fortunate with his own publishing house: He went belly-up after a few years, exhausting his mother's fifty thousand franc seed capital.

Around the same time in Russia, Fyodor and his wife, Anna, founded the Dostoyevsky Publishing Company and The F.M. Dostoyevsky Bookstore. His 1869 title from Stellovsky, *The Idiot*, tanked, and the fact that Tolstoy earned twice what he did annoyed him. In the first year of business, the couple sold three thousand copies of their debut title, *The Possessed*.

Virginia Woolf started The Hogarth Press for her own work and that of her Bloomsbury friends.

Then there were the many masters who moonlighted as editors for their own publishers. To name a few: Gide at Gillimard, Michener at Macmillan, Doctorow at Dial, and Toni Morrison at Random House. At Faber and Faber, T.S. Eliot himself said: "I suppose some editors are failed writers; but so are most writers."

Finally, the wave of the future: James Frey's Full Fathom Five writer's sweatshop. The *Million Little Pieces* author employs unpublished MFAs in an Andy Warhol-like factory, giving each a few hundred dollars for a manuscript or Hollywood concept with a promise of participation in back-end profits. Among Frey's most promising recent collaborative brainstorms is his animated *Fart Squad* concept for eight-to-ten-year-old boys. He characterized Fathom Five with his customary modesty: "This is the future," he told *Esquire* magazine. "Every writer I know is scared of the future," he added. "I'm *making* the future. I'm gonna be a part of who determines what the future *is*! Same as Henry Miller!"

Oprah's pick is nothing if not plucky. "I believe in myself almost more than anybody I ever met, which is how I'm able to do things," he went on. "It's not because I'm smart. It's not 'cause I'm gifted ... [or] went to great schools. It's because I get up every day and I go to work."[8]

---

8 John H. Richardson, "'There Is No Truth,'" He Said," *Esquire* magazine, October 13, 2011.

CHAPTER 18

LSP TRIFECTA

"One of the signs of Napoleon's greatness is that he once had a
publisher put to death."
—**Siegfried Unseld**

For those who are too impatient or fainthearted to weather multiple
submissions, one historic way of avoiding dues to the muse remains: In
short, avoiding rejection entirely.

Play the Luck, Suck, & Pluck Trifecta: Conquer your own country, kill all competitors and critics, and make your work mandatory
national reading.

Jack London, H.G. Wells, Upton Sinclair, James Michener, Norman
Mailer, Gore Vidal, and Hunter Thompson, among others, all ran for
office. Fortunately, all lost and returned to the private sector without
resorting to arms (except for Mailer and Thompson).

Only three part-time writers have made the LSP Trifecta a reality in modern times: Mao, Saddam Hussein, and Muammar Gadhafi.
The trio was indebted to a certain rejected German art student for
laying the strategic groundwork for such a literary coup—part of

his "grandiose" scheme, according to necrographer Mark Seinfelt, to "conquer all the arts."[1]

Hitler didn't pen his autobiographical title from one of his later fuehrer "wolf lairs" but from his suite at Landsberg Prison. Here the once homeless painter served eight months of a five-year stretch for treason. In this time he managed to finish *Four and a Half Years of Struggle Against Lies, Stupidity, and Cowardice*. He had no problem finding a publisher, Max Amann, who inveigled him to change the title to the punchier *Mein Kampf (My Struggle)* and to cut nearly five hundred pages from the original manuscript.

Hitler's commanding officer in World War I, Amann, had had his arm blown off and later became the publisher of the *SS Monthly*. *Kampf* became an instant hit, allowing its author—whose motto was "Words build bridges into unexplored regions"—to buy a Mercedes even before being paroled. His tax tab on the bestseller topped 405,000 Reichsmarks ($8 million in today's U.S. currency). When the ex-con became chancellor in 1933 he waived the tax, thus avoiding paying dues to the muse or to the state. But later the patriot compensated Germans by donating a copy of his title to every soldier and newlywed couple.

By 1945, Hitler had distributed 10 million copies of the three official editions: the People's Edition, the Wedding Edition, and the Portable Edition. Not long after its original publication, he dashed out *Zweites Buch (Second Book)*. But Amann persuaded him to shelve the sequel for fear that it would diminish the feeding frenzy on *Kampf*. Also, *Zweites* laid out his plan to overrun the world by 1980, and Amann decided it would be premature to let that cat out of the bag.

Assisting Amann was Hitler's lit agent, Joseph Goebbels. After completing his doctorate on romance writer Wilhelm von Schutz, he wrote an autobiographical novel, *Michael*, which he couldn't get published until he became the Minister of Propaganda in 1929. Then he started burning most everybody else's books except his and his boss's.

While Germans who valued their lives were universal in their praise for Hitler's title, an Italian romance novelist took exception, as Italians will. *Mien Kampf*, he charged, was filled with "little more than

---

1 Mark Seinfelt, *Final Drafts: Suicides of World-Famous Authors* (Prometheus Books, 1999).

commonplace clichés," rendering it unreadable. The Fuhrer might have had the critic gassed had he not been his ally, Benito Mussolini.

Mussolini, a former newspaperman, had himself burst onto the literary scene fifteen years before Hitler with his serialized romance, *The Cardinal's Mistress*. Although a fascist, Mussolini never made his potboiler required state reading, nor did he release a Wedding Edition. In fact, he later removed the anticlerical screed from circulation in order to gain the Vatican's favor during the War. But privately, like most heretics, he remained unrepentant. "The history of saints is mainly the history of insane people," he wrote.

After Adolf swallowed cyanide and Benito was hung from a gas station roof by a meat hook, Mao pinched a chapter from their playbook, but with a wise alteration: He didn't try to publish too early. The former librarian waited until he finished executing all the Chinese critics during his Cultural Revolution before releasing his poems and aphorisms. In thinning out the intellectuals and Fahrenheit 451-ing their books, he was flattered to be compared to Qin Shi Huang, the First Emperor, who did the same in 210 B.C. but on a more modest scale. "He buried 460 scholars alive; we have buried forty-six thousand scholars alive," the Blessed Leader boasted to the readers who were left. "We have surpassed Qin Shi Huang a hundredfold!"[2]

The Chairman's titles outsold Rowling's Potter series. Even without Oprah or a Barnes & Noble signing tour he became the best-selling author of all time, moving six billion units in forty years (second only to the Bible at 6.5 billion in 2,500 years). The author expected each citizen not only to buy his masterpiece but to carry it at all times lest his literary agents, The Red Guard, more efficient than even CAA or William Morris, recycle them with the 46,000 critics and the three million other armchair quibblers.

To the regret of Harlequin fans, however, Mao never tried his hand at romance, though he'd had four wives, three thousand concubines, and—thanks to powdered deer antlers— never needed Viagra to keep them satisfied. Nor did he need to bathe, brush his teeth, or floss.

---

2 Kenneth Lieberthal, *Governing China: From Revolution to Reform* (Second Edition) (New York: W.W. Norton, 2003).

Mao's literary successor, Saddam Hussein, picked up the slack in the genre. While the CIA thought the Middle Eastern Saladin was stockpiling WMD's, the dictator was actually penning romances, leaving Muammar Qaddafi's story collection, *Escape to Hell*, in the Libyan dust, though the colonel had, like Mao, made his work required reading.

Saddam's debut, *Zabibah and the King* (2000), was about a beautiful but abused Tikrit town girl.[3] The second, *The Fortified Castle*, was a Romeo and Juliet vehicle involving an Iraqi GI and a Kurdish virgin. Following Joe Klein's lead in *Primary Colors*, Saddam published both anonymously as "THE Author." Seeming to suspect who this might be,[4] Iraqis flocked to the bookstores in bulletproof vests.

The Iraqi strongman's last title, *Demons Be Gone*, would surely have topped the Baghdad bestseller list, too, had Bush and the infidels not invaded the very day after the ms. was finished in 2003.

Three years later, Saddam's dutiful daughter, Raghad, in gratitude to him for executing her husband, secured a contract for his swan song. After the Butcher of Baghdad was hung, the Jordanian publisher, who had promised a first run of 100,000, backed out of the deal. Undiscouraged, Raghad went viral with queries and SASEs. But not even Judith Regan would touch *Demons*. At the time, Murdoch's maverick editor was rounding out her list of *Private Parts, How to Make Love Like a Porn Star*, and O.J.'s *If I Did It*.

So, in the end, only Mao Tse-tung won the Luck, Suck, & Pluck Trifecta, paying no dues to the muse but still winning an adoring communist audience.

Critics agree that Mao's LSP feat may never again be achieved in the truth-stranger-than-fiction annals of publishing.

---

3 The novel was the basis for Sacha Baron Cohen's 2012 movie *The Dictator*.

4 According to a *New York Times* article—"C.I.A. Sleuths Study a Novel for the Thinking of Saddam Hussein" (May 25, 2001)—U.S. intelligence agents concluded that the dictator likely used ghostwriters. The *Zabibah* introduction revealed that the author declined to identify himself "out of humility."

PART V

"THE BUILT-IN, SHOCK-PROOF, SHIT DETECTOR"

"The most essential gift for a good writer is a built-in, shock-proof, shit detector."
—Ernest Hemingway

CHAPTER 19

TALENT

**"I see the notion of talent as quite irrelevant. I see instead per-
severance, application, industry, assiduity, will, will, will, desire,
desire, desire."**

—Gordon Lish, aka Captain Fiction

Is the fourth ingredient of literary success talent?

Many publishers say yes. The unpublished may say no. Let's examine the question.

First, a definition of terms: What is talent?

In ancient days, it was a weight of gold. Money. The Book of Matthew
gives an example: A rich merchant (say, a publisher) gives his first servant (a writer) five Talents, his second two Talents, his third one Talent.
The first two servants put their Talents to work and double their money;
the third buries his and makes nothing. The master blesses the first two
as "good and faithful," inviting them to "come and join my happiness."
He curses the third as "wicked and worthless," takes away his one
Talent, and throws him "into the darkness, where there will be weeping
and gnashing of teeth."

For our purposes, the first servant was J.K. Rowling, the second Stephen King, and the third an MFA graduate who tries to make a living writing the next *Finnegans Wake* or *Gravity's Rainbow.*

The ancient definition of talent has been revived in today's Babylon: Hollywood. The million-dollar star is called "The Talent." Similarly, in publishing, if you make Talents, you've got talent. If you make a million Talents, you're a genius.

But as one genius, Stephen King, points out, "Talent is cheaper than table salt. What separates the talented individual from the successful one is a lot of hard work." Which brings us back to Pluck.

Practically speaking, what is literary talent? Most would agree that it is the ability to write well and tell a story well. Twain, Dickens, Stendhal, Tolstoy, and others could do both. Today, many good writers are not good storytellers, and many good storytellers are not good writers.

On one hand is the *Me Talk Pretty One Day* school; on the other, the hard-boiled Patterson storyteller school. The first focuses on the How: voice, imagery, nuance. The second on the What: blood, semen, and surprise.

The stylist enriches; the storyteller entertains. The stylist is nutritious, offering organic eggs and fresh produce; the storyteller is delicious, serving Chicken McNuggets, biscuits, and pie.

Is talent essential to literary success?

Storytelling talent, yes; stylistic talent, no. The latter can sometimes be a handicap. As Elmore Leonard writes in *10 Rules of Writing:* "If it sounds like writing, I rewrite it."

Most experts agree that the art of writing cannot be taught, but the craft can; that by following the right rules, a writer can polish his or her talent and, in doing so, have a better shot at publication. So, for nearly a century now, publishers, adopting a No Writer Left Behind educational program, have been mass-producing instruction manuals. Academics have started schools. Entrepreneurs have gone mail order.

CHAPTER 20

"AN APPEAL
TO THE GULLIBLE"

In 1969 Robert Byrne released *Writing Rackets*.[1] Of the 182,505 fiction manuscripts submitted to U.S. publishers annually in the late 1960s, he reported that 560 (0.003%) were accepted, and the average freelance writer earned $3,000 a year.

In light of these numbers, Byrne—who as an amateur stage magician knew a thing or two about hoaxes—turned his attention to The Famous Writers School. The Connecticut-based mail-order operation was founded by Random House owner Bennett Cerf in 1961 and run by former president of William Morrow Publishers John Lawrence. Its brochure assured prospective students: "You couldn't consider breaking into writing at a better time than today. Everything indicates that the demand for good prose is growing much faster than the supply of trained talent."

The correspondence school boasted a sales force of eight hundred field reps and fifteen personal tutor "celebrity" writers. Among them was Paul Engle, Nobel nominee and Iowa Workshop pioneer. Another

---

1 Robert Byrne, *Writing Rackets: An Expose of Phony Writing Schools, Agents, and Others Who Exploit Would-Be Writers* (New York: Lyle Stuart, 1969)

.was Faith Baldwin, a best-selling romance novelist who in 1936 earned over $300,000 (about $5 million in today's currency) and whose titles became movies (*Men Are Such Fools!, An Apartment for Peggy*).

Another instructor, J.D. Ratcliff, pledged that he and his colleagues would help spare students "the sheer blood, sweat, and rejection slips" they themselves had suffered in their early careers. To this end, the school published a "Writers Worth Watching" quarterly that featured student work. Contributors were assured, "Each issue of the magazine is received and read by some two thousand editors, publishers, and other key figures in the writing world." They were also told that 75 percent would publish in their first year.

The Famous Writers School tuition for its three-year course started at $785, twenty times what university correspondence courses cost at the time. But for this, students received no-nonsense professional texts, including, "How to Turn Your Writing Into Dollars." The school ran testimonial ads in *The New York Times Magazine* in the vein of, "I've just received a big, beautiful check from the *Reader's Digest!*"

Bilking dreamers became big business. In its first year, Cerf's operation netted $7 million and its stock cost $5 a share; by 1969 it was making $48 million and its stock had jumped to $40 a share. All fifteen famous writers on the faculty were stockholders, including *Twilight Zone* creator and host Rod Serling. By 1970, FWS boasted an enrollment of sixty-five thousand (two thousand of whom were veterans covered by the GI Bill) and received three hundred thousand requests for information.

Business boomed at FWS until Jessica Mitford arrived to do an article for *McCall's*. Today's best-selling author, J.K. Rowling, calls her "my most influential writer, without a doubt," and named her daughter, Jessica, after her. Mitford had made waves in 1963 with *The American Way of Death* about how, with entrepreneurial spirit, corpses can be recycled as cash cows. Her study of morticians proved invaluable to her study of the FWS.

When Mitford turned in "Let Us Now Appraise Famous Writers," *McCall's* refused to publish it for fear of blowback from Cerf. *The Atlantic Monthly* ran the exposé in July 1970.

The magazine soon received three hundred letters from FWS students who felt defrauded and wished to cancel their contract.

When the author asked Cerf about this, he told her, "Once some-body has signed a contract with Famous Writers he can't get out of it, but that's true with every business in the country." Mitford found that the drop-out rate had varied between 66 and 90 percent, and she attributed much of the school's success to this since tuition was nonrefundable.

She also wondered about the faculty (fifteen) to student (65,000) ratio: one to 4,333. How could each famous author, while maintaining his or her career, personally read and appraise 4,333 manuscripts?

Cerf told Mitford that "anyone with common sense" should know this was impossible. "Oh, come on, you must be pulling my leg," he protested. "No person of any sophistication, whose book we'd publish, would have to take a mail-order course to learn how to write." He called his school's marketing strategy "an appeal to the gullible." But "for God's sake, don't quote me on that 'gullible' business," he begged the burial and embalming expert—knowing that writers, after all, suspend disbelief for a living and so are inclined to gullibility.

Unfortunately for the moonlighting Random House head, Ms. Mitford was an English baron's daughter and a communist. And her husband, Robert Treuhaft, was a Don Quixote civil rights lawyer who was representing a broke elderly woman who demanded a refund from FWS. Treuhaft persuaded several state attorney generals to file suit against the school.

Refund checks went out, enrollment at FWS tanked, and the opera-tion filed for bankruptcy in 1972. Before filing, Cerf, according to a school insider, urged his fifteen famous writers to sell their stock. The publisher and "What's My Line?" regular emerged unscathed because, as he impressed on Mitford, "I've nothing to do with how the school is run."

Today, the Famous Writers School has been revived on the Internet, under new management. Prospective students are assured: "Thousands of people like you with the desire to write have developed their talent with a Famous Writers Course ... prepared by some of America's most successful professional writers. And you're person-ally guided every step of the way by a skilled instructor who's a pro-fessional writer or editor." The new FWS offers a "How to Turn Your Writing Into Dollars" sequel, plus instructive texts. The two-volume "Principles of Good Writing" includes such cloud-parting chapters as:

"What to Write About," "Ways to Use Words," and "Why Grammar?"
The fiction texts teach students "how to capitalize on the fact that readers like to be thrilled, amused, terrified, angered, saddened."[2]

Graduates of the eighteen-lesson curriculum are awarded a Certificate of Recognition, "a document you will be proud to own and to display."

---

2 http://www.famous-writers-school.com/fws.html/Fiction1-2.html

CHAPTER 21

THE ELEMENTS
OF BILE

"Any fool can make a rule and every fool will follow it."
—Henry Thoreau

Rather than drinking the Kool-Aid and spending hundreds for an FWS diploma or a hundred thousand for an MFA, many frugal do-it-yourselfers have invested in a writing self-helper. The benign kings of publishing have released almost more of such titles than cookbooks.

Among the first and most venerable titles was *The Elements of Style*, self-published by Cornell professor William Strunk, Jr. in 1918 and picked up forty years later by Macmillan. In the introduction, Professor Strunk's student E.B. White boasted that the seventy-page primer fit "the rules and principles on the head of a pin," concisely cataloging stylistic high crimes and grammatical misdemeanors. The *Stuart Little* author went on to reveal the purpose of what he called his teacher's *parvus opum*, or "Little Book": to rescue the writer "floundering in the swamp … delivering his man up on dry ground … or at least throwing him a rope."

The Elements of Style became a best-selling classic, reportedly delivering drowning scriveners to dry ground. With the serial adjectives he spurned, White concluded, "Longer, lower textbooks are in use nowadays, I daresay—books with upswept tail fins and automatic verbs." But—indulging himself in not one, but two, adverbs— he insisted that none "come to the point as quickly and illuminate it as amusingly."

Many other lines have been tossed into the high seas of literature since the *Elements*. Today's writer, now with more ropes on him than Gulliver under the Lilliputians, must decide which are lifesavers and which are nooses.

In *On Writing*, Stephen King says that, unlike other books, *The Elements of Style* contains "little or no detectable bullshit."

But the shockproof shit detector of linguist Geoffrey K. Pullum[1] sounded off: "Both authors were grammatical incompetents…. The book's contempt for its own grammatical dictates seems almost willful, as if the authors were flaunting the fact that the rules don't apply to them."

On the other hand, most would agree that Professor Strunk's stylistic rules are bulletproof and timeless. But does Shakespeare, his exemplar, flaunt the fact that the professor's rules didn't apply to him either?

> Don't overstate, overexplain, or pontificate.
> Omit needless words: Be clear and concise.
> Don't use a twenty dollar word when a ten center will do.
> Don't affect a breezy manner.

Some might say that, in their bloviations, Hamlet, Othello, Lear, and Falstaff not only bend these rules but bury them.

Was the arbiter of style blinded by the Emperor's New Clothes? Shakespeare turned the King's English into Elizabethan Ebonics. For every page of a published play, half is devoted to explanatory footnotes. Did the Bard commit Strunk and White's own "most unpardonable sins": "showing off" and "using mannerisms, tricks, adornments"?

Shakespeare's subjects insist he created the deepest, most dramatic, eloquent characters in history. His detractors call them breast beaters and Chicken Littles. Stylistically, he tops Thomas, Yeats, Joyce,

---

1   Geoffrey K. Pullum, "50 Years of Stupid Grammar Advice." *The Chronicle of Higher Education,* April 17, 2009. Pullum is co-author (with Rodney Huddleston) of *The Cambridge Grammar of the English Language* (Cambridge University Press, 2002).

and others as a verbal dandy.

According to the shit detector, is Shakespeare's style exemplary? Or is it much ado about nothing?

The latter, charged Voltaire. He called *Hamlet*, "a vulgar and barbarous drama which would not be tolerated by the vilest populace of France or Italy."

Grading the Bard's composition, Samuel Johnson said he had to red pencil every "six consecutive lines." Dickens found his stories "so intolerably dull that it nauseated me." Tolstoy, who rarely criticized anybody, called the tragedies and comedies "rude, vulgar, and senseless." And George Bernard Shaw threatened to "dig him up and throw stones at him" for "his monstrous rhetorical fustian, and unbearable platitudes."

»»

The premise of Strunk's Little Book boils down to this: "A careful and honest writer does not have to worry about style." Does this imply that the careful and honest don't need the manual and the careless and dishonest do? Anyway, most authorities agree on the importance of honesty. Gordon Lish told Dick Cavett, "The secret of good writing is telling the truth." But, the legendary Knopf editor seemed to change his mind later: "Never be sincere—sincerity is the death of writing."[2]

This sort of mixed message or apparent contradiction is what gives the student writer indigestion—the elements of bile, not style.

Experts generally agree that good writing—publishable writing— should be clear, concise, and compelling. The Three Cs. But beyond that, it's a free-for-all of conflicting rules and regulations worthy of an Islamic state.

Death to adjectives, adverbs, verbs-to-be, colons, semicolons, the second person, ellipses, exclamatories, passives, parataxis; *i* before *e* except after *c*.

But not always.

Never use multiple points of view. But, for some, the more points of

---

2 Alexander Neubauer, *Conversations on Writing Fiction: Interviews with Thirteen Distinguished Teachers of Fiction* (Perennial, 1994).

view the better—especially the Russians.

Never start at the beginning—instead, begin *in medias res.* But, sometimes the beginning should begin at the beginning.

Beyond usage and mechanics, the debate heats up on the weightier issues.

"Less is more," said Robert Browning and so many after him. "I don't believe that less is more. I believe that more is more," Stanley Elkin—speaking for Melville, Faulkner, Joyce, and so many more—told *The Paris Review.*

Most story gurus insist that the indispensable building blocks are plot, character, setting, and theme. "The true enemies of the novel are plot, character, setting, and theme," novelist John Hawkes told his students at Brown.[3]

"Never try to make anything up—neither plot nor narrative," Dostoyevsky advised young writers. "If you want to be true to life, start lying about it," John Fowles countered.[4] And according to critic Grigory Yeliseyev, Fyodor did too: He called *Crime and Punishment* "the most stupid shameful fabrication."

Even the audience question is a bone of contention among the masters. "I write to please myself," Tobias Wolff told *The Paris Review.* "What shit. ... Write for yourself—why?" objected his friend Richard Ford.

The late, great novelists were especially vehement in their stylistic denunciations of one another. Trollop called Dickens' work "jerky, ungrammatical, and created by himself in defiance of the rules. ... No young novelist should ever dare to imitate it." H.G. Wells charged that Henry James "splits his infinitives and fills them up with adverbial stuffing. ... His vast paragraphs sweat and struggle. ... And all for tales of nothingness." Faulkner called Mark Twain "a hack writer who would have been considered fourth-rate in Europe."

But experts today continue to tout these masters as style role models who speak with a single voice. What really causes young writer indigestion is the party-line double standard: The Great X, Y, or Z did it,

3 "Remembering John Hawkes," *Providence Phoenix,* April 8, 1999. http://www.providencephoenix.com/archive/books/99/04/08/HAWKES.html

4 http://www.iwise.com/John_Fowles

but you can't.

In his *10 Rules of Writing*,[5] Elmore Leonard says: "Avoid detailed descriptions of characters, which Steinbeck covered." Might this not lead to underdeveloped, 2-D, or stereotypical characters—the great pitfall of storytelling? And because Steinbeck offered such detail, and Dickens before him, all the way back to Homer, nobody else should be allowed?

"Never use a verb other than 'said' to carry dialogue," Leonard goes on. Death to "he jested," "ejaculated," "trumpeted," "chortled," "chirped," "hissed." Good. But might one thousand *saids* lead to another universally acknowledged pitfall—monotony?

Exclamation points are even more horrifying than semicolons to the bare-bones school. Leonard's Rule 5: "You are allowed no more than two or three per 100,000 words." But some masters loved them, especially the Europeans. Not to mention a certain best-selling American. Okay, then, "If you have the knack of playing with exclaimers the way Tom Wolfe does, you can throw them in by the handful," allows the *Get Shorty* creator. "YOU ARE HEREBY EMPOWERED!!!!!!!!!!!!!!" wrote the man in full in his *Electric Kool-Aid Acid Test.*

With his dispensations, Leonard is more lenient than many an MFA or writers conference mentor. Most will red pencil a sentence or passage that violates current canon. "But Tolstoy did it," the student protests. Which activates the professor's implacable shit detector: "So, you're Tolstoy?" he demands. Which of course is the same question Tolstoy got when his teacher caught him imitating Shakespeare.

The greatest style disagreements have always arisen between the two schools of writing: The More-Is-More Montagues versus The Less-Is-More Capulets. The first camp writes by addition, the second by subtraction.

MM stylists like 1,000-word sentences (Faulkner through Bolaño). They make editors cut hundreds of pages (as Perkins did for Wolfe). Or, loading their Royal with a 120-foot scroll, they type 150 words a

---

5 Elmore Leonard, *Elmore Leonard's 10 Rules of Writing* (New York: William Morrow, 2007).

minute for twenty-one sleepless days. That's how Kerouac wrote *On the Road.* Some called it genius. Truman Capote said, "That's not writing, that's typing."

The LM stylists follow the Hemingway credo: "Every first draft is shit"; "Writing is rewriting." Their sentences are clean and well lit, their words served in carefully budgeted food groups. Nouns are meat and potatoes. Verbs, water. Adjectives and adverbs, sugar and fat trimmed in the second draft. The result is a muscular, fat-free LM narrative.

In spite of their religious fervor, insider spats have erupted in each writing school. Hemingway said of his rose is a rose co-founder, Gertrude Stein: "She learned to write dialogue from a book called *The Sun Also Rises.* I thought it was splendid she had learned to write conversation."[6]

Her shockproof shit detector sounding, Ms. Stein knew that the big game hunter was again dangling his modifier. She insisted that he'd learned not just dialogue, but everything, from *her.*

According to Christina Gombar, the Lost Generation matriarch only credited learning one lesson from one master: punctuation, from her poodle, lapping water.[7]

Like Hemingway and Stein, some novelists learn far more from reading each other than they do from professors or style manuals. "I have played the sedulous ape to Hazlitt, to Lamb, to Wordsworth, to Defoe, to Hawthorne," said Robert Louis Stevenson. "That, like it or not, is the way to learn to write."

The same goes for sports. Countless titles have been written about how to improve your golf game. But the best way is to shelve the book, forget all the rules, and watch Tiger or Mickelson on the tee, in the traps, on the green.

Like golfers, some writers are long-game specialists, swinging for the fences with breathtaking, unpunctuated drives; others are short-game specialists, laying up, then sinking chips and surgical putts. Different strokes for different folks.

The writer decides which is most suited to his own natural abilities

---

6 George Plimpton, *The Paris Review* interview with Ernest Hemingway, *The Art of Fiction* No. 21.

7 Christina Gombar, *Great Women Writers, 1900-1950* (Facts on File, 1996).

and inclinations; then he imitates one, playing the sedulous ape; then he parrots a few others; then he cross-pollinates and, with luck, creates his own eclectic golf game.

Of Hemingway, Gore Vidal once said: "I detest him. ... I thought his prose was perfect until I read Stephen Crane and realized where he got it from."[8] In fact, the Hemingway recipe was not so simple. In addition to three cups of Crane, he is two cups Twain, one cup Stein, and a pinch of Pound. All of which, when baked, make something that is more than the sum of its parts: Hemingway.

Though some novelists have been called "sui generis," neither Gore Vidal nor anybody else has reinvented the wheel. The few who tried have regretted it. The dying words of Joyce, though he had read everybody and experimented with every style, were: "Does no one understand?"

STYLE TIPS FROM THE MASTERS

"There are three rules for writing a novel. Unfortunately, no one knows what they are."
    —**W. Somerset Maugham**

"The best technique is none at all."
    —**Henry Miller**

"Let the writer take up surgery or bricklaying if he is interested in technique. There is no mechanical way to get the writing done, no shortcut. The young writer would be a fool to follow a theory. Teach yourself by your own mistakes; people learn only by error. The good artist believes that nobody is good enough to give him advice."
    —**William Faulkner**

---

8 Gerald Clark, *Paris Review* interview with Gore Vidal, The Art of Fiction No. 50.

"Forget grammar and think about potatoes."

—Gertrude Stein

"The moment a man begins to talk about technique, that's proof that he is fresh out of ideas."

—Raymond Chandler

"Every style that is not boring is a good one."

—Voltaire

"Listen carefully to first criticisms of your work. Note just what it is about your work the critics don't like—then cultivate it."

—Jean Cocteau

"Sound like yourself. ... Pity the reader."

—Kurt Vonnegut

"The difference between the right word and the almost right word is the difference between lightning and a lightning bug."

—Mark Twain

"Style is knowing who you are, what you want to say, and not giving a damn."

—Gore Vidal

CHAPTER 22

THE KENTUCKY-FRIED BESTSELLER

"If a novel is not an entertainment, I don't think it's a successful book."

—Stephen King

If the subject of style is controversial among the experts, the subject of storytelling is even hotter. Countless plot critics have weighed in over the years, providing their own foolproof guidelines for a great story. But why haven't any followed their own formulas and written a bestseller?

As with style experts, story experts disagree on many issues. There's only one consensus rule among them. It dates back to *Beowulf*: Don't bore me. But as novelist and lit professor Sandra Newman points out, this can be particularly challenging for the serious artist: "Paradoxically, the most interesting works of literature are often also the most boring."[1]

Today's reader bores more quickly than yesterday's. He warns the author: You've got thirty seconds to terrify me, thrill me, break my heart, or give me enlightenment or an orgasm.

---

1 Sandra Newman, *The Western Lit Survival Kit: An Irreverent Guide to the Classics From Homer to Faulkner* (New York: Gotham, 2012).

The late David Foster Wallace is among the few who have challenged the ultimatum. In his foreword to *The Pale King*, he warned: "The very last thing this book is is some kind of a clever metafictional titty-pincher." Indeed, the unfinished, heavily footnoted 548-page novel (which he worked on for almost a decade and wearily referred to as "the long thing") is all about boredom: Its characters are Midwestern IRS auditors. Calling Wallace's swan song "breathtakingly brilliant and stupefying dull," *The Times'* Michiko Kakutani wondered if his intent were to "test the reader's tolerance for tedium." But *Entertainment Weekly* found the boredom study "entertaining, not-at-all-boring," *Publisher's Weekly* called it "one hell of a document," and it became a finalist for the controversial 2012 no-win Pulitzer. Before abandoning the work and reaching the end of his rope on the patio, Wallace told his wife that he was considering retiring and opening a dog shelter.[2]

But the *Infinite Jest* author was the exception, not the rule. When an editor or agent rejects a manuscript saying—Where are the plot points? What's so-and-so's motivation? Where is the character arc? What is the message here?—what they mean is: You're boring me.

South to north, a good story engages: the groin, the heart, the head, the soul. Yesterday's titles focused on the last pair. Today's tend to stimulate the first. But, if the head is targeted, it must be the prefrontal lobe, or what scientists call the "medulla oblongata."

In addressing the reptilian brain, the sensible writer chooses a genre—Creeper (Horror, Fantasy), Jeeper (Sci-Fi, Thriller), Reaper (Murder Mystery), Peeper (Romance), or Bleeper (Erotic).

Most storytelling experts agree that the engaging novel, regardless of genre, contains three elements: jeopardy, conflict, and surprise. For this reason, some call popular fiction "formulaic." But not all jeopardy, conflict, and surprise are created equally. What is conflict for one reader is catatonia for another; what is surprise to one is a snore to another. Two writers tell their stories around the campfire: the facts are the same, but one bores, the other grips. Which brings us back to the *How*. The delivery. The voice. The *je ne sais quoi*.

---

2 D.T. Max, "The Unfinished (David Foster Wallace's Struggle to Surpass *Infinite Jest*)," *The New Yorker*, March 9, 2009.

"Some of us tried pretty hard to break out of the formula, but we usually got caught and sent back," wrote Raymond Chandler, the pioneer of hard-boiled pulp fiction, in the introduction to his 1950 story collection, *Trouble Is My Business*. "To exceed the limits of a formula without destroying it is the dream of every writer."

As with the stylists, there are two schools of storytellers: the Less-is-Mores, and the More-is-Mores. The first are born of the Just-the-Facts, Jack, *Dragnet* school. Elmore Leonard's anti-writing writing school, popularized by Hemingway. They are *trompe l'oeil* realists, not impressionists or expressionists. They hide brush marks. They cut all words that call attention to themselves, that fog up the story or weigh down the action. Sentence by sentence, they bulldoze plot speed bumps—whatever seems clever, thoughtful, or ornamental.

Many literary editors now prefer the anti-writers. Algonquin's Chuck Adams told *Poets & Writers* that he joked about putting a sign above his desk that read, "Quit writing and tell me a story."

Style comes from the head, a story from the heart. So, for popular fiction: Give heart, not head. Feel, don't think. Then pray that the implacable captains of publishing will be persuaded that the fickle reader will be moved beyond words.

»

The decisive battle of the shit detectors was waged in 1998: Three pedigreed but aging stylists versus one feisty storyteller with a bastard style.

Swords had crossed ten years before when Tom Wolfe made millions on *The Bonfire of the Vanities*, but Mailer, Updike, and Irving called the novel "populist shit." Wolfe counter-attacked with his 1989 *Harper's* essay, "Stalking the Billion-Footed Beast," about a fictional Old Guard too fossilized to appreciate his revolutionary "fictional nonfiction".[3]

Resentments seethed for a decade and erupted again with Wolfe's bestseller, *A Man in Full*.

---

3 David Foster Wallace and Sven Birkerts reinforced Wolfe with their 1997 *New York Observer* "Twilight of the Phallocrats" denouncing "our arts-bemedaled senior novelists [Updike, Mailer, Bellow, and Roth]... as Great Male Narcissists." In turn, the *Observer's* Anne Roiphe denounced the young literary guns for "urinating" on G.M.N.S.'s out of their own "primitive" male competitiveness. ("Literary Dogs Snap Savagely at Top Dogs," *New York Observer*, October 27, 1997).

"Entertainment, not literature," sniped Updike in his *New Yorker* review,[4] "even literature in a modest aspirant form."

"At certain points, reading the work can even be said to resemble the act of making love to a three-hundred-pound woman: Once she gets on top, it's over. Fall in love, or be asphyxiated,"[5] argued Norman Mailer, speaking from the experience of tackling his own 1,200-page Amazon, *Harlot's Ghost*. *A Man in Full* tipped the scales at a mere 742. Mailer went on to coronate his colleague as "the most gifted bestseller writer ... since Margaret Mitchell."

Wolfe dismissed the creators of *Rabbit* and *The Dear Park* as "two piles of bones."[6] Their comrade-in-arms John Irving flew over the ropes and spelled the hyperventilating tag team. "I can't read him," he said of Wolfe, "because he's such a bad writer."

Now it was three against one—the hoopster, the headbutter, and the wrestler—against the diminutive dandy in full. "I think of the three of them now—because there are now three—as Larry, Curly, and Moe," he said. "It must gall them a bit that everyone—even them—is talking about me."

"If I were teaching freshman English," Irving fumed, "I couldn't read a sentence [of his] and not just carve it up." When the Canadian TV *Hot Type* host asked if he was at war with the little man in white, Garp's creator bristled, "I don't think it's a war because you can't have a war between a pawn and a king, can you?"

But in the end the southern gentleman had the last word, aware that Irving and his stooges were the best PR reps he'd ever had. "Why does he sputter and foam so?" Wolfe wondered.[7]

In the mid-'60s, the thirty-four-year-old heretic published *The Kandy-Kolored Tangerine-Flake Streamline Baby*. The title, a collection of his pieces from *The Washington Post* and elsewhere, replete with exclamations, ellipses, and neo-street speak, spawned The New Journalism. To create a buzz by tossing a Molotov cocktail over the battlements of

---

4 John Updike, "AWRIIIIIGHHHHHHHHH!" *The New Yorker* magazine, November 9, 1998.

5 Norman Mailer, "A Man Half Full" *The New York Review of Books*. December 17, 1998.

6 *The Charlotte Observer*, November 1999 interview.

7 Jim Windolf, "It's Tom Wolfe Versus the 'Three Stooges," *New York Observer*, February 7, 2000.

the Bastille, he strode into his editor's office at the *Herald-Tribune* one morning and asked, "How about blowing up *The New Yorker*, Clay?"

So the *Tribune* ran "Tiny Mummies! The True Story of the Ruler of 43rd Street's Land of the Walking Dead," Wolfe's assault on the alma mater of his Moriartys—Larry, Curly, and Moe. It featured a portrait of *The New Yorker* editor William Shawn as head funeral director, surrounded by his dutiful retainers and embalmed guardians of literature, the Tiny Mummies. The satire had been inspired by *The New Yorker's* invitation-only fortieth anniversary party at the St. Regis, which the stooges had attended and Wolfe crashed.

Shawn, who received an advance copy, fired a letter off to the *Tribune's* owner, Jock Whitney. He called the article "murderous and certainly libelous," and demanded that it be pulled from Sunday's upcoming edition. Jock declined.

The magazine called in its cavalry. The *Tribune* was barraged with diatribes from Muriel Spark to J.D. Salinger to Strunk's Sancho Panza, E.B. himself. Then the magazine's enforcer, Dwight Macdonald, fired off a 13,000-word polemic, "Parajournalism, or Tom Wolfe & His Magic Writing Machine," for its sister publication, *The New York Review of Books*. MacDonald called Wolfe's style "a bastard form, having it both ways, exploiting the factual authority of journalism and the atmospheric license of fiction."[8]

When the smoke cleared, the magazine had a shiner, and Wolfe's new *Streamline Baby* was a sensation.

From this the gonzo provocateur learned an important lesson in not boring an audience, which he revealed in his "The New Yorker Affair" essay. "You can be denounced from the heavens," he wrote," and it only makes people interested."

But years before, the best-selling nonfiction novelist had learned the greatest lesson about the postmodern elements of bile and Hemingway's built-in, shock-proof, shit detector.

"Bullshit reigns!" he proclaimed in *Bonfire of the Vanities*.

---

8 Dwight Macdonald , "Parajournalism, or Tom Wolfe & His Magic Writing Machine," *The New York Review of Books*, August 26, 1965.

PART VI

SCHMOOZING
THE MUSE

CHAPTER 23

THE MFA MAFIA

"Everywhere I go I'm asked if I think that university stifles writers. My opinion is that they don't stifle enough of them."
—Flannery O'Connor, Iowa MFA grad

University of Iowa launched the first writers' workshop in 1936. By 1972 there were seventy-three creative writing programs in the United States; by 2009, 822.[1] Before the arrival of MFA programs, every serious writer was an autodidact. Some still are.

Had an MFA program been available, would Charles Dickens, Mark Twain, Jack London, or any of the other high school dropouts have attended? Had they done so, would their work have been different, or better? Had O'Connor, Irving, Wallace, or any other noteworthy MFA graduates not attended, would their work have been as good or as celebrated?

The practical question for the 99 percent author is this: Like the original masters, shall I self-teach craft while attending the business school of hard knocks? Or, shall I spend $100K I don't have and get an MFA?

---

1 Louis Menand, "Show or Tell: Should Creative Writing be Taught?" *New Yorker,* June 8, 2009. http://www.newyorker.com/arts/critics/atlarge/2009/06/08/090608crat_atlarge_menand?

More and more are deciding to go the second route. In the last
two decades, 150,000 creative writing MFA diplomas have been
issued.[2] Competition has become increasingly keen. If nothing else,
academia provides an early introduction to the one inevitability of the
profession: rejection.

The national rejection rate for MFA programs averages 95 percent.
At top universities, the rate is higher. Iowa receives 1,300 annual applications for fifty slots. Johns Hopkins had 260 applications for their two
fiction openings in 2009.

Before winning the Pulitzer and selling more than 75 million books,
James Michener was turned down by every writing program to which
he applied. In the early nineties, he gave the University of Texas $20
million to start the Michener Center for Writers MFA program (which, in
2009, processed five hundred applicants for five openings, as did the
University of Michigan and University of California at Irvine).[3]

Other highly competitive programs include those offered by
Columbia, Boston University, Syracuse, NYU, University of Michigan,
University of Virginia, Cornell, Brown, and Princeton. All tout the pub-
lishing successes of their alumni.

BU, for example, advertises that "our graduates have won every
major award in each of their genres," and that they release a novel or
poetry collection with a major publisher every month. Moreover, they
earn tenure-track professorships at noted universities. "We make, of
course, no such assurances," BU concludes. "Our only promise to those
who join us is of a fair amount of time in that river-view room."

Most programs weigh applicants according to four criteria: talent,
ambition, teachability, and collegiality. So the selection process is subjective. Addressing ambition in their interview or written self-descrip-
tion, most aspiring authors will, without compromising the truth, make
clear they are ready to sacrifice a limb for publication. This is important
for the application committee to know since alumni deals and prizes
propagate the program, no less than the literary stars on staff. The
resident and visiting faculty roster at the best programs (many being

---

2 Paul Vidich, "The Future of the Book -- Publish Or Perish: The Short Story," *The Millions,* May 26, 2011.

3 Jessica Murphy Moo, "Writers in Training," *The Atlantic,* July 2007.

alumni) reads like a PEN/Pulitzer Who's Who.[4]

The dream MFA postgrad Affirmative Action career goes like this. He debuts with a story in a magazine where his professor publishes; he wins a magazine contest judged by said publisher or is included in a short fiction anthology edited by him.[5] Next, represented by his mentor's agent, he wins a debut fiction contract with the teacher's publisher or an associated house. Then, on the merits of this title and sequels, he wins grants or awards overseen by his benefactor or a colleague. Such accomplishments win him a faculty position at his alma mater. Now, with the incest cycle coming full circle, he teaches and promotes the next generation of great American novelists.

Sometimes an MFA student will break into the market with material produced before graduation. Iowa profs John Cheever and Stanley Elkin placed their student Allen Gurganus's short story "Minor Heroism" with *The New Yorker* and didn't tell him about the submission until it was accepted. Alice Sebold started her debut autobiographical novel, *Lucky*, at Irvine. Michael Chabon's advisor at Irvine, MacDonald Harris, sent the young man's master's thesis, *The Mysteries of Pittsburgh*, to his agent, who soon landed a $155,000 advance from William Morrow for the coming-of-age novel.

Granted, most MFAs do not enjoy such good fortune. Some are undone by the competitive pressure. Rick Moody, now an NYU professor, complained of this in the Columbia writing program he attended in the eighties. His classmates would, he wrote, "eviscerate their enemies and lionize their friends. I was often among the eviscerated."[6]

---

4 For example, the Iowa Writing Program: Wallace Stegner, Kurt Vonnegut, John Irving, John Gardner, Flannery O'Connor, Raymond Carver, Andre Dubus, Denis Johnson, Thom Jones, Charles Wright, Richard Bausch, T.C. Boyle, Allan Gurganus, Ron Hansen, Jayne Anne Phillips, Bob Shacochis, Curtis Sittenfeld.

5 MFA students who became teachers who became editors for *The Best American Short Fiction* series: Raymond Carver (Iowa), Gail Godwin (Iowa), Jane Smiley (Iowa), Ann Patchett (Iowa), Richard Ford (Irvine), Michael Chabon (Irvine), Alice Sebold (Irvine), Amy Tan (Irvine), Tobias Wolff (Stanford), Geraldine Brooks (Columbia), Louise Erdrich (Johns Hopkins), Lorrie Moore (Cornell), E.L. Doctorow (Columbia).

6 Rick Moody, "Writers and Mentors," *The Atlantic*, August 2005.

Still, the writer who perseveres and earns an MFA, as Moody did, has a leg up in the submission process. All other things being equal, an overworked editor or agent is naturally more apt to pick an MFA ms. from the slush pile over another GED, BA, or BS ms.

Some teachers today warn their students not to overestimate this advantage. Novelist Dani Shapiro, who has taught at Wesleyan, Columbia, and the New School, tells her students that a degree will "entitle them to nothing"—that, unlike law or med school, "writing school guarantees them little other than debt." *The Best New American Voices 2010* editor emphasizes this first lesson not to be "sadistic," much less "unpopular," but "because it's the truth."[7]

The caveats of other prominent MFA professors relate to a fundamental flaw in the educational approach itself.

E.L. Doctorow, who taught at Yale, Princeton, and NYU, told *The Paris Review*, "The great danger is that you are creating and training not just writers but teachers of writing ... teachers of writing begetting teachers of writing, and that's bad."

When the magazine asked Wallace Stegner, namesake of the prestigious Stanford University fellowship, about the proliferation of MFA programs, the Iowa Workshop grad and Pulitzer Prize winner called it "dangerous" because the training is "all analytical, all critical. It's all a reader's training, not a writer's training."

Susan Sontag, who taught at Sarah Lawrence, found that the programs could be no less damaging to teachers than to students. "I've seen academic life destroy the best writers of my generation," she told *The Paris Review.*

Many such Prestige writers don't make enough on their novels and are obliged to teach. Few like it. Wages are low: The average non-tenured professor earns between $8,000 and $15,000 per semester.[8] Moreover, creative teaching approaches are often discouraged: When a loaded Barry Hannah packed a revolver to class to demonstrate the six movements of a short story, he was fired. But worst of all, the

---

7 Dani Shapiro, "A Writing Career Becomes Harder to Scale," *Los Angeles Times*, February 2, 2010.

8 Matt McCue, "Because Writers Who Can Write, Teach," *New York Magazine*, December 20, 2010. http://nymag.com/news/articles/reasonstoloveny/2010/70053/

classroom takes the master away from his work and cuts his focus, and nothing is more intolerable to most artists. "When I did finally do some teaching, it completely ate me up," said Jonathan Franzen.[9] More than that, as pointed out by William Gass, who taught many years in spite of his choleric disposition, "Creative-writing teachers, poor souls, must immerse themselves in slop and even take it seriously." But even more trying for him early in his career was his feeling that "I wrote far worse stuff than I see from my students."[10]

In his 1991 title, *On Writing*,[11] crime novelist and Boston University professor George V. Higgins echoed his colleague. He complained that most writing students recycle the same six stories: "Old man dies; old woman dies; why I hate my mother; why I hate my father; how I lost my virginity; how I tried to and failed. That's it."

Stephen King covered his share of this territory and far more. While some of his contemporaries were doing grad work, he worked at a motel laundromat by day and on shorts for men's magazines by night. He believed that one learns to write by reading and that classrooms do little more than teach terminology and promote exclusivity. "The keepers of the idea of serious literature have a short list of authors who are going to be allowed inside," he declared in his 2006 *The Paris Review* interview, "and too often that list is drawn from people who know people, who go to certain schools, who come up through certain channels of literature. And that's a very bad idea—it's constraining for the growth of literature."

---

9 David Amsden, "The Write Start," *New York Magazine*, July 21, 2003.

10 Thomas LeClair, *The Paris Review* interview with William Gass, The Art of Fiction No. 65. July, 1976.

11 George V. Higgins, *On Writing: Advice for Those Who Write to Publish (Or Would Like To)*, (New York: Henry Holt, 1991).

CHAPTER 24

CONTESTS & GRANTS

Heads We Win, Tales You Lose

"There is no way of being a creative writer in America without being a loser."

—**Nelson Algren, namesake of the** *Chicago Tribune* **short story award**

Many colleges or universities with creative writing graduate programs publish a literary magazine. Readers are generally MFA students, some of whom also correct papers for their advisor's undergraduate classes. Screening magazine submissions gives the grad pupil a preview of what it's like to be an editor or agent, should she decide to move to the other side of the desk later on. Exposed to a morass of unsolicited short stories, she will discover firsthand just how awful 99 percent are. Still, something must be salvaged from the slush lest outsiders suspect that a university lit mag is a vanity press for its MFA franchise or, worse, that academia is less an open-armed meritocracy than a Skull and Bones society.

To further ward against ignorance and prejudice, many periodicals hold an annual fiction contest. Scholarship MFAs screen the entries for free while the contest fees bring much-needed capital into the editorial office, though some insist that they run their lotto in the red. Circulation is often boosted, too, as many publications throw in a subscription to the losers for their competition fee. But usually also-rans must pay extra for a copy of the story that beat them. Sometimes they get a discount since editors realize they're the only ones who'll be reading the story anyway.

An acclaimed judge attracts contestants. But this judge only sees the finalist manuscripts—the ten or twenty from hundreds or thousands winnowed by the mind-numbed screeners. The readers themselves are ineligible, precluding nepotism. For the same reason, some contests require that manuscripts be submitted anonymously.

Other competitions are sponsored by independent journals—*Glimmer Train, Tin Roof, Narrative*, etc.—and are an excellent source of revenue and publicity. Sadly, some great contests, such as *The Paris Review*'s Aga Khan and the *Chicago Tribune*'s Nelson Algren, are defunct.

Some master awards and prizes—the Faulkner, the Flannery O'Connor, the Hemingway, the Wolfe, the Steinbeck, the James Jones, etc.—are run by foundations, others by universities. Only the sore loser or heretic wonders if any of these writers might, in a parallel universe, prove unable to win their own award today.

Major contests offer winners $500 to $2,000; lesser ones, ten or twenty free journal copies for family and friends. Some competitions boast extras: a chance for representation by a top-flight New York or Hollywood literary agency, a free trip to read one's story to a narcoleptic audience, a possible Pushcart nomination. (Hemingway never entered a short fiction competition, but his story collection, *Winner Take Nothing*—published four years after his bestseller, *A Farewell to Arms*—sold only 12,500 copies.)

No matter the contest, an entrant usually gets a form snail or e-jection like this: *We received an unprecedented volume of brilliant work this year. Unfortunately yours, in spite of its evident merit, was not a finalist. But keep writing and don't forget to apply next year!*

Finally, lest anyone think the search for the next Hemingway is anything but energetic and equal opportunity, there are cattle calls such as the Amazon Breakthrough Novel Award (ABNA), which draws nearly as many contestants as *American Idol* and Southern pie cook-offs.

>>>

Grants and fellowships generally offer more money than contests and, with it, resumé gold. The majors include the Guggenheim, the Fulbright, the MacArthur Genius, the MacDowell, the National Endowment for the Arts—all overseen by the usual suspects. In the late 1980s, Wallace Stegner refused an NEA National Medal because he believed the organization had become "too politicized."

Unlike a contest, a grant application is seldom anonymous. It's all about who the applicant is (i.e., whom she knows). Winning rests heavily on recommendations and endorsements. The best are from former grant recipients themselves, many of whom are writing program chairs. The best of the best are from former grant jurors or honorary board members.

Whether the writer is applying for an NEA, a Guggenheim, or a Fulbright, a letter from his award-winning thesis advisor will carry more weight than one from his psychiatrist or parole officer. Such a grant in turn rescues a winner from slush piles and can be parlayed into publication. And, if luck and suck hold, one may eventually become a Nobel, Pulitzer, Booker, or National Book Award nominee.

As for scoring the latter, *New York Magazine*'s publishing reporter, Boris Kachka, provided a helpful checklist:[1]

1. Don't be a young debut novelist.
2. Don't write short stories.
3. Do aim for world-historical significance.
4. Do be a literary insider.
5. Do expand your demo.

---

1   Boris Kachka, "How to Win a National Book Award in Five Easy Steps," November 13, 2007. www.vulture.com/2007/11/how_to_win_a_national_book_awa.html

CHAPTER 25

KUMBAYA CONFERENCES

"The first value of a writers' workshop is that it makes the young writer feel not only not abnormal but virtuous."
—John Gardner

Hawthorne helped Melville; Pound helped Joyce; Emerson, Thoreau; Capote, Harper Lee; Burroughs, Kerouac; Cheever, Updike; Edmund Wilson, Mary McCarthy (his wife); Kingsley Amis, Martin (his son); William Buckley, Christopher (his son); Susan Sontag, David Rieff (her son); and so on.

Nowadays, legendary sponsors are seldom stumbled upon at the local bar or salon or, for most, in the family tree. But, luckily, some of today's Melvilles and McCarthys materialize at writers conferences.

The best conferences, like the best substance-abuse retreats, are in scenic spots: from the Green Mountains to the high Sierra to the Northwest's Puget Sound to the white beaches of Maui.

First to the podium is usually the founder—a university MFA head, an Ivy League emeritus, what-have-you. They speak about the importance of community in a lonely profession and how all present are equal and united in the noble struggle with the muse. They introduce faculty writers who expand on these themes and conclude with words on passion, persistence, and optimism.

Finally, the Pulitzer keynote emerges *deus ex machina* from the wings to warm applause. After reminiscing about the trials and tribulations of his own early career, he climaxes on passion, persistence, and optimism.

The next day students learn about How to Find the Story, How to Create 3-D Characters, How to Write the Bones, and the many other aspects of their craft. Missing from the curriculum are introductory and advanced marketing courses.

Students must fall back on their own resources when turning to the real business of the conference: the schmooze.

»»

If the resident Ford, Franzen, or Oates hasn't already dematerialized, you track them down on the beach, on the chairlift, or in the bathroom.[1] But you find them already surrounded as if they were Mick Jagger or Lady Gaga. Those in front are editors and agents hoping to land the great one's next tome; in second position are the publish-or-perish faculty looking for an endorsement; in third are the conference organizers. Finally, at the fringes are the bottom feeders—everyone who paid retail for the conference.

Protagonist revelation: The Darwinian food chain here is the same as in New York; except here you can ride the gondola, learn to sail, or polish up on your boogie boarding.

But, passionately persistent, you drop in on the Bodhisattva's chalet or aloha hut at midnight. A party is in progress with the Parnassians and their retainers. Refusing to go home empty handed, you now adopt a more realistic MO: schmoozing a junior agent who covers the slush and brings Chinese takeout back at the office. Except they're too busy schmoozing to get schmoozed themselves.

---

1 In *Some Writers Deserve to Starve!: 31 Brutal Truths about the Publishing Industry*, veteran conference coordinator Elaura Niles warns workshop participants against following VIPs here. "Stalls are not confessionals [and] urinals are not meant for impromptu pitches," she advises. But she adds that conference sex is abundant and okay, just as long as participants don't violate the "pecking order."

But the conference organizers realize that, for purposes of morale no less than the future of their franchise, at least one flounder must be elevated. So, by the end of the week, one lucky attendee has a contract with an agent or editor and is attending readings and sing-alongs in the great one's chalet, and the news of this spreads like wildfire among the nonCinderellas.

Meanwhile, talk about honesty and authenticity dominates the conference. Everyone from the Pulitzers on down agrees: If a writer doesn't strive for these virtues in his work, he should sell life insurance.

CHAPTER 26

% OF YOUR BACK END

Hollywood's Return of the Screw

"The only sad part of being a hack is that one is called upon to
adapt the work of more successful hacks."
—**Gore Vidal**

But suppose nothing pans out: You can't get into an MFA program or, if
you did, the training and degree were of no help. Your efforts to score
a grant or fellowship have also proved fruitless, and your attendance at
Breadloaf, Squaw, or Maui was also a dead end.

What now? Is there any other rope that might, as E.B. White put it,
"deliver the writer to dry ground?"

Yes. It is called Hollywood.

Granted, the emerald palace in the City of Angels is, indeed, harder
to break into than Iowa, Yaddo, or the NEA. Here, even the suck of
sleeping with somebody has a twenty-four-hour statute of limitations
before a restraining order is issued.

But, again: nothing ventured, nothing gained.

This is the belief of some agents nowadays. If they're not getting any
nibbles in New York, they'll send a treatment out to the coast or pitch
the idea over the phone. A greenlight from DreamWorks or Miramax

can be parlayed into a package deal from one of the big houses worth much more than it would have had the book been marketed in the standard way.

Getting a table in Hollywood, however, can be a daunting task. Estimates of spec screenplay registration and submissions vary dramatically. A median annual figure of new Writers Guild and U.S. Library of Congress copyright registrations is forty thousand. In 2011, TheWrap reported eighty-six spec script sales. But only a fraction of these reach the big screen. So the odds of a spec homer are not far from the odds of being struck by lightning. But let's say you're Spielberg's rabbi or Cruise's Scientology auditor and you've got a novel that could be the next *Schindler's List* or *Mission Imposssible*. What next?

Two choices: Either send the ms. directly to Steven's or Tom's people and let them spec out the script, or cut the middleman and do the script yourself.

Three acts. One hundred twenty pages. One hundred four-letter words per page, plus conjunctions. With a car chase, a scene with the ex and the kids for character development, a dismemberment, several sex scenes, then a fade to black.

How hard can that be?

For the original California gold rushers—Faulkner, Huxley, Heller, Vonnegut, Maugham, Mailer, Saroyan, Vidal—"hard as hell," according to their leader, F. Scott Fitzgerald.

Each was assigned to translate another's novel to the screen. Fitzgerald tried to adapt Mitchell's *Gone with the Wind*; Vidal, Faulkner's *Barn Burning*; Faulkner, Chandler's *Big Sleep*; Chandler, Cain's *Double Indemnity*; Huxley, Brontë's *Jane Eyre*; Heller, Fleming's *Her Majesty's Secret Service* and Helen Gurley Brown's *Sex and the Single Girl*.

As we will see in the next chapter, writers tend to be mad. The greater, the madder, and, often, the most masochistic. Besides their appetite for punishment, why did the masters answer the MGM siren call?

John Cheever provided the answer to *The Paris Review*. "I went to Hollywood to make money. It's very simple. The people are friendly and the food is good, but I've never been happy there … my principal feeling about Hollywood is suicide."

F. Scott, who made three pilgrimages west to escape bankruptcy, the last being the death of him, felt the same way: "I hate the place like poison." Between 1927 and 1940, he worked on sixteen scripts, five of which were rejected outright, the others for which he received no credit, save one (*Three Comrades*).

Of his and Zelda's first trip, the novelist told his daughter, Scottie, "Hollywood made a big fuss over us. ... I honestly believed that with no effort on my part I was a sort of magician with words, an odd delusion." By the third go-round, he'd forgotten the words and only talked about the money. In his notes for *The Last Tycoon*, he jotted out the Hollywood weekly payscale:

Junior writers: $300
Minor poets: $500
Broken novelists: $850–$1,000
One play dramatists: $1,500
Sucks: $2000–$2,500

Neither Fitzgerald nor any of his colleagues broke through the Broken Novelist glass ceiling. Faulkner, too, peaked at $1,000 per week. But soon Jack Warner of Warner Brothers was boasting about how he was paying "America's greatest novelist" hardly enough to cover his bar tab. Later, Marilyn Monroe spoke for herself and the masters when she said, "Hollywood is a place that pays you a thousand dollars for a kiss and fifty cents for your soul," neglecting to add that the soul is usually DOA by the time you start getting paid.

At the end of their tenures in America's dream factory, all the literary icons were well acquainted with the industry's definition of a screenwriter: "The first draft of a human being."

When a human rough draft had the audacity to stand up to a producer or director, he was promptly reminded who he was. His five major novels behind him, plus screenwriting Oscars, Raymond Chandler was put in his place by Alfred Hitchcock while writing *Strangers on a Train*.

Hitchcock had paid $7,500 for the rights from debut novelist Patricia Highsmith, who at Truman Capote's urging had finished the novel at Yaddo. The filmmaker had hired Chandler to adapt Highsmith's murder

mystery after nine other writers had declined the job, including John
Steinbeck, Thornton Wilder, and Dashiell Hammett.[1]

Like his colleagues, Chandler, a retired oil executive, had a reputation for getting difficult when lubricated. Which he almost always was,
especially when dealing with the likes of Hitchcock. When Chandler
complained of the director's "god-awful jabber sessions," which
allowed him no time to write, much less rehydrate during happy hour,
Hitchcock gave him his all-writers-are-cattle scowl. In response, the
wordsmith called him "a fat bastard." In response to this, Hitchcock
deposited Chandler's *Strangers on a Train* drafts into the trash while
holding his nose.

Afterwards, the *Double Indemnity* adaptor wrote his screenwriting
epitaph: "If my books had been any worse, I should not have been
invited to Hollywood, and if they had been any better, I should not
have come."

What was and still is the serious novelist's great quandary about
Hollywood is this: Producers find little or no truth in the truism *If it ain't
broke, don't fix it.*

The studio will have a script rewritten many times, then the director
will take a shot, then the actors, then the key grip. Finally, the whole
thing may explode and the "collaborative" process starts all over again.
If you wrote the original script, you may not get credit for it. You may not
even get fully paid. A hired gun like Shane Black or David Mamet will
collect your million for tweaking the third act.

If you file a copyright infringement suit, now you're really screwed.
Copyright law protects expression, not idea. So Hollywood can keep
all your car wrecks, dismemberments, and sex scenes—that's just
idea—shuffle your sentences, pump up your modifiers, toss your prep-
ositional phrases—and that's their new expression.

But suppose a judge finds the Studio Scrabble inadequate and
awards you your million (though this has never happened). First, to
have reached this point, you will have spent about the same amount

---

1 Donald Spoto, *The Dark Side of Genius: The Life of Alfred Hitchcock,* (New York: Ballantine Books, 1983).

in legal fees, not to mention years of your life; in short, you'll be bankrupt and in a nursing home. Second, you won't be able to collect your million award anyway since Hollywood, like New York, zeroes out its books so even successful ventures don't show profit. So goldbricker writers, no less than the IRS, are SOL.

Which is the reason the only writer to leave L.A. with his balls and liver intact—plus a cut of Paramount's $288 million for ripping off his *Coming to America* treatment—was Art Buchwald.

Then, in 2012, E.L. James arrived with her S&M blockbuster *Fifty Shades of Grey* and Lena Dunham with her Twixter comedy *Girls*.

After unloading 65 million copies of her originally e-published FanFiction, James sold *Fifty Shades* to Universal for $5 million. A British TV programming executive in her own right, the reigning queen of romance also demanded from Universal powers which Fitzgerald and the others didn't even dream of: final approval of screenwriter, screenplay, director, cast, locations, and marketing campaign. The studio agreed to everything. *American Psycho* Bret Easton Ellis, hoping to again tap into the zeitgeist and return to cultural relevance, lobbied aggressively to adapt the novel to the screen, telling James that her bondage billionaire hero, Christian Grey, was "a writer's dream." Though they shared a publisher (Vintage), James declined Ellis' services and gave the nod to her fellow Brit writer Kelly Marcel.

Meanwhile Lena Dunham was and is making millions from HBO as creator/writer/director/producer of *Girls*. Inspired by HBO's previous hit, *Sex in the City*, the comedy features the romantic and career misadventures of four New York Twixters so self-absorbed they make the *Seinfeld* four look like UNICEF workers. Dunham's three co-stars are David Mamet's daughter, Zosia; Brian Williams' daughter, Allison; and Bad Company drummer Simon Kirke's daughter, Jemima (her former schoolmate). According to *Rolling Stone*, Dunham's casting has led to "endless nepotism debates."[2] The 2008 Oberlin College creative writing grad began her screenwriting career with the autobiographical *Tiny Furniture*, shot in her parents' TriBeCa loft, followed by her Web

---

2 Brian Hiatt, "Girl on Top: How Lena Dunham Turned a Life of Anxiety, Bad Sex, and Countless Psychiatric Meds into the Funniest Show on TV," *Rolling Stone*, February 28, 2013.

podcast comedies, *Tight Shots* and *Delusional Downtown Divas*. The first indication that Dunham might have a brighter future in screenwriting than her legendary predecessors was when her *Tiny Furniture* producer covered her bill at a restaurant, saying: "Lena, you made a hit movie—we can pay for your nachos."[3]

Dunham's inspirations are fellow autobiographical writer/producer/director/actors Nora Ephron and Tina Fey. The daughter of two screenwriters, Ephron adapted her hit novel, *Heartburn*, for the screen and went on to become a Hollywood VIP. Fey received a $6 million advance from Little Brown for *Bossypants*, an account of her early days as a *Saturday Night Live* writer and, later, as the *30 Rock* creator. In the best-selling autobiography she shares her hard-won wisdom about the industry: "The definition of 'crazy' in show business is a woman who keeps talking even after no one wants to fuck her anymore."

So the four Bossypants have proved to entertainment moguls what the Fitzgerald fraternity couldn't: They're more than first drafts of human beings, so they expect to be paid accordingly on both the back and the front ends.

Usually manuscripts migrate east to west. Novels that become movies enjoy exponential sales. But occasionally a manuscript will fly from the City of Angels to The Big Apple. This was the case with Rex Pickett's *Sideways*.

The novel—about a failed novelist on a Holy Grail Pinot Noir quest in Santa Barbara wineries with his randy former college roommate—had been purchased in 2000 by director/producer Alexander Payne. But when production began three years later in California, the ms. had been shot down one hundred times in New York with what Pickett called "splenetic, downright hateful" editorial rejections such as: "*Sideways* is nothing more than a glorified screenplay, and if it was made into a film it would stink to high heaven with the rot of Pickett's

---

3 David Carr, "Young Filmmaker's Search for Her Worth Is Rewarded," *New York Times*, March 19, 2010.

writing."[4] Thinking the novel "roadkill," a bummed and broke Pickett "sweetly fantasized" about suicide until at last his agent scored a $5,000 advance from St. Martin's. His mild relief evaporated when his new editor told Pickett that he needed to hire a line editor, then foot the bill for his own PR.

After *Sideways* won the 2005 Academy Award for best adapted screenplay, St. Martin's still refused to bankroll any marketing for the novel, leaving, according to Pickett, "millions on the table because of their ostrich-like ignorance of the movie's phenomenon."[5] Having earned less than $100,000 on the book, he called himself "a bona fide member of the 99 Percent."

Pickett's agent, hoping to capitalize on his "ephemeral heat," persuaded him to novelize an old script of his, "The Road Back." Though gun shy after his St. Martin's experience, he submitted a one-page proposal. Knopf fronted $75,000 for the novel. After two deadline extensions, Pickett turned in a 175,000-word first draft. Six months later his editor, now co-president of Knopf, responded with cursory "unhelpful" revision notes. Pickett submitted a second draft. Knopf apparently failed to review it and instead exercised the contract's kill clause—a cancellation his agent failed to tell him about for five months. Pickett considered suing both his agent and publisher but bitterly surrendered, knowing the Random House legal department would bury him financially before any proceeding went to trial.

"I was an established writer with a track record and I ended up getting treated more execrably than in Hollywood, where writers are notoriously abused," he concluded. "And I lived—barely—to tell the real truth of traditional publishing."[6]

---

4 Rex Pickett, "The Sideways Publishing Saga—Part I: Rejection," *Huffington Post*, January 27, 2012. http://www.huffingtonpost.com/rex-pickett/sideways-book-rejection_b_1232398.html

5 Rex Pickett, "The Sideways Publishing Saga—The St. Martin's Press Nightmare (Part II)," *Huffington Post*, February 20, 2012.

6 Rex Pickett, "The (Un)Romantic Path of Literary Fiction: Alfred A. Knopf (Part IV)," *Huffington Post*, May 9, 2012.

PART VII

THE MAD, MAD, MAD, MAD WRITER

"This sickness, to express oneself. What is it?"
—Jean Cocteau

CHAPTER 27

THE CUCKOO'S NEST

"The good writing of any age has always been the product of someone's neurosis."
—**William Styron**

"This is what I find most encouraging about the writing trades: They allow lunatics to seem saner than sane."
—**Kurt Vonnegut**

This much should be clear now: Given the professional hardships, one cannot want to write literature for a living and still be sane. Not just a little off—serious writing requires professional crazy. In his own life, no less than in his books, the novelist cannot let reality stand in his way.

Johns Hopkins professor William Egginton will soon release his eagerly awaited *The Man Who Invented Fiction: A Biography of Miguel de Cervantes*. Cervantes' fictional alter ego, Don Quixote, fought giants that sane men saw as windmills. "Too much sanity may be madness," he cried. In the end, he abandoned his crusades, surrendered his lance, and died sane as the doddering Alonso.

"How do you take away from a man his madness without also taking away his identity?" wondered William Saroyan, an admirer of the
inventor of fiction and his hero.

Kerouac called the loss of reason "the highest perfect knowing."
He rhapsodized in his automatic writing travelogue, *On the Road*:
"...the only people for me are the mad ones, the ones who are mad to
live, mad to talk, mad to be saved ... the ones who burn, burn, burn
like fabulous yellow roman candles exploding like spiders across the
stars and ... everybody goes 'Awww!'" Allen Ginsberg, a Bellevue
psych ward alumnus, praised Jack, the Rocky Mountain Sanitarium
grad: "Your stories of the madhouse are so actual that I feel again as I
did in the Navy nuthouse—scared and seeing through heads. I used to
sit with the worst ones to learn."[1]

All of life's mysteries are explained when we realize everybody is
nuts, said Mark Twain. Beckett's hero, Estragon, agreed: "We are all
born mad. Some remain so."

Given the rich history of literary madness, is it possible for today's
creative writer to be well balanced? Theoretically, yes. But such a writer
is at a disadvantage in the essentials of art: imagination and energy.

Artists agree that there are two kinds of crazy: Creative = good,
Destructive = bad. But the first can morph into the second slowly or
suddenly in spite of every effort to stop it. "We have a high rate of
self-destruction," Doctorow told *The Paris Review*. "Do we mean to punish ourselves for writing? For the transgression?"

In the end, Maupassant was chained to an asylum wall, Virginia
Woolf walked into a river, Plath turned on the oven. Or the fire is lost
altogether, so Jerzy Kosinski put a bag over his head, Inge gassed
himself, and Hunter Thompson, Richard Brautigan, and Hemingway
painted walls. Before reaching the end of his own rope, David Foster
Wallace said, "Ever notice that most writers shoot themselves in the
evil uncontrollable command center—the *head*?"

Hemingway, whose physician father also blew out the command
center, wrote, "The real reason for not committing suicide is because
you always know how swell life gets again after the hell is over." Losing

---

1 Paul Maher, Jr., *Kerouac: The Definitive Biography* (Taylor Trade Publishing, 2004).

hope that his muse would ever return, *The Sun Also Rises* master was convinced his hell would be eternal. In the final irony, he said his asylum electroshock treatments "put me out of business."

Norman Mailer idolized Hemingway. His debut novel, *The Naked and the Dead*, was hailed as the greatest war novel since *For Whom the Bell Tolls*. When, six years after its publication, Hemingway shot himself, Mailer told *The Paris Review* that the tragedy had a message:

"Listen all you novelists out there. Get it straight: When you're a novelist you're entering on an extremely dangerous psychological journey, and it can blow up in your face."

In the following chapters, let's examine the conditions that can inspire and guide that dangerous journey, and may lead to the ultimate madness: *fame.*

CHAPTER 28

MEGALOMANIA

"Writers write for fame, wealth, power, and the love of women."
—**Sigmund Freud**

One of the leading nineteenth-century head cases was Edgar Allan Poe—short, hydrocephalic, moody. "It is my crime to have no one on Earth who cared for me, or loved me," he wrote. After his actor father vanished and his actress mother died of TB, the three-year-old orphan was adopted by the implacable tobacco tycoon Mr. Allan. At age sixteen, the boy wrote his first poem, "Oh, Tempora! Oh, Mores!" but Allan forbade its publication for fear Edgar might get a "swelled head." His classmates already described him as "ambitious" and "inclined to be imperious."[1]

Allan discouraged his stepson from "eating the bread of idleness"—writing. After the young man was expelled from West Point for reporting to dress parade undressed, he turned full-time to literature. "For God's sake pity me," he wrote home, "and save me from destruction!"

---

1 Kenneth Silverman, *Edgar A. Poe: Mournful and Never-ending Remembrance* (New York: Harper Perennial, 1992).

Allan disinherited him.

Edgar moved in with his surrogate mother, Aunt Muddy, a seam-
stress, and like Jerry Lee Lewis, he married his thirteen-year-old
cousin, Virginia, whom he called Sissy. For the next two decades, the
threesome lived on molasses sandwiches and laudanum. Poe's average
annual income was $100. In 1845 he earned a record $699, $9 of which
came from "The Raven."

After R&R at a Utica asylum in 1846, the novelist/poet/critic/editor
resolved to make a fortune on "Eureka." He wrote a friend that in
this essay on the origin of the cosmos he would "question the sagacity
of many of the greatest and most justly reverenced of men (such
as Aristotle and Bacon) … with no unwarranted fear of being taken for
a madman."

"My whole nature utterly *revolts* at the idea that there is any Being in
the Universe superior to *myself*!" he told his publisher. Adding that he
had eclipsed Isaac Newton himself, he told Putnam to print a million
copies, 50,000 at the very least. Putnam advanced him $14, ran 750 cop-
ies, and sold 500 at 75¢ apiece.

After the "Eureka" debacle, Sissy died of TB. On the rebound, Poe
dated mother surrogates. The first, poetess Jane Locke, was smitten. "I
felt as if in the presence of a god!" Then, realizing he had psychological
issues, she dumped him. Fearing that he mightn't be canonized in his
own lifetime, much less deified, the poet now drank thirty times his
maintenance dose of laudanum.

To his disappointment, Poe survived. Complaining again of
"brain fever," he declared, "I became insane, with long intervals of hor-
rible sanity."

In the end, the father of the murder mystery and horror genre
was carried from a Baltimore bar to a hospital, wearing one shoe, and
somebody else's clothes, babbling incoherently.[2]

Literary history teaches us that declaring one's godlike genius is

---

2 Kenneth Silverman, *Edgar A. Poe: Mournful and Never-ending Remembrance* (New York: Harper Perennial, 1992).

mandatory for the megalomaniac.

Explaining his depression to a friend one day, Oscar Wilde said, "I'm sad because one half of the world doesn't believe in God, and the other half doesn't believe in me." Another time, asked to name his hundred favorite books, he declined "because I've only written five." When entering America, he told the customs official, "I have nothing to declare but my genius." After dying penniless and disgraced, the genius was laid to rest in Paris under a stone angel whose genitals were cut off and used as paperweights by the cemetery guards.

When Theodore Dreiser was asked how he wrote *Sister Carrie* at age twenty-nine, he replied, "Genius, I suppose." Later, he wrote his autobiographical novel *The Genius*.

While some writers decide that they're geniuses before creating a work of genius, the humble wait.

"I am about to become a genius," said Balzac after finishing *La Comédie Humaine*.

"By God, I think I have genius," said Thomas Wolfe after finishing *Look Homeward, Angel*.

At age fifty-three, Truman Capote preceded his own declaration with modifiers: "I'm an alcoholic. I'm a drug addict. I'm homosexual. I'm a genius."

Sometimes a fellow genius will disagree. After Wolfe was nine years in the ground and defenseless, Hemingway wrote their publisher, Charles Scribner: "Tom Wolfe was a one-book boy and a glandular giant with the brains and the guts of three mice." Then he weighed in on another self-proclaimed genius, F. Scott Fitzgerald, who had connected him with Scribner in the first place. "Scott was a rummy and a liar ... with the inbred talent of a dishonest and easily frightened angel."

By then Fitzgerald had been thrown from his *Gatsby* high horse and was drinking himself to stupor. "His [Hemingway's] inclination is toward megalomania and mine toward melancholy," he wrote.[3]

Papa's original mentor, Gertrude Stein, had provided a role model for self-aggrandizement. The Montparnasse matriarch had written literary scholar Samuel Putnam: "20th century literature *is* Gertrude Stein. The big American writers are Poe, Whitman, James, myself. The line of

---

3 Jeffrey Meyers, *Scott Fitzgerald: A Biography* (New York: HarperCollins, 2004).

dissent is clear."[4] In her journal she added, "It takes a lot of time to be a genius, you have to sit around so much doing nothing." Hemingway had no patience with such gasconade. His mentor's talent, he wrote, had "gone to malice and nonsense and self-praise ... But, I swear, she was damned nice before she got ambitious."

Sinclair Lewis, whom Hemingway had also dismissed as a fake, called Papa "a monosyllabic simpleton." At a cocktail party, the *Arrowsmith* author informed H.L. Mencken, "Let me tell you something. I'm the best writer in this here goddamn country!" Mencken, a grandiose self-advertiser himself, called Lewis a "jackass."[5]

Sinclair had the last laugh, becoming the first American to win a Nobel. Faulkner—who had declared, "I am the best in America, by God!"—collected his own nineteen years later. Five years after that, in 1954, Hemingway—who had declared, "I don't like to write like God. It is only because you never do it, though, that the critics think you can't do it"—was finally beatified by the Academy.

Like Nixon, Gadhafi, Hemingway, and other egomaniacs, John O'Hara referred to himself in the third person, at least when composing the epitaph on his tombstone.

> Better than anyone else,
> he told the truth about his time.
> He was a professional.
> He wrote honestly and well.

Brendan Gill, the novelist's nemesis at *The New Yorker,* wondered, "*Better than anyone else?* Not merely better than any other writer of fiction but better than any dramatist, any poet, any biographer, any historian? It is an astonishing claim."[6]

---

4 Noel Riley Fitch, *Sylvia Beach And The Lost Generation: A History Of Literary Paris In The 20s And 30s* (New York: W.W. Norton, 1985).

5 Mark Schorer, *Sinclair Lewis: An American Life* (New York: McGraw-Hill, 1961).

6 Brendan Gill, *Here at the New Yorker.* (New York: Random House, 1975).

The first rock star American novelist, Mark Twain, like O'Hara and Faulkner, wrote that he wished to "outrival those whom the public most admires."[7]

Twain was Hemingway's idol. Convinced that he was without match in the United States, Hemingway took on dead European heavyweights. He claimed to have KO'ed Turgenev, Maupassant, then Stendhal. With characteristic modesty, he concluded, "But nobody's going to get me in any ring with Mr. Tolstoy unless I'm crazy or I keep getting better."[8]

At the outset of his career, Tolstoy, embarrassed by his own arrogance, whipped himself. His friend, Dostoyevsky, spoke for the two of them when he told his brother, "I have a terrible vice: a boundless pride and vanity."[9]

Steinbeck agreed. "The whole early part of my life was poisoned with egotism," he confessed. He believed that good writing came from "an absence of ego."[10] This helped him become a master of characterization, a difficult skill for the narcissist.

Fitzgerald admitted that all of his characters, even his women, were himself.[11] Hemingway refused to admit the same. Of his last novel, *The Old Man and the Sea*, he wrote: "It will destroy the school of criticism that claims I can write about nothing except myself and my own experiences."[12] But the only thing different about his old man was that he was penniless, hadn't been on the covers of *Life, Time,* or *Argosy,* and hadn't tried to gaff his fellow fishermen.

One of the few colleagues Hemingway hadn't found it necessary to cannibalize was Ezra Pound, because Pound was a poet and never bad-mouthed him. But, in private, to Archibald MacLeish, Papa wrote, "If Ezra has any sense he should shoot himself. Personally I think he

---

7 Ron Powers, *Mark Twain: A Life.* (New York: Free Press, 2005).

8 James R. Mellow, *Hemingway: A Life Without Consequence* (New York: Houghton Mifflin, 1992).

9 Geir Kjetsaa, *Fyodor Dostoyevsky: A Writer's Life* (New York: Viking, 1987).

10 Jay Parini, *John Steinbeck: A Biography* (New York: Henry Holt, 1995).

11 According to his biographer, Jeffrey Meyers, Fitzgerald wore falsies and make-up in Princeton plays. One classmate recalled: "He looked exactly like a beautiful lady and acted like one."

12 Carlos Baker, ed., *Ernest Hemingway Selected Letters 1917-1961.* (New York: Scribner, 2003).

should have shot himself somewhere along after the twelfth *Canto*, although maybe earlier."

Pound spent twelve years in St. Elizabeth's psychiatric hospital in Washington, D.C. He composed his later *Cantos* there, on toilet paper. T.S. Eliot described meeting his friend, surrounded by inmates frothing at the mouth. Deciding that he was just a "narcissist," the doctors moved the poet to a private room. He became so comfortable at the hospital that he resisted leaving. Colleagues who were trying to spring him—Hemingway, Eliot, Auden, and others—were baffled.

After his release, Pound was asked by a reporter if he felt free. He said no. "When I left the hospital I was still in America, and all America is an insane asylum."[13]

---

13 John Tytell, *Ezra Pound: The Solitary Volcano* (New York: Doubleday, 1987).

CHAPTER 29

MISERABLE & MANIC

"I have been ecstatic; but I have not been happy."
—Edna St. Vincent Millay

According to *Scientific American* (1995), writers are ten times more likely to be depressed than civilians and eighteen times more likely to kill themselves.

"I think a lot—not just a little, but a lot—about killing myself," said Truman Capote. "I wake up hoping that I will die."

Said Hemingway, "Happiness in intelligent people is the rarest thing I know."

The mystery, as George Orwell, the creator of *Animal Farm*, once pointed out, is how people ever got the crazy idea that the object of life is happiness.

So, the age-old question: Must the writer suffer?

Not long ago, *The New Yorker* fiction editor Deborah Treisman was asked why most stories in her magazine were dark and depressing. "I fear this goes back to the basic rules of narrative structure: Without some form of conflict, you have no plot," she replied. "Happiness doesn't provide progression or development. It's very difficult to write an entirely cheerful story and have it be interesting."[1]

From the writer's personal perspective, there's another reason as well. To the extent that he is bummed—feeling helpless, insignificant, alienated, pissed off—creating an alternate reality, especially with a protagonist alter ego, is a power trip.

It might be argued that authors are the characters in God's novel who create their own novel and characters so they don't go off the deep end of God's novel. In which case writers work at cross-purposes with the Almighty. Sometimes they get a taste of their own medicine: They lose control of their own Adams and Eves and become bipolar.

"Oh, I am so unhappy, so unhappy!" Dostoyevsky wept to his brother. "I am tortured, killed! My soul quakes. I have suffered for so long. ... I have endured the most unimaginable tortures, but there must be some bounds! I am not made of stone!" Then he would yo-yo with an epileptic attack. "I experience a joy that is unthinkable ... complete harmony with myself and the whole world. This feeling is so bright and strong that you could give up ten years for a few seconds of that ecstasy."

The author of *The Air-Conditioned Nightmare* went further. "I discovered that this suffering was good for me, that it opened the way to a joyous life," Henry Miller wrote in his *Rosy Crucifixion*. "I have no money, no resources, no hopes. I am the happiest man alive." As an afterthought he added, "To be joyous is to be a madman in a world of sad ghosts."

Miller's idol, Dr. Louis-Ferdinand Céline, was less upbeat. By day, he started out delivering babies, then, to escape depression, became a TB and syphilis specialist. By night, he wrote novels.

"When in your life were you happy?" *The Paris Review* asked the ex-pediatrician in 1960.

Céline: "Bloody well never."

Interviewer: "Do you detest life?"

Céline: "Well, I can't say I love it, no. I tolerate it because I'm alive."

Writing *Death on the Installment Plan* and *Journey to the End of the Night* helped him tolerate it.

---

1   http://www.newyorker.com/online/blogs/ask/2008/12/questions-for-treisman.html

A Céline fan, Kurt Vonnegut wrote the introductions to his last three novels, *Castle to Castle, North,* and *Rigadoon.* "Compulsively ... understanding that many people will believe that I share many of his authentically vile opinions," Vonnegut began, "I continue to say good things about this man." Aside from a few political differences, he and the Frenchman felt much the same about being on the planet.

"How's life?" David Brancaccio of PBS asked Vonnegut in 2005.[2]

"Well, it's practically over, thank God," said the eighty-two-year-old, who kept a sign on his refrigerator which read: *Your planet's immune system is trying to get rid of you.*

The year before, the chain-smoking novelist told the *Spokesman Review* that he'd filed suit against Brown & Williamson (now R.J. Reynolds) for failing to live up to the promise on their Pall-Mall packs to kill him.[3] The author of "God Bless You, Dr. Kevorkian," called smoking "a classy way to commit suicide."

In 2000, Vonnegut nearly died in a house fire and expressed regret for not doing so. Speaking for like-minded colleagues, he told a reporter, "We all would like to have died as young as F. Scott Fitzgerald, but we didn't manage it."

Is there no way of making such writers happier?

"To cheer yourself up, read biographies of writers who went insane," suggests Irish novelist and British Top 300 Intellectual Colm Tóibín.

Meantime, "Resign yourself to the lifelong sadness that comes from never being satisfied," recommends Zadie Smith, NYU creative writing prof and *New Yorker* luminary.[4]

---

2 PBS Interview with Kurt Vonnegut, Oct. 7. 2005. http://www.pbs.org/now/transcript/transcript-NOW140_full.html

3 *Spokesman Review* interview with Kurt Vonnegut, April 14, 2004. http://www.spokesmanreview.com/breaking/story.asp?id=1997

4 "Ten Rules for Writing Fiction," *The Guardian,* February 19, 2010. http://www.guardian.co.uk/books/2010/feb/20/10-rules-for-writing-fiction-part-two

CHAPTER 30

MASOCHISTIC

"I do think that the quality which makes a man want to write and be read is essentially a desire for self-exposure and is masochistic."

—**James Jones,** *The Paris Review* interview

"When God hands you a gift, He also hands you a whip; and the whip is intended solely for self-flagellation."

—**Truman Capote, Preface to** *Music for Chameleons*

As every student who had to do a book report or a "My Summer Vacation" memoir knows, writing is rarely fun. When *The Paris Review* asked William Styron if he "enjoyed" writing, the *Darkness Visible* author said, "I certainly don't." But many make it a profession though it offers no holidays, no retirement, no health care—for minimum wage. It does, however, provide a chance at ulcers or liver failure.

So the writer's family and friends are, understandably, mystified. There are many other far more rewarding professions for a crazy. Not just in the arts.

Why writing?

As Freud pointed out, it's the power, fame, and sex. At least posthumously.

But the father of psychoanalysis forgot one thing: immortality. Unlike banking, law, sales, etc., literature promises immortality. Busts, memorials, pantheons, postage stamps, fellowships in your name. At least, for .000001 percent of writers.

The more one thinks he's got a shot at legacy, the more compulsive he tends to be about creating. Whether it's a painful pleasure, or a pleasurable pain, the more the OCD uses Capote's whip on himself.

To the nonprofessional this may seem like bondage and discipline. And, for some, like the Marquis de Sade, there may be an element of this. The greatest pain he endured was when the terrorists of the French Revolution destroyed his magnum opus in progress, *120 Days in Sodom*, and threw him in the nuthouse. But he rewrote the masterpiece in his cell.

The other eponymous half of the S&M pair was Austrian novelist Leopold von Sacher-Masoch. He published his popular *Venus in Furs* after becoming the legal slave of the Baroness Fanny. In mink, she flogged Masoch regularly. When they traveled, she rode first class, he rode third. His last novel, *Fierce Women*, was penned in an asylum on the Rhine.

Serious authors have no illusions about the mercilessness of their calling. As Anne Lamott pointed out in *Bird by Bird*, "It's not like you don't have a choice, because you do, you can either type or kill yourself." And she dedicated the book to a colleague who did just that.

T.C. Boyle compares himself and his colleagues to "trained dogs ... and Kafka's Hunger Artist, performing astonishing feats for a nonexistent audience." When *The Paris Review* asked him why, then, he kept writing, the PEN/Faulkner winner and USC Distinguished Professor of English replied, "Because writing is an obsessive-compulsive disorder."

OCD author records are impressive. In his lifetime, Asimov cranked out 300 titles, Lewis Carroll 255, Defoe 250. George Simenon completed 400 in his seventy years, though he was said to have regularly vomited from the strain. Kerouac holds the short-story gold, having finished 200 in eight weeks.

In some cases, the whip was supplemented by cocaine or caffeine. Voltaire, Dumas, and Balzac each consumed up to seventy cups of coffee a day. Original coke records include Stevenson doing *Dr. Jekyll and Mr. Hyde* in six days and Stephen King completing *The Running Man* in three. Mark Twain racked up 1,600 pages in four months. Though his output slowed after *Huck Finn*, he wrote with his left hand after his right cramped up.

Dumas, the author of *The Three Musketeers* and 271 other titles, is the sprint champion. In 1844, he wagered 100 Louis that he could complete volume one of *Le Chevalier de Maison-Rouge* in three days. Downing French roast and eating the grounds, he cranked out all 34,000 words with six hours to spare, then retired to his harem for R&R.

The adventure novelist was no less prolific in bed. "I need several mistresses," he said. "If I had only one, she'd be dead inside eight days."

CHAPTER 31

MAD

"When they want to know about inspiration, I tell them it's mostly animus."
— **Robert Frost,** *The Paris Review* **interview**

"I went briefly apeshit in the 1980s in an effort to get out of life entirely, and wound up playing Eightball in a locked ward for thirty days instead. I was pissed off."
— **Kurt Vonnegut,** *Fates Worse Than Death*

Given the difficulties of the profession, is it any wonder that some writers have been pissed? Thankfully, most lock themselves in a room and hammer out a *Crime and Punishment* or *American Psycho* rather than going Mr. Hyde or Charlie Manson on anybody. Still, nobody on death row can beat Ellis, King, or other mild-mannered men of letters when it comes to murder and mayhem melodrama. Where does that talent come from?

"I do think many writers have what you might call a demonic nature," ventured Henry Miller.

Mad usually starts out small. With irritation. "I go from exasperation to a state of collapse, then I recover and go from prostration to fury, so that my average state is one of being annoyed," said Flaubert even before the syphilis and epilepsy kicked into high gear.[1]

His annoyance went to misanthropy. "I detest my fellow-beings and do not feel that I am their fellow at all," he continued. So, like many of his colleagues, he lived with his mother and dated hookers who looked like her.

But since misanthropy can be a handicap to character-driven fiction (it took Flaubert eighteen years to make *Madame Bovary* sympathetic), other annoyed writers have taken it down a notch.

"I've always been interested in people, but I've never liked them," said Henry James, though he wrote tens of thousands of letters to acquaintances.

When bailing from his writer-in-residence post at U of Michigan, Vonnegut told the program director, "I've realized the only thing I hate more than listening to people is talking to them."

"I love humanity, but I hate people," said Edna St. Vincent Millay who, like the Brontës, Dickinson, and O'Connor, rarely left the house.

There is also the I'm-mad-as-hell-and-not-going-to-take-it-anymore mad. Vendetta mad. Grudge mad. "Getting even is one reason for writing," said William Gass. "I write because I hate. A lot. Hard." The American Book Award winner added: "I want to rise so high that when I shit I won't miss anybody."[2]

After being panned by critic Kenneth Rexroth, Kerouac raged, "I'll bombard you with … works that make you all go mad, you bunch of … no good bastards!" He wrote in his journal that due to his "melancholia and maniacal appearance," he'd soon be thrown in the nuthouse. His friend Allen Ginsberg suggested he "lay down his wrath" and discover his "untroubled and tender" true self. "Beware of meeting me on the street!" Jack warned. But twice he was nearly beaten to death by street thugs and made no attempt to defend himself.

Which brings us to loser mad. Humiliation mad. "Why has the South produced so many good writers?" wrote Walker Percy. "Because we got beat." In his National Book Award-winning *The Moviegoer,* he

---

1 Geoffrey Wall, *Flaubert, A Life* (New York: Farrar, Straus, and Giroux, 2002).

2 Thomas LeClair, *The Paris Review* interview with William Gass, The Art of Fiction No. 65.

added, "All the friendly and likable people seem dead to me; only the haters seem alive."

Before the South got beat, the preternaturally pissed Mr. Poe wrote of hanging cats and hearing bloody hearts beating under floorboards. The poet called his hypersensitivity "an over-acuteness of the nerves."

Another sensitive southerner was Mark Twain. Unlike Poe, the humorist became rich and famous. But, shortly before his death, he admitted to being "full of malice, saturated with malignity." He used his "pen warmed up in hell" on, among others, Bret Hart, Robert Louis Stevenson, James Fenimore Cooper, Jane Austen, and George Eliot, and, according to his anthologist, Bernard De Voto, he was involved in more lawsuits than any other author. Like Poe, the satirist flew off the handle regularly. Once, discovering a button missing on one of his countless pressed shirts, he flung them all out the window.

As for the other Confederate master, "Faulkner had a mean small Southern streak in him, and most of his pronunciamentos reflect that meanness."

So said Norman Mailer[3] who, besides savaging many of his colleagues, shanked his wife at a cocktail party. His arraignment statement to the magistrate read, "Naturally, I have been a little upset but I have never been out of my mental faculties. ... It's important for me not to be sent to a mental hospital, because my work in the future will be considered that of a disordered mind. My pride is that I can explore areas of experience that other men are afraid of. I insist I am sane."[4] The judge, declaring that the novelist couldn't "distinguish fiction from reality," sent him to Bellevue for a seventeen-day evaluation. After charming his shrinks and begging his wife not to press charges, Mailer returned home. His next novel, *An American Dream*, opened with his hero, Rojack, strangling his wife.

Capitalizing on in-house talent such as Mailer, the long overdue Bellevue Literary Press was founded in 2007. The "micro-Knopf," as

---

3 Steven Marcus, *The Paris Review* interview with Norman Mailer, The Art of Fiction No. 32.

4 http://realitystudio.org/bibliographic-bunker/william-burroughs-and-norman-mailer/

New York Magazine calls it,[5] has published seven novels to date. One—Andrew Krivak's 2011 *The Sojourn*—was a National Book Award finalist. Another—Paul Harding's 2009 *Tinkers,* about an epileptic father and crazy grandfather, a manuscript rejected by all other publishers—won the Pulitzer. The publisher's sister operation, *The Bellevue Literary Review,* has featured work by Charles Bukowski, Amy Hempel, Rick Moody, and Sharon Olds.

The oldest public hospital and psychiatric facility in the United States (founded in 1736), Bellevue has treated its share of artists over the years: Eugene O'Neil was admitted after his 1912 suicide attempt; in 1935 Malcolm Lowry was treated for advanced alcoholism; in 1949 Allen Ginsberg pleaded insanity and checked in; in 1957, *New Republic* poetry editor Delmore Schwartz arrived in a straightjacket after attacking art critic Hilton Kramer, whom he dreamed had cuckolded him; etc.[6]

Saul Bellow immortalized his mentor, Schwartz, as the exquisitely mad hero of his 1976 Nobel Prize-winning novel, *Humboldt's Gift*: "From Bellevue he phoned me," wrote Bellow. " ... He yelled, 'Charlie, you know where I am, don't you? ... This isn't literature. This is *life.*'"

---

5 Boris Kachka, "Because a Once-Notorious Mental Hospital Is Now a Publishing House,"*New York Magazine,* December 11, 2011. http://nymag.com/news/articles/reasonstoloveny/2011/bellevue-publishers/

6 Mark Harris, "Checkout Time at the Asylum," *New York Magazine,* November 16, 2008.

PART VIII

BARDS
BEHAVING BADLY

"It's very hard to be a gentleman and a writer."
—W. Somerset Maugham

CHAPTER 32

WRITERS ROUGHHOUSING

An Introduction

While writers have long battled publishers, editors, and critics, many have fought even more fiercely with the competition—themselves. If editorial rejection is bad, peer criticism can be even more upsetting.

This is particularly true in the United States where competition is king. The works of fully mature artists are incomparable—apples and oranges. But some have struggled to be recognized, through sales or prizes, as The Greatest.

"I started out very quiet and I beat Mr. Turgenev," wrote Hemingway. "Then I trained hard and I beat Mr. de Maupassant. I've fought two draws with Mr. Stendhal, and I think I had an edge on the last one."

Dispensing with metaphor, Hemingway and his colleagues came to real blows about who was the titleholder. The one-upsmanship often deteriorated into character assassination. In a letter to Harvey Breit, Hemingway called Faulkner "a strange sort of phoney." In a note to Malcolm Cowley, he described his rival as lacking "conscience" and "moral fiber." But lest Cowley think he begrudged Faulkner his earlier Nobel, Papa conceded that his foe had natural, if undisciplined, talent.

"I wish to Christ I owned him like you'd own a horse and train him like a horse and race him like a horse—only in writing," the sportsman went on. He concluded with a takes-one-to-know-one compliment. "He is almost as much of a prick as Poe. But thank God for Poe and thank God for Faulkner."[1]

The great southern novelist himself could be no less competitive. "The good artist ... has supreme vanity," he told *The Paris Review.* "No matter how much he admires the old writer, he wants to beat him."

In 1955, against his better judgment, Faulkner accepted a dinner invitation from Steinbeck in New York. By then the latter was in his prime and his guest twenty years past it. Three sheets to the wind on arrival, Faulkner managed a few monosyllables during the course of the evening. Otherwise, he grunted, glared, and drained the bar. "We had a dreadful time with him," recalled Elaine Steinbeck. Months later the Sound and the Fury ran into the Grapes of Wrath at a literary affair.

"I must have been pretty awful that night," Faulkner said.

Steinbeck, not always an easy person himself, winked. "You were."[2]

Mark Twain, whom Faulkner dismissed as "fourth rate," could be awful himself. In his critical reviews, he eviscerated many of his colleagues with ill-concealed gusto but reserved his greatest spleen for his first editor and mentor, Harte Crane. "He trimmed and trained and schooled me patiently," he admitted. Within a few years, Crane was written out, broke, and begging his now rich and famous student for a handout. Twain offered him $25 for a play collaboration. Soon he branded Harte "a liar, a thief, a swindler, a snob, a sot, a sponge, a coward" and said he never "had an idea that he came by honestly." After his teacher surrendered to throat cancer, he provided the eulogy: "Not a man ... but an invertebrate without a country."[3]

Meanwhile, a literary free-for-all was in progress. Thackaray was trashing Dickens; Conrad, Melville; Wells, James; Orwell, H.G Wells; Poe, everybody.

Nor was it all just boys being boys. George Eliot jumped into the fray with her essay, "Silly Novels by Lady Novelists." Later, Dorothy

---

1 Carlos Baker, ed., *Ernest Hemingway: Selected Letters 1917-1961* (New York: Scribner).

2 Jay Parini, *John Steinbeck: A Biography* (New York: Henry Holt, 1995).

3 Anthony Arthur, *Literary Feuds: A Century of Celebrated Quarrels—from Mark Twain to Tom Wolfe* (Thomas Dunne, 2002).

Parker, observed, "As artists, women novelists are rot, but as providers they are oil wells—they gush."

Then Lillian Hellman and Mary McCarthy squared off. Even before the heat of it, the former observed, "Writers are interesting people, but often mean and petty." Proving it, Ms. McCarthy announced on the *Dick Cavett Show*, "Everything she [Hellman] writes is a lie, including the 'and' and the 'the'." The author of *Julia* sued for $2.5 million, including $1.7 for "pain and anguish." In *The New York Times*, pugilist-turned-peacemaker Norman Mailer scolded the defendant for hitting her opponent "when down" and appealed for truce. Instead, Hellman had a heart attack and the libel suit was dropped.

Dueling preceded boxing as the gentleman's way to resolve serious literary and extra-literary disputes.

After publishing *Pleasures and Days*, Proust challenged critic Jean Lorrain to a duel for a review depicting him as "one of those pretty boys who've managed to get themselves pregnant by literature."[4] The two managed to rise before dawn and find a free meadow. But both shot over each other's heads, returning home for hot compresses and cognac. Proust staged several other such duels, health permitting.[5]

Then came the Turgenev-Tolstoy showdown that didn't happen, a bitter disappointment for Dostoyevsky. It all started when Ivan badmouthed the motherland in *Smoke*, and Fyodor suggested the novel be "burned by the public executioner." Ivan in turn called the newly patriotic gulag con a "madman" and a "petty, dirty gossip." Fyodor then parodied him in *The Devils* as "the most written-out of all written-out authors"; whereupon Ivan called him "the Russian Marquis de Sade."[6]

Tolstoy found all this deeply disturbing since he liked both the fussy dilettante and the excitable epileptic. He'd even called *The House of the Dead* "the finest work in all of Russian literature." In turn, Dostoyevsky heaped praise on Tolstoy (though, in private, he found

4 Edmund White, *Marcel Proust* (Fides, 2002).

5 William C. Carter, *Marcel Proust: A Life* (Yale University Press, 2000).

6 Myrick Land, *The Fine Art of Literary Mayhem* (New York: Holt, Rinehart, Winston, 1963).

his masterpiece, *Anna Karenina*, "rather tedious"). So, diplomatically, Tolstoy was between a rock and a hard place.

The scales were tipped one day when Tolstoy scolded Turgenev about his poor treatment of his daughter born to his mother's slave: "If she were your legitimate daughter, you would educate her differently." Ivan threatened to slap Leo's face. Instead Leo suggested a duel. But soon, conscience getting the best of him, Leo apologized to Ivan and called the whole thing off so as not to interrupt his work on *War and Peace*.

At last, master dueling gave way to what Joyce Carol Oates called "The Sweet Science."[7] Boxing. The writer didn't have to compete at dawn with a hangover, he didn't have to find a second, and he didn't risk life and limb, only humiliation and a concussion.

Literary sparring is still alive and well. In 2012, Bret Easton Ellis went ballistic on David Foster Wallace. He notified his 300,000 Twitter followers that the Pulitzer nominee was "the most tedious, overrated, tortured, pretentious writer of my generation." He added that anybody who considered the MacArthur Genius a genius belonged in "The Literary Douchebag-Fools Pantheon."

Wallace might have defended himself except he was dead.

He'd bloodied The Lit Brat Packer with his own broadsides back in 1987. After the tradition of Hemingway's *Torrents* and Mailer's *Advertisements*, Wallace critiqued his Twenty-Something rivals in a *Review of Contemporary Fiction* essay, "Fictional Futures and the Conspicuously Young." He argued that many suffered from "Workshop Hermeticism," "Catatonia," and/or "Yuppie Nihilism" and that Ellis held the Triple Crown, writing "trash" no better than television. The polemicist compared the *Less Than Zero* author to a hooker, charging that he "titillates, repulses, excites, transports—without demanding any intellectual or spiritual or artistic responses." At the time, Ellis was at work on his second trick, *American Psycho*, the hero of which dismembers and eats prostitutes while playing the stock market.

A larger issue was at stake between the X-Generation novelists, as there often is with such literary showdowns. Their editor, Gerald Howard, alludes to it in "I Know Why Bret Easton Ellis Hates David

---

7 Joyce Carol Oates, *On Boxing* (New York: Doubleday, 1987).

Foster Wallace." Minimalism against Maximalism. The new Pop vs. the
new Proust. Commercial vs. Purist.

When he wrote "Fictional Futures," Wallace, twenty-five, had one
novel (*The Broom of the System*), which concerned symbolic language
and Wittgenstein's philosophy: It sold 2,200 copies. Ellis, twenty-three,
had one novel (*Less Than Zero*) about partying yuppie junkies and
sex slaves in L.A: It sold over 50,000 copies in the first year and would
be made into a major motion picture. In 1990, Wallace wrote his best-
selling friend Jonathan Franzen: "Right now I am … a failed writer at 28,
who is so jealous, so sickly searingly envious of you and Vollmann and
Mark Leyner and even David F--kwad Leavitt … that I consider suicide
a reasonable … option."

By the time he took that option in 2008, he had eclipsed his peers.
Especially Ellis. Wallace's last complete novel, *Infinite Jest*, sold well
and earned a slot on *Time's 100 Best Novels* list; Ellis' last, *Imperial
Bedrooms*, a *Less Than Zero* sequel, tanked critically and commercially.
Rattling Ellis further, the martyred Wallace was canonized in D.T. Max's
2012 biography, *Every Love Story Is a Ghost Story*. So, before his rival
was beatified, the L.A. novelist delivered the Pale King one last blow:
He called him a "fraud" and his fans "Douchebags."

As for Franzen's relationship with Wallace, the National Book Award
winner told *The Paris Review*, "Our friendship was haunted by a competition between the writer who was pursuing art for art's sake and the
writer who was … getting public attention and money."[8]

Historic author battles which we will now review were fueled by the
same sort of competition: Art versus Popularity. But these feuds mustn't
make us lose sight of the kindness and generous support already noted
among other authors.

"Cheever continues to do what the best fiction has always done: give
us back our humanity, enhanced," John Updike wrote of his friend's novel,
Falconer. In turn, Cheever had the highest praise for Updike's *Rabbit Is
Rich*: "Superb—the most important American novel I've read in years."

---

8 Jonathan Franzen Interview, *The Paris Review*, Winter 2010.

"Barth isn't simply another writer, he's a point on the compass," Frederick Barthelme said of his older colleague. The National Book Award Winner Barth enthusiastically returned the compliment to his young admirer, calling him "… a bright star in the constellation of new American short story writers."

Examples of such magnanimity between authors abound. But the other side of the coin cannot be ignored. As Norman Mailer told *The Paris Review*, "What's not understood sufficiently about novelists is how competitive we all are. We're as competitive as star athletes." As we have seen in the cases of Curtis Sittenfeld, Nell Freudenberger, Lena Dunham, and others, this competitiveness is all the more keen today, given the writer population explosion, the proliferation of prizes, the enormous— though rare—jackpots, and the increasingly uneven playing field.

As the following bouts show, writing is not, and never was, a Special Olympics. Everyone is not a winner, people do get hurt, and otherwise high-minded, civilized artists can be reduced to their lowest instincts in their attempt to distinguish and elevate themselves.

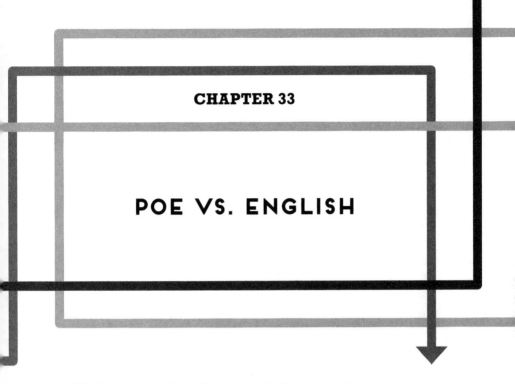

CHAPTER 33

POE VS. ENGLISH

"His jealousy of other writers amounted to a mania."
—Frederick Saunders, Poe's publisher

Edgar Allan Poe had many unwilling sparring partners. His early favorite was Henry Wadsworth Longfellow. Longfellow had done nothing in particular to piss off Poe other than outselling him, being an esteemed professor, and having a rich wife.

Initially Poe had called Longfellow a genius and begged him for an endorsement of his work so "my fortune will be made." When Longfellow declined, Poe dismissed him as "the GREAT MOGUL [his caps] of the Imitators" and a plagiarist.[1]

Henry played rope-a-dope with Edgar, stoically taking his most devastating shots and saying only, "Life is too precious to be wasted in street brawls."

Beside himself, Poe threw haymakers at his rival's *Poems on Slavery*, saying they were written "for the especial use of those

---

1   Kenneth Silverman, *Edgar A. Poe: Mournful and Never-ending Remembrance*. (New York: HarperCollins, 1991).

negrophilic old ladies of the north, who form so large a part of Mr. LONGFELLOW's friends."

Returning to his corner at the bell, the father of Horror cooled down. He then counted himself one of his opponent's "warmest and most steadfast admirers" and regarded him as "the principle American poet." Ignoring the olive branch, Henry still stubbornly refused to endorse Edgar's work.

Poe soon traveled to Boston to deliver his lecture "On Reason." Receiving a chilly reception from Bostonians, he called everyone in the audience a plagiarist. He then took a carriage across town to the Lyceum to read "The Raven," only to realize, en route, that he'd forgotten to pack his popular poem. So he recited it by heart with some stammering and hyperventilation. As audience members walked out, he hectored the stage, cackling that he had "demolished" the Walden "Frogpondians."

Back in New York, Poe courted patronesses while his wife/cousin, Sissy, was in the last stages of TB at home. He boasted that one, Mrs. Ellet, was sending him love letters. She charged him with libel and enlisted gentlemen to protect her honor. Poe hurried to his colleague, T.D. English, asking to borrow his pistol.

T.D. had recently published a parody of "The Raven." Poe felt that the least he could do, by way of making amends, was to lend him a piece to protect himself against Mrs. Ellet's champions. But English insulted him again, suggesting that he apologize to the widow. Poe had recently finished "The Cask of Amontillado," in which his hero, Montresor, making good on his motto—"*Nemo me impune lacessit*" (No one insults me with impunity)—buried his rival, Fortunato, alive.

Instead of walling up T.D. in a wine cellar, Edgar boasted that he "gave English a flogging which he will remember to the day of his death… [and] had to be dragged from his prostrate, rascally carcass."

English had a different take on the bout. He said he flattened the poet's nose with a signet ring punch, sending him "to bed from the effect of fright and the blows he received from me."

Poe wrote "Literati," a caricature of the work and physical peculiarities of English and his allies. After its publication, the author announced his plans for a sequel, "American Parnassus," which would discredit the entire American literary population. According to biographer

Kenneth Silverman, he vowed that the title would be "a culmination of his work as a critic, aesthetician, and tastemaker."

Rebutting "Literati" in *The New York Evening Mirror,* magazine publisher Charles Briggs described his former editor and book critic as a self-confessed forger and a loan cheat. Adding insult to injury, Briggs described Poe as: "5 feet 1. ... His tongue too large for his mouth ... his head ... of balloonish appearance."

The poet sued the *Mirror* for libel, insisting that his character was unimpeachable. Furthermore, he described himself as 5 feet 8, English a dwarf by comparison, and the *Mirror*'s owner, Hiram Fuller, "a fat sheep in reverie."

Two years later, Poe was in a Baltimore ER watching, according to his physician, Dr. Moran, "spectral and imaginary objects on the walls." In a brief moment of coherence, he told Moran "the best thing my best friend could do would be to blow out my brains with a pistol."

The next day he muttered, "Lord help my poor soul" and expired.

On a raw, cloudy Baltimore morning, the poet was buried beside the father who had abandoned him as an infant. Only a few attended the brief service. His aunt, whom he called Mother, was not present, nor his supposed fiancée, Elmira, nor English.

"This death was almost a suicide," said his admirer and translator, Baudelaire. "A suicide prepared for a long time."

CHAPTER 34

LEWIS VS. DRIESER

This rivalry began in much the same way as that between Poe and Longfellow. The elder Dreiser asked Sinclair Lewis to endorse his 1925 novel, *An American Tragedy*. Lewis declined. But, by way of consolation, he assured his colleague that it deserved the Nobel.

Five years earlier, the publication of *Main Street* was "the most sensational event in twentieth-century American publishing history," wrote Lewis's biographer, Mark Schorer.[1] The title sold 300,000 copies. By contrast, Frank Doubleday destroyed the 1,000 copies of Dreiser's own first major novel, *Sister Carrie*, because his wife found it "immoral." Devastated, Dreiser was forced to take a job as a day laborer, like his poor protagonist.

Lewis was canonized after the publication of *Babbitt* (1922) and *Arrowsmith* (1926). He refused the Pulitzer for the latter work, peeved that *Main Street* hadn't won the prize. Though *Sister Carrie* (reissued in 1912) and his other novels were well received, Dreiser grew furiously jealous of his younger colleague, now the rock star of American letters.

Despite this commercial disparity, both artists were considered the leading candidates for the first American Nobel in Literature. Lewis

---

1 Mark Schorer, *Sinclair Lewis: An American Life* (New York: McGraw-Hill, 1961).

won the honor in 1930. Dreiser feigned indifference. But according to friends he was suicidal. He believed, as did others, that Lewis had been recognized because his novels were critical of American capitalism, making them more popular in Sweden.[2]

Again, Lewis tried to console his rival. "You are the father of us all," he told him.

After the Nobel snub, Dreiser tried to seduce his rival's journalist wife, Dorothy Thompson. Though she rebuffed him, he boasted that she had surrendered to his charms. Moreover, he charged that Thompson had plagiarized him when in fact the opposite was the case. On hearing of the malicious gossip, Sinclair's wife exploded, "That swine!"

This set the stage for the 1930 Lewis-Dreiser prizefight. The venue was a Nobel celebratory dinner for Lewis in New York.

After toasts, the star of the evening was asked to say a few words. Lewis rose to announce he could not do so "in the presence of a man who has stolen 3,000 words from my wife's book."

The man in question invited his accuser to the next room. Here the bell sounded and the lumbering, meat-faced Sister Carrie squared off with the skeletal, pop-eyed Arrowsmith.

Refusing to withdraw his charge, Lewis began floating like a butterfly and stinging like a bee: He called his opponent an "ignoramus" and "crazy." Unshaken by the combination, Dreiser challenged, "Say it again, and I'll slap you." So his opponent did so and got slapped. Before the Nobel laureate could reciprocate, the literati rushed in and separated the two.

The next day, the newspapers whipped up a popular frenzy for a proper rematch between the reigning American realists. A New York fight promoter proposed a Dreiser "Heavyweight Champ of American letters" versus "Kid Lewis" fifteen-round bout at Ebbets Field. When the two declined to participate, the promoter suggested they hire ghostwriter fighters.

---

2 Even Mark Shorer was ambivalent about Lewis's triumph, concluding in his biography, "He was one of the worst writers in modern American literature, but without his writing one cannot imagine modern American literature."

CHAPTER 35

HEMINGWAY VS. EVERYBODY

> "The minute he began to have some sort of obligation to you of love or friendship ... then is when he had to kill you."
>
> **—Donald Ogden Stewart, Hemingway friend**

In his *Paris Review* interview with George Plimpton, Norman Mailer again spoke with reverence of Hemingway but concluded: "I think if we had met it could have been a small disaster for me."

Meeting the legendary novelist had indeed been disastrous for many of his contemporaries.

Steinbeck met him in 1944. He was finishing *Cannery Row* at the time and riding high from *The Grapes of Wrath*. But, to his annoyance, many still dismissed him as "the poor man's Hemingway." As for Hemingway, his *For Whom the Bell Tolls* had come out in 1940, but he was entering an eleven-year drought.

With great expectations, John O'Hara and John Hersey arranged a summit at a Manhattan restaurant. After shoptalk and a few rounds, Hemingway bet $50 that he could break O'Hara's prize blackthorn walking stick—a gift from Steinbeck—over O'Hara's head. Papa promptly did so, triumphantly threw the pieces down, and demanded his money. Head in hands, O'Hara was on the edge of tears.[1]

As a point of honor, Steinbeck prided himself in not criticizing colleagues. The walking stick incident moved him to change his policy: He launched into diatribes about Hemingway.

Earlier, Ernest Walsh, Sinclair Lewis's editor, had called Papa's *Torrents of Spring* hatchet job on his competitors "The Cheapest Book I Ever Read." In another essay, Walsh failed to include Hemingway in his list of "the six greatest living literary artists."[2] When, months later, the editor died of TB at age thirty-one, Hemingway wrote Pound, "I have known too many good guys die to be able to sweat much from the eyes about the death of a shit."[3]

While they were still on speaking terms, Hemingway had assured Walsh that his other title that year, *The Sun Also Rises*, would contain "no autobiography and no complaints." But it contained all the characters and events of bullfighting season in Pamplona the year before. The Jewish antihero, Robert Cohn, was his former traveling companion and boxing sparring partner, Robert Loeb, was Peggy Guggenheim's cousin. After the publication of the novel, he avoided his former "friend" for fear of being shot.[4]

With *Death in the Afternoon* (1932), Hemingway introduced bullfighting as a sacrificial passion play. Bristling at the parodies that followed, he told one of his picadors, William Saroyan, "We've seen them come and go. Good ones, too. Better ones than you, Mr. Saroyan."

The next year, he vented to his editor, Max Perkins: "You see what they [critics] can't get over is (1) That I *am* a man; (2) That I can beat the shit out of any of them; (3) That I can write. The last hurts them the worst. But they don't like any of it. But Papa will make them like it."

However, he failed to make them like his follow-up, *The Green Hills of Africa* (1935). Now he wanted to do more than beat the shit out of his

---

1 Steve Newman, "John Steinbeck Meets Ernest Hemingway," *The Bookstove*, December 15, 2010.

2 Ezra Pound, James Joyce, Robert McAlmon, Carl Sandburg, William Carlos Williams, and Emanuel Carnevali.

3 Carlos Baker, ed., *Ernest Hemingway: Selected Letters 1917–1961* (New York: Scribners).

4 James R. Mellow, *Hemingway: A Life Without Consequence* (New York: Houghton Mifflin, 1992).

detractors. "I would like to take a tommy gun and open up at 21 [Club] or in the N.R. [*New Republic*] offices or any place you name and give shitdom a few martyrs and include myself," he wrote his friend John Dos Passos, whom he called a money-grubbing "pilot fish."

By 1951, fearing that James Jones' *From Here to Eternity* was overshadowing his own war novels, Hemingway wrote to their publisher, Charles Scribner, Jr.: "I hope he kills himself as soon as it does not damage his or your sales."

In his otherwise laudatory and diplomatic memoir,[5] Scribner wrote, "Working with Hemingway was rather like being strapped to an electric chair," adding that he was "a two-timer and not above despicable tricks."

Had the *Life* and *Argosy* celebrity sportsman been deprived of Spanish bulls and African trophies,[6] one imagines that he might have adorned his Ketchum hunting lodge walls with the heads of Sherwood Anderson, Gertrude Stein, Ford Maddox Ford, and the others imprudent enough to help him.

"Ernest would always give a helping hand to a man on a ledge a little higher up," wrote F. Scott Fitzgerald, explaining his friend's idea of camaraderie. Fitzgerald had indeed been higher up in 1925 after *Gatsby* but was overtaken by Hemingway's *Sun* the following year.

This is how things stood when the American heavyweight faced off with the Canadian Morley Callaghan, with Fitzgerald filling in as ref. A former *Toronto Star* colleague of his opponent, Callaghan had only one novel[7] to his credit before their bout at the American Club of Paris, where they sparred regularly.

Though four inches shorter and forty pounds lighter, Callaghan knocked Hemingway down late in the second round. Regaining his feet, Papa struggled to stay up until the three-minute bell from Fitzgerald. But the three minutes seemed to him the longest he had ever endured

---

5 Charles Scribner Jr., *In The Company of Writers*, (New York: Scribner, 1991).

6 In *Papa: A Personal Memoir*, Gregory, who inherited his father's passion for hunting, wrote, "I went back to Africa to do more killing. Somehow it was therapeutic." Gigi, as Papa had called Gregory, had a sex change and called himself Gloria. He died in a Florida women's detention center after being arrested for indecent exposure. He called his father's swan song, *The Old Man in the Sea*, "sentimental slop." Papa had always called the youngest of his three sons "the mean one."

7 Morley Callaghan, *Strange Fugitive* (New York: Scribner, 1928).

in the ring. Callaghan delivered a barrage of haymakers that returned him to the mat several times. When at last Fitzgerald counted him out, through swollen eyes Hemingway saw that the clock was closing in on four minutes. Scott apologized profusely.

"If you want to see me getting the shit knocked out of me, just say so," bellowed Ernest. "Only, don't say you made a mistake!"

The relationship of the two masters was never quite the same. Some years later, Hemingway began publicly denouncing his former friend for cowardice and self-pity.

"Please lay off me in print," Scott wrote him. "If I choose to write *de profundis* sometimes it doesn't mean I want friends praying aloud over my corpse."

CHAPTER 36

MAILER VS. CAPOTE VS. VIDAL

In his title on writing, *The Spooky Art*, Mailer wrote about the affinity of writers and fighters. Boxing figures prominently in his other work, including *The Fight*, about his hero Mohammad Ali's showdown with George Foreman in 1975.

His editor, E.L. Doctorow, once observed, "It was almost as if each [Mailer] book was a round in a fight." After his book bouts came his bouts with reviewers. When encountering a book critic, the 5'8", 170-lb. Pulitzer winner would drop into his crouch and work the air speed bag just as his idol, Hemingway, had done while walking the Montparnasse years before.

Algis Valiunas described him as "the perfect mama's boy cruising for a bruising."[1] Like Hemingway, Mailer had been a pampered child. His mother, Fanny, a nurse, considered boxing barbaric and blamed the Light Heavyweight champion Jose Torres for teaching him the sport.[2]

---

[1] *Commentary* (2009).

[2] John G. Rodwan, Jr., "Mailer's Victory," *Open Letters Monthly*, November, 2011. www.openletters monthly.com/norman-mailer-on-boxing/

Unlike his mentor, Mailer fell into the habit of sparring at cocktail parties and outside bars. One of his early matches was held in his own venue, *Advertisements for Myself* (1959). Here he took on his rivals one by one.[3]

"Prizefighting," wrote Mailer, "offers a profession to men who might otherwise commit murder in the street." He would later champion two such men, Gary Gilmore and Jack Abbot. And he came near to following their footsteps upriver.

It was the year after *Advertisements*. Venue: a launch party for the novelist's New York City mayoral campaign. On the invitation list were the literati who had not excommunicated him, homeless people, and "the power people," as he called them. His 1 percent friend George Plimpton was responsible for mustering the third group. Disappointed more didn't show for his fete, Norman swatted *The Paris Review* editor with a rolled newspaper at the weigh-in.

By 4 A.M. only about twenty diehard partiers were left. Their host had ordered them to form two lines: those *for* him and those *against* him. His second wife, Adele, led the second, larger group. According to her memoir,[4] the bell rang when she challenged her lubricated lesser half, dressed in a torn matador's shirt: "Aja Toro, aja! … Where's your cojones? Did your ugly whore of a mistress cut them off, you son of a bitch!"

Mailer didn't KO Adele. Instead, he shanked her in the chest with a pocketknife.

Later, in *Tough Guys Don't Dance*, he wrote: "I was thinking that surgeons had to be the happiest people on earth. To cut people up and get paid for it—that's happiness."

But, after doing Adele, he was more desperate than happy. At the hospital, he begged her, on bended knee, not to press charges, although he had told his party guests not to call an ambulance and to "let the bitch die." Showing herself to be a sport, she didn't. She told her doctors

---

3 In this order: James Jones, William Styron, Truman Capote, Jack Kerouac, Saul Bellow, Nelson Algren, J.D. Salinger, Paul Bowles, Gore Vidal, Anatole Broyard, Ralph Ellison, James Baldwin, Herbert Gold, William Borroughs.

4 Adele Mailer, *The Last Party: Scenes from My Life with Norman Mailer.* (Blake Publishing, 1997). Simultaneously, Mailer released his first-person novel, *The Gospel According to the Son,* in which Jesus corrects the apostles' record vis-à-vis his miracles, his love life, his crucifixion.

she fell on glass. This allowed her husband to do *The Mike Wallace Show* days later to flesh out his mayoral platform. To combat increasing city crime and juvenile delinquency, he suggested that potential felons blow off steam by jousting on horseback.

Mailer went on to pass his court-ordered psych evaluation at Bellevue, perhaps handing out to his examiners signed copies of *The Naked and the Dead* or his "No More Bullshit" campaign buttons.

As a result of "the Trouble," as he called the stabbing of his wife, the novelist found himself unable to write anything but poetry. In 1962, he released his four-hundred-piece collection, *Deaths for the Ladies*. At a pre-pub reading, he told the crowd: "So long as you use a knife, there's some love left."[5]

》》

By this time, Mailer's top contenders for the American self-promoter crown were Gore Vidal and Truman Capote. "Out of all those people who began publishing when I did," said the latter, "there are only three left that anybody knows about—Gore, Norman, and me."[6]

Gore Vidal spoke for them all when he said, "Whenever a friend succeeds, a little something in me dies."

Early on, Capote and Mailer were Brooklyn neighbors and friends. In a 1967 *New York Post* interview,[7] Truman praised Norman as "a fantastic talent," though undisciplined. In turn, Norman praised Truman for "having a lovely poetic ear" and for crafting "the best sentences" of their generation.[8]

The pushing and shoving started in 1968 when Mailer won the Pulitzer and National Book Award for his "nonfiction novel" about Vietnam, *Armies of the Night*. Two years before, with the publication of *In Cold Blood*, Capote had declared himself father of the nonfiction

---

5 Mary V. Dearborn, *Mailer: A Biography* (Houghton Mifflin, 1999).

6 Gerald Clarke, *Capote: A Biography* (New York: Simon & Schuster, 2010).

7 Jerry Tallmer, "Truman Capote, Man About Town," *New York Post*, December 16, 1967.

8 Robert Emmet Long, *Truman Capote? Enfant Terrible* (Continuum, 2008).

George Plimpton, *Truman Capote: In Which Various Friends, Enemies, Acquaintances, and Detractors Recall His Turbulent Career* (New York: Talese/Doubleday, 1997).

novel, ignoring such minor earlier works in the same genre as the *Iliad*, the *Odyssey*, and the Bible. So he had thrown himself a celebratory "party of the century" at the Plaza. But the Pulitzer committee had ignored him. He doubled his medications in 1979 when Mailer landed a second Pulitzer for *The Executioner's Song*.

Capote accused Mailer of pirating his new fiction genre. "Now I see that the only prizes Norman wins are for that very same kind of writing," he sniped. "I'm glad I was of some small service to him."

Holding his Pulitzer belts high in the ring, the TKO winner didn't bother finishing the 5'2" featherweight off. He just laughed in his face and sat on him at a cocktail party.

"He has no talent! None, none, none!" protested the unheralded father of The New Journalism.

>>>

Capote might have mounted a stiffer defense if the third rail of the postwar American trinity, Gore Vidal, hadn't been softening him on the ropes, too.

The two had been bickering for years. Truman called Vidal a poor man's Somerset Maugham, devoid of sensitivity and suited only for glib essays. Worse, in 1976 Truman told *Playgirl* magazine that Bobby Kennedy had once "kicked Gore out onto Pennsylvania Avenue" for manhandling his stepsister, Jackie, at a White House party.

"Truman Capote has made lying an art. A *minor* art," Vidal rejoined, filing a $1 million libel suit. As for his rival's writing, he told *Playboy* magazine it was "ruthlessly unoriginal" and lifted from Carson McCullers and Eudora Welty.

"I'm always sad about Gore—very sad that he has to breathe every day," parried Truman. He countersued, hoping to "destroy his career" to exact "the greatest single revenge in literary history" and to write his epitaph: "Here lies Gore Vidal: he messed with TC!"

Though furious with Mailer for stealing his *In Cold Blood* thunder, Capote was giddy when Mailer flew over the ropes and headbutted Gore before their joint appearance on *The Dick Cavett Show* in 1971.

"You're absolutely mad," gasped the victim. "You *are* violent."

But Mailer wasn't finished. He stumbled out, took a seat beside Cavett, and started working Gore's gut. What was inside, he announced to America, was "no more interesting than the contents of the stomach of an intellectual cow."[9]

Mailer and Vidal had also been friendly early on. The relationship soured at the 1968 Democratic convention. Norman was there to research a book. Gore was there to needle William Buckley. The ABC face-off climaxed with the novelist calling the *Crossfire* host a "pro-crypto Nazi," and Buckley then threatened to "sock [him] in the goddamn face."

Afterwards, Vidal saw the conservative champion chumming it up at a Chicago Happy Hour with the self-described "Marxian anarchist"— Norman Mailer. Vidal, like Capote, was miffed that Mailer had just won the Pulitzer, whereas his own 1968 bestseller, *Myra Breckinridge*, had been ignored. Worse, Buckley called Vidal "an evangelist for bisexuality" and labeled the controversial novel "pornography." More upsetting still, Mailer had accused Vidal of seducing Jack Kerouac and driving him to suicidal drinking.

To see his detractors schmoozing at the bar drove Vidal to the offensive. He soon shot one over his former friend's bow. "No one reads Norman, they *hear* of him," he sneered.[10]

So Mailer responded with the 1971 headbutt. According to Boris Kachka, he threw a cocktail in his Moriarty's face, chased with a haymaker. "Words fail Norman Mailer yet again," stammered Vidal, regretting by now that writers don't get workers' comp and can only file libel suits.

But in the end Gore Vidal had the last laugh. He was elected president of the American Humanist Association in 2009 and died in peace three years later at the age of eighty-six, outliving Mailer, Capote, and Buckley.

---

9 In his 2007 *New York Times* replay, "In This Corner, Norman Mailer," Cavett wrote that Mailer's "mission ... was to eviscerate Vidal" for the latter's *The New York Review of Books'* piece on *The Prisoner of Sex*, likening the title to "three days of menstrual flow" and comparing him to Charles Manson for his violent misogyny.

10 Susan Shapiro, "The Punch Lines," *The Village Voice*, April 11, 2000.

THE LAST SCRIBE STANDING:
BON MOTS, BROADSIDES, & SUCKER PUNCHES

"Trash suitable only for the slums."

—Louisa May Alcott, of Twain's *Huckleberry Finn*

"God, what filth!"

—Dostoyevsky, of Zola's *Le Ventre de Paris*

"The whole thing reminds me of an interminable stomach ache. God save us from it during cholera season!"

—Ivan Turgenev, of Dostoyevsky's
Crime and Punishment

"Melville knows nothing of the sea."

—Joseph Conrad, of *Moby Dick*

"One must have a heart of stone to read the death of Little Nell by Dickens without laughing."

—Oscar Wilde, of *A Christmas Carol*

"A queasy undergraduate scratching at his pimples."

—Virginia Woolf, on James Joyce

"He [Aleksandr Solzhenitsyn] is a bad novelist and a fool. The combination usually makes for great popularity in the U.S."

—Gore Vidal

"Flat as cardboard … crude … and unreal."

—Virginia Woolfe of Hemingway's characters

"…Something about bells, balls and bulls. I loathed it."

—Nabokov, of Hemingway's *For Whom the Bell Tolls*

"Hemingway has never been known to use a word that might send a reader to the dictionary."

—William Faulkner

"Faulkner said more asinine things than any other major American writer. I can't remember a single interesting remark Faulkner ever made."

    —Norman Mailer

"Wrote it to destroy Sherwood and various others. ... It's the first really adult thing [I] have done. Jesus Christ, it is funny."

    —Hemingway, of *Torrents of Spring*, in a letter to
    Ezra Pound

"He never knew one human being from another ... and never much cared."

    —Ezra Pound, of Hemingway

"I don't think writers are comfortable in each other's presence. We can talk, of course, for five minutes or so, but I don't think we want to socialize."

    —Joseph Heller

PART IX

AGENTS

Bouncers at the Bastille

CHAPTER 37

AGENT GENTS

The first agent was a gentleman. His name was Paul and he worked pro bono for disciples who were finishing the early drafts of their memoirs. The retired tent maker sent out queries to the Corinthians, Galatians, Philippians. He pitched the chapbook-in-progress as the first nonfiction novel that married Inspirational with True Crime with Magic Realism: *The Purpose Driven Life* meets *The Celestine Prophesy* meets *The Three People You Meet in Heaven*—but bigger.

Getting no bites, the disciples' rep submitted over the transom to the Romans. Nero decapitated him before reading the query. Editorial assistants remaindered his clients before they got into sequels, much less resurrections. Their roman à clef was later released as a print-on-demand title that climbed the Roman Catholic charts and became the world's biggest bestseller.

Paul's experience put a chill on agenting for the next two millennia. Nobody wanted to get blinded, imprisoned, shipwrecked, stoned, or decapitated for 15 percent—not even for a title they really believed in. No author—medieval, Renaissance, or Enlightenment—could find an agent more interested in heavenly, rather than earthly, awards. So, as we have seen, they got exiled, pilloried, and burned without representation.

Then came capitalism and gentile agents. Among the first was another Paul: Paul Revere Reynolds (a descendent of the Revolutionary Paul), who founded the Society of Authors' Representatives. He represented Stephen Crane, George Bernard Shaw, and Joseph Conrad. His successor and son, Paul R. Reynolds, wrote titles about publishing.[1] In one, he warned: "A number of the people listed [in the SAR Directory] as agents are not really agents, but predatory sharks."

That fewer agents were gentlemen, much less saints, became a common criticism in years to come, both among the writers they represented and those they refused to represent.

Another pioneering agent, Harold Ober, was a notable exception. In 1908, he signed Jack London and struck 10 percent gold on the ex-prospector's Klondike adventures. Later, he took on F. Scott Fitzgerald. For the next thirty years, the novelist begged and borrowed from Ober to cover his Gatsby extravagances and his wife Zelda's psychiatric tab. By the 1950s, Ober Inc. had Faulkner and Salinger in the stable, plus history's No. 1 best-selling novelist, Agatha Christie, whom he helped unload four billion units.[2]

By that time, most published writers were represented.

---

1 *The Middle Man: Adventures of a Literary Agent, `The Writing and Selling of Nonfiction, The Writing and Selling of Fiction, The Writer and His Markets*. Reynolds Jr., whose career ran from 1926 to 1978, represented Alex Haley, Richard Wright, William Shirer, Irving Wallace, Howard Fast, Malcolm X, and the estate of Henry and William James.

2 Barbara Cartland is No. 2 at 1 billion, Harold Robbins No. 3 at 750 million.

CHAPTER 38

AGENTS AND GENTLE WOMEN

Where in the old days most agents were men,[1] if not gentlemen, now the majority of the 1,500 American reps are women, as are editors.

Publishing today is a matriarchy. There are many reasons for this, not the least of which is that nearly two-thirds of all books are purchased by women. A recent Associated Press survey found that they account for 80 percent of the fiction market.

British novelist Ian McEwan confirmed the fact for himself when, conducting an experiment in 2005, he gave away thirty copies of his novel *Saturday*: Most were snapped up by women, whom he called "eager and grateful," while the men "frowned in suspicion, or distaste."

"When women stop reading," the Booker Prize winner wrote in *The Guardian*, "the novel will be dead."[2]

Waxman agent Jason Pinter begs to disagree or to at least qualify the argument. He suggests that perhaps men read less because the titles available to them are chosen by women agents and editors. "I

---

1 In addition to Reynolds and Ober, pioneers included: Allan Collins (Curtis Brown), Carl Brandt, A.P. Watt, David Lloyd. Notable exceptions: Madeleine Boyd, Ann Watkins, Mavis McIntosh, among others.

2 Ian McEwan, "Hello, Would You Like a Free Book?" *The Guardian*, September 19, 2005

hope it doesn't get worse," he said. "If 85 percent [of the industry is female]—it's hard to think that acquisitions aren't in some way affected by that." George Gibson, president of Bloomsbury USA, agrees: "Women and men see the world differently, and therefore I think it would be healthier to have more men in the business."[3]

Explaining what is known in the industry as "The Fiction Gap," Louann Brizendine, author of *The Female Brain,* writes, "Reading requires incredible patience, and the ability to 'feel into' the characters. That is something women are both more interested in and also better at than men." Cognitive psychologists agree, asserting that women are more empathetic than men and possess greater emotional range.

Binky Urban, the queen of literary agents, is nothing if not empathetic. "With fiction of course, you just fall in love," she told *Haaretz* magazine in 2009. She added that it is imperative that, when falling in love, the agent must trust her own judgment and taste but that this is "the hardest thing to learn."

Earlier in her career she had done this with Richard Ford and Cormac McCarthy, both published novelists but still obscure. Later, she scored an $8 million advance for Charles Frazier's *Cold Mountain* follow-up, *Thirteen Moons.* She had hoped to top this with Woody Allen's memoirs, but publishers' auction bids fell $4 million short of his $10 million asking price, so he continues to make movies and play clarinet.

Today, Urban says she's "more desperate than ever" to find a great new novelist. Though he or she may not be an apostle, the International Creative Management vice president would represent a new greatest story ever told and spread the gospel with an evangelical fervor rivaling Paul's, just as she did with Donna Tartt's *The Secret History* and Nell Freudenberger's "Lucky Girls."

Urban's original ICM mentor, Lynn Nesbit, is equally zealous in promoting her clients, dead or alive—Hunter Thompson, Tom Wolfe, Michael Crichton, Joan Didion, Ann Beatty, and Jayne Anne Phillips. She told *Poets & Writers* in 2008 that an agent must possess four qualities

---

3 Rachel Deahl, "Where the Boys Are Not," *Publishers Weekly,* September 20, 2010. http://www.publishersweekly.com/pw/by-topic/industry-news/publisher-news/article/44510-where-the-boys-are-not.html

above all: enthusiasm, energy, commitment, and taste. She helped nurture them in Urban as well as in Esther Newberg, the Wheaton College classmates who became vice presidents at ICM, replacing Nesbit when she joined Mort Janklow, agent for the pope and four presidents.

Today Nesbit, Urban, and Newberg form the literary trinity of the agenting matriarchy. *New York Magazine* editor Clay Felker identified the secret of Nesbit's success and those of her students when he called her "the toughest, bitchiest agent in town." The members of the trinity and their alpha colleagues—Melanie Jackson, Nicole Aragi, Jane Dystel, Carol Mann, Sandra Dijkstra, etc.—all express a burning desire to represent the next great novelist even though, as Lynn Nesbit points out, fiction is "an endangered species." But, as a practical matter, they simply don't have the time to wade through the countless great American novels submitted to them daily.

"I'm beginning to think there are more writers than readers," Nesbit frets. "It's because of the memoir. Everybody thinks they have a story."

So, the only stories she and other top-level reps consider are those recommended by a client—a pontiff, a president, a Prestige. If the cover letter shows promise, they turn the ms. over to a junior colleague. But if it is from a backlister, it is turned away with regret because an undersold second novel is "a huge black spot on that writer's career," says Nesbit. She attributes this to the conglomerate takeovers. "The corporate thing," as she calls it, has everybody "too scared" about losing money and their jobs.

Many remaindered literary editors, says Nesbit, were "the big characters" and "the eccentrics" who fronted monster advances to the next Hemingway or Harper Lee. "Who is a madman now in publishing?" she and other literary agents now wistfully wonder.

Nesbit went on to explain that fewer young people, sane or not, are pursuing an editorial career because the job offers little money and less freedom in exchange for longer hours and constant stress. Instead, moving from the Prosecution to the Defense, they are becoming agents or "Baby Binkys" as they are known in the business. Agent Molly Friedrich told *Poets & Writers* that the editor exodus started years ago when she and everybody else at Anchor—"aside from Bill Strachan, who has no sense"—left to become author advocates.

Though agent numbers have grown exponentially in the past decades, the increase has still not been enough to keep pace with the writer population explosion.

Agent and former editor Betsy Lerner documents the common predicament of one such Baby Binky. "Sarah," who opened her own agency but declined to give her last name, receives four hundred queries a month and has accepted only one-quarter of a percent of submitting authors, though she is actively building a list. The young Michelle Brower, with Folio Agency, which receives eight hundred queries a month, can process nineteen in fourteen minutes. An author's odds of winning representation by Brower or one of Folio's other eight agents are 1 in 11,111.[4]

Still, both agents and editors "get off on the thrill of discovering a new writer … as a junkie craves a fix,"[5] Lerner insists.

So, what gives? Are they waiting for the next *Rabbit Redux* from the ghost of Updike, the only recent master who never had an agent? Or are they too preoccupied with their midlisters on life support, waiting for the second coming of Max Perkins or another legendary but long-gone editorial madman?

"The question is really how you keep authors alive until they break through and garner a large readership," the empathetic Nesbit concludes. "That's what I stay awake at night and worry about."

---

4 Michael Bourne, "A Right Fit: Navigating the World of Literary Agents," *The Millions,* August 15, 2012. www.themillions.com/2012/08/a-right-fit-navigating-the-world-of-literary-agents.html

5 Betsy Lerner, *The Forest For The Trees: Editor's Advice to Writers* (New York: Riverhead, 2005).

CHAPTER 39

THE AUTHOR-AGENT
MATING RITUAL

In the agenting matriarchy, as in publishing generally, tough love still outweighs nurturing. When approaching a Binky or Baby Binky, the writer—emerging, midlist, or Sub-Performing Marginal—must abandon illusions about what she should be but, regrettably, is not:

She is not your analyst, your cheerleader, or your mother.

This is nonnegotiable, unless you make her a million dollars, in which case she may consent to pick up your dry cleaning. If a deal falls through, some empathetic agents who are also writers may provide counseling at no extra charge. "In college I had been good at talking people down from bad acid trips, and my skill returned in force," confided Betsy Lerner. Bonnie Nadell of Hill Nadel Agency consoled David Foster Wallace and even gave him a haircut while he was detoxing at Harvard's McLean Psychiatric Hospital.

But professionals mostly stick to business. Though often said, it is seldom understood: An agent is, above all, a salesperson. A Suck surrogate. But that doesn't take the author off the hook for being a salesperson as well. Some turn to writing because they mistake it for a profession that will deliver them from the purgatory of sales. Most authors hate the business of the business. Many hope to get around the Woody Allen Showing Up Rule by getting an agent and having *her* show up.

It doesn't work that way. Writing is a car dealership: No matter how many salespeople are out on the lot, the manufacturer has to hump, too.

The current publishing process is a Byzantine sales loop. The author sells her title to an agent. The agent sells it to an editor. An editor sells it to her house's editorial board. The board sells it to their sales and PR departments. Sales sells it to stores, distributors, and book clubs, while PR sells it to reviewers, radio, and television. The stores sell to people. Finally, coming full circle, the author tries to boost sales with book signings, media spots, and viral blogging or Tweeting. Meanwhile, everybody's trying to sell to Hollywood.

The critical link in the chain is of course the first: the author selling to the agent. Today it is nearly impossible to be published without one. The agent is the liver of the publisher digestive system. No shit gets past her. Theoretically. To ensure this, most use prefilters—agency trainees fresh out of a BA or MFA program. The trainee shovels through the agency's daily ms. shit storm, and the next morning she deposits a few promising pieces on her boss's desk. Using her judgment, taste, and marketing ESP, the boss weeds out the ones that have slipped past the trainee. Then she sends out the piece she has fallen in love with, hoping the beleaguered editor—then the board, then the sales depart-ment, then the distributors—will get a crush on it, too, perform publish-ing alchemy, and turn it into *NYT* bestseller list gold.

Now, the age-old question: How does the writer clear that all-important first hurdle and steal the heart of an industry gatekeeper?

>>>

Landing a good agent is like scoring Charlize Theron or George Clooney at a singles spot. They may be nice people, but it's their job to play hard to get. And they've heard every pickup line. The writer's job is to come up with a new one without sounding pathetic, desper-ate, or dangerous.

The catch-22 of the agent hunt is this: The lower your Suck and Luck quotient, the higher your need for an agent, but the lower your chances of getting one. So you must show extraordinary Pluck.

Let's assume the most challenging scenario of the suck-challenged author. She is six-degrees of F-separation from an agent: She is not Family, not a Friend, not Fucking him or her, not a Familiar face, and she is not even a Fone or Fax acquaintance. In short, she's a true Outsider in the Insider industry.

How does such an illegal immigrant get past the border?

First, get a coyote directory. INS AAR agent Jeff Herman offers the most helpful. In this guide, each of his colleagues defines "The Client From Hell." Six types are identified: The Pest, The Complainer, The BS Artist, The Screw-up, The Sun God, The Liar. Though many writers may fit into one or more of these profiles, when seeking an agent, a cover-up, or at least an airbrush, is imperative.

Agents are unanimous on the single virtue of "The Dream Client": She makes big money. In short, she is Biblically Talented, as earlier discussed. But, since the agent-shopping author usually hasn't made a dime yet, she must show promise.

Now there are two possibilities: (1) The agent may sign him/her but be unable to make a sale, so the author will become a Complainer and a Pest; or (2) The agent may score a six-figure advance, so the author is now free to throw off the masquerade and become a Sun God or a Screw-up.

But reps have a hustle of their own. What makes a good one? Their reply is almost unanimous. The good rep will:

- Answer client phone calls or return them promptly.
- Regularly update the client on who she is submitting to, and their response.
- Continue submitting until every likely publisher is exhausted.
- Help with subsidiary rights and tie-ins.
- Help with PR and marketing.

For Franchises, Bread-and-Butters, and Prestiges, this may be true. But for most midlisters, backlisters, and newcomers, less so. As Janklow & Nesbit vice president Eric Simonoff told *Word Smitten* a few years ago, "I'm often approached by people who are leaving their agents. What I hear cited as the number one reason for dissatisfaction from authors is—'My agent never returns my telephone calls.'"

So when entering a singles spot and hoping to score, the writer must know that, just as she must be a bit of a BS artist, the agent might be one, too.

After the bachelorette has done her best to look like a Dream Date, the next step is to decide whom to hit on. This requires more boning up. Print and online agent profiles answer important predate eHarmony questions:

- Does she consider unsolicited submissions?
- Is she actively seeking new clients?
- Does she specialize in a genre?
- What is her track record?

The writer must decide if she will approach a big Manhattan office with more muscle but less individual attention or a boutique operation with less clout but more TLC.

Practically nothing can be lost by shooting high and then working down as necessary.

Say you've just finished a *Look Homeward, Angel* sequel that is a shoe-in for the Thomas Wolfe Award or a *Dracula* follow-up destined to take the Bram Stoker. You enter the Four Seasons' Grill Room, ms. in hand. Holding audience here is the Trinity: Lynn, Binky, and Esther. In the interest of equal opportunity, let's say Mort Janklow, Andrew Wylie, and Sterling Lord are also on hand. Before them stand MFAs and refugee midlisters, each with a deli number. Noting that each agent holds a Bloody Mary in one hand and a can of mace in the other, you decide to learn more about your prey before striking.

CHAPTER 40

HOW TO BAG AN AGENT WITHOUT GUNPLAY

"Unfortunately, many writers who strive to make an impression on agents and editors aren't aware of the social hierarchies and cut-throat practices that have existed for decades."

—Elaura Niles[1]

Insiders agree that compatibility and the right fit are essential in the writer-agent relationship. "Chemistry," as it is called. But in most cases it's simple biology: The writer is looking for anybody with a pulse and a Rolodex.

Since agent hunting is among the most popular American sports now, the industry offers many How-to-Bag-Your-Ten-Pointer type primers. They reveal where a given rep can be found in rut or hibernation—mostly Manhattan, a few coveys in Westport and Sag Harbor, some California transplants, and a sprinkling of herds from D.C. to Dallas to the Dakotas. The guides also include agents' higher education (Harvard BS, Wharton MBA, Yale Law, community college, etc.)

---

1 *Some Writers Deserve To Starve! 31 Brutal Truths About the Publishing Industry* (Writer's Digest Books, 2005).

and career histories. Revealed, too, is what they'd be if they weren't an agent—some say ballerina, others Buddhist monk, cellist, chanteuse, or catcher for the Mets. Most importantly, the directories detail each rep's genre specialty, their kill rate, plus their favorite TV program.

After deciding which species of agent to pursue, then researching his or her feeding grounds and preferences, you're ready for the hunt. As any sportsman knows, you have better luck when the quarry comes to you, rather than you going to it.

To draw game, especially one as wary as a trophy agent, you need good bait. The bait is your book. But another catch-22: She doesn't want to see your etchings—at least not on the first date. She prefers a log line in the bait package—the query. Professionals assume, reasonably, that if you can't write an interesting sentence, you probably can't write an interesting book. Unless you're James Frey or E.L. James.

But the writer must beware of using a meaty log line for a tofu, soy extender, or bioengineered payoff—a boring or clichéd or impossible plot climax. The bait-and-switch angers an agent. The 007 will use her license to kill.

Another trapping caveat: Use fresh bait. The agent refuses to feed on ABC meat—Already Been Chewed by her rivals (or, worse still, by her office mates). Germophobic agents, no less than editors, have a sixth sense about anything that has been "making the rounds."

Today, fiction is being eclipsed by reality-based "creative nonfiction." But agents are also leery of canned MREs, Meals Ready to Eat. Like a father's story about his balloon boy. Or somebody who claims to have been kidnapped, tortured, and raped, but never was. Or somebody who swears they're from Bangladesh but is actually from Beacon Hill. This is a letdown and rip-off for all readers, not just the publishing professional.

The best agent bait is manna: a true triumph of the human spirit tale that drops from the heavens and onto the bestseller list. Like a new *High and Mighty*: a pilot landing his iced Airbus on the Hudson. An upbeat *Into the Wild* spin-off and Hollywood tie-in about an adrenaline junkie who cuts his arm off with a dull knife. Or a *David Copperfield* update about a Bombay boy who becomes a game-show millionaire.

》》

Whether your novel is reality-based, magic realism, or pure genre fantasy, you must telegraph its uniqueness and irresistibility to the agent in a query not much longer than a Tweet.

Since the ability to craft such a morsel is indispensable, of the many titles about writing and publishing, the most popular are about "attention-grabbing" and "rocking" queries—ones that make editors and agents "miss their subway stop" and "beat a path to your door." But many authors, even veterans, still seem unable to compose the perfect query.

Let's deconstruct this vital first communication to an industry gatekeeper piece by piece, providing Dos and Don'ts for each.

Salutation

- Do open with *Dear*—not *Hi*, *Hey*, *Yo*, or *Wassup*.

- Don't address the agent by just a first name (too familiar)—a full name or last name with *Mr.* or *Ms.* indicates a sign of respect.

- Don't address the agent by a handle (*Binky*, *Boots*, *Jackal*) or by honorific title, be it too much or too little in the honor department (*Madam*, *Esteemed Sir*, *Bro*, *Ho*, *Dude*, *Dog*).

Icebreaker

- Remind the rep that one of her clients is a relative, friend, or friend of a LinkedIn friend of yours; that you met her at Yaddo, Bennington, or a Pro-Choice rally; or that she is in your Pilates Class or AA Group.

- If you are unable to claim any such personal connection, compliment her own or one of her client's recent books, blogs, or interviews. Don't just say you loved it, showing you didn't read it. In a few words, describe how it changed your life.

Synopsis of Your Novel

- Model this after a bestseller back-cover blurb while at the same time avoiding self-serving superlatives and sensationalism.

- Introduce a conflicted, demented but deeply sympathetic hero or heroine like Larsson's Lisbeth or James' Christian Grey.

- Since professionals rarely appreciate self-delusion, much less psychosis, don't promise your novel will outsell *The Girl with the Dragon Tattoo* or *Fifty Shades of Grey.*

- Instead, dramatize a plot point or MacGuffin just short of your climax, leaving the agent breathless.

Your Credentials

- When listing your degrees, publications, grants, awards, etc., avoid a Google, BookScan, or Wikileak bust: Don't outright lie.

- Don't list the other agents you've had. Appear like a virgin who is saving herself for a real and lasting relationship.

- If you have no credits to speak of, don't tell them how many times your literary efforts have been unfairly spurned in the past.

- Don't use the Mohammad Ali "I am the Greatest" approach—i.e., claim to be the next Hemingway, Rowlings, or The Rock. (As the truism goes in the profession: Only bad writers think they're good.)

- Don't use the Kafka "I am a bug" approach, either. Professionals like pathos, not pathetic. (But if you're a paraplegic or have had your face chewed off by a chimpanzee, mention that if it pertains to your plotline or platform.)

Your Audience

- Proving that you already have a built-in readership, direct the agent to your Twitter or Facebook page (but only if you have at least several thousand real—not virtual—followers).

- Identify your demographic and use statistics to prove how vast, yet underserved, it is.

Closing

- Do close with a simple *Thanks*—not a promise of your firstborn, your kidney, or your remaining nut for their representation.

- Don't say *Cheers, Ciao, Adieu,* or *Hasta la vista.*

- Do sign *Sincerely.* Use no other —*ly* words followed by a *Yours* (*Audaciously, Desperately, Helplessly Yours*).

Length & Appearance

- Keep the query under one page, in 12-point font, single-spaced, with at least 1" margins.

- Avoid excessive CAPS, italics, underlines, exclamations, uncommon punctuation, typos (obviously), foreign phrases, ebonics, or— to discourage agent speed-reading—Braille.

PS

- Pitch the agent only one book at a time, even if you have ten ready to go.

- Don't send her a ms. already coffee-stained, dog-earred, or graffitied. That's her job.

- If some publishers have already seen and rejected the ms. because another agent already made the rounds for you and later dropped the project, chances are the new agent will find out, and fast. Either admit it up front or change the title and take a pseudonym.

Finally, and most importantly:

- If you write poetry—don't mention it.

CHAPTER 41

ON THE ROCKS

The Author-Agent Divorce

Thomas Pynchon has been happily married to his agent, Melanie Jackson, for decades, just as John Irving has been happily married to his, Janet Turnbull. But thick-and-thin romances are more the exception than the rule in the industry. Even the seemingly most solid literary marriages often end in an irreconcilable difference: The agent decides that the author is no longer talented, or never really was, and/or the author decides the agent doesn't appreciate real talent, or never really did.

Many lit weddings are shotgun and consummated in Vegas. Drunk on a hit at the pub house tables or slots, the delirious couple hurries to the drive-through. Confident of a bright, till-death-do-us-part future, many forget the prenup representation contract.

Thankfully, neither bride nor groom has any illusions about God being involved, sickness and health, or monogamy. The author knows that her agent has as many significant others as Zsa Zsa Gabor and Newt Gingrich. And the agent knows that the author will bed anybody and everybody for professional reasons. That is to say, for art.

Still, during the honeymoon, the faithful author has eyes only for the agent, especially if she springs for lunch. The honeymoon climaxes when, in his book acknowledgments, the author expresses eternal gratitude to the agent as not only an exemplary professional but a peer-less human being.

Soon, the couple has their first lovers' quarrel (about run, royalties, hardcover/softcover, sub rights, marketing, whatever). Then they patch up. Then a more serious misunderstanding over the next title (auction or no auction? Hollywood tie-in or no? digital rights rate? etc). Finally comes the annulment or divorce.

As with romantic divorces, author-agent proceedings revolve around alimony. On her deals, the agent gets her 15 percent in perpe-tuity. The publisher still sends her 100 percent of the royalties, and she forwards 85 percent to the author. So she may still hear from her ex on the back of her checks.

»»»

The author must make every effort to be the Dumper, not the Dumpee. If he is a Franchise, a Bread-and-Butter, or a Prestige, statistically he has a 98 percent chance of being the first. If an Albatross or Debut, he has a 99.9 percent chance for being the second.

The Dumpee-to-be must stay alert for signs of a blow off so he can pull out with honor. As General MacArthur said, "I'm not retreating, I'm advancing in a different direction."

Of the many dump MOs, even Jewish agents overwhelmingly prefer papal excommunication to confrontation. They know too well that every author has paper-thin skin. In short, he is a hemophiliac in a razor fac-tory. He may develop calluses or scar tissue after his first couple hun-dred rejections. But he remains a bleeder to the end.

So, the Fifth Avenue Freeze-Out is the least messy option for the agent. Some may be tempted to tackle a breakup head-on—tell the writer he's just not viable "in today's competitive market" but not to take it personally. Of course everyone knows that writers take everything personally. Or else they wouldn't be writers.

The first phase is the phone freeze. Whereas the rep was chatty during the honeymoon, she's now all business, increasingly given to monosyllables, pregnant pauses, or throat clearing. Then she starts saying she's got somebody else on the line. She puts her client on hold. He gets disconnected. He calls back. The assistant picks up. "Let me

see if she's in. What did you say was your name again?" she asks. After
the novelist holds for another five or ten, the assistant, without offering
to take a message, tells him, "She's stepped out."

This can be disconcerting to an artist. From his point of view, he's
calling for a good reason. In the manuscript submission phase, he has
pressing concerns. Has his agent scored the seven-figure deal yet?
What editors has she contacted? Any bites? Nibbles? No? Then why is
she not trying Editor X, Y, or Z?

In the postpub phase, the author has even more urgent questions.
When will she call Spielberg, the Coens, or the Weinsteins? Why is
he getting shafted on subsidiaries? Why can't she forward his royalty
statement, even though his Amazon sales ranking is 2,000,000?

These questions can be even more vexing to an agent. So, the next
time her client calls, she's on maternity leave or a Mongolian bike trek.

At this juncture in the Fifth Avenue Freeze-Out, the agent is wondering (since writers are sensitive to nuance), "Why can't he take a HINT?"

For his part, the author is wondering (since publishing is a please-
and-thank-you enterprise), "Why can't she show some MANNERS?"

After his politely persistent e-mails and Comanche smoke signals
have been ignored, the scribe finds that gentle irony is impossible to
avoid in a certified return-receipt letter.

Dear Binky,
Having trouble getting through.
When you get a minute, could you please answer a few questions?
(See attached doc from my attorney.) Thanks as always!

The agent now must abandon Cold War diplomacy. After looking into
plastic surgery or a witness protection program, she uses his last SASE
to forward the help-wanted ads from another city. This way she avoids
the embarrassment of flagging a cab next week and getting picked up
by her former client, Travis Bickle, in a Mohawk.

After being served with her restraining order, the writer, smelling
the coffee, can now send his agent a pink slip and fire her before she
fires him.

PART X

MS. IMPOSSIBLE

The Challenge for Today's Novelists

CHAPTER 42

ANATOMY
OF A 21ST-CENTURY
BLOCKBUSTER

The Twenty-First Century Mission: Write and publish a story better than anything on Fox, HBO, ESPN, Comedy Central, or the Net. Not even Dickens or Twain could do it. But that just makes the challenge more challenging.

Today, truth—nonfiction—is stranger than fiction. So the hurdle for the debut novelist is to make her fiction stranger than nonfiction but still believable. Franchise, B&B, and Prestige authors are excused from this mission because they won fans before the bar was set so high.

The newcomer most qualified for a Ms. Impossible is the six o'clock news victim du jour who has survived something unimaginable—a formerly unknown who suddenly has a built-in audience desperate to hear the details of the nightmare. It's a matter of getting the horror out before the public starts feeding on the next tabloid believe-it-or-not.

The heart of a story remains the same today as yesterday: Something bad has to happen, or be about to happen, to somebody. The worse, the better. As Vonnegut advised in *Bagombo Snuff Box*, "Be a Sadist. No matter how sweet and innocent your leading characters, make awful things

happen to them." Plot gurus call this "stakes." Regardless of the genre—
romance, horror, thriller, YA, chick lit—the hero or heroine must have
something serious to lose: career, family, sanity, salvation, life and limb,
the world itself.

The novelist mustn't forget that her reader is an ADD rubbernecker.
So she must stage her disasters engagingly and without interruption.

The challenge is to create stakes that are new in a world where,
as the cliché goes, nothing is new. Occasionally, a writer thinks she's
on to a fresh story line only to Google it and find out it's not. "Make it
new!" was Ezra Pound's command a century ago, though, four centu-
ries before that, even Pascal said, "Everything is written." Robert Frost
agreed: "There are no new ways to be new."

So today's MI writer is left with only one option: to retread or reor-
ganize the old, even the classic, so it looks new.

The first steps in this direction are FanFictions such as *Little Vampire
Women* and the *Adventurers of Huckleberry Finn and Zombie Jim*.

But now this is old. So what's left for today's Alcotts or Twains?

»»»

The two building blocks of old literature and new genre remain the
same: character and plot. Since nobody cares about a plot if they don't
care about a character, the novelist, in trying to make the old new,
must concentrate first on beefing up her protagonist. The hero is often
an author alter ego, but the author must try to avoid boring personal
details no less than stereotypes.

Here are a few that are played out: international spies or private
dicks of any kind; homicidal maniacs; deranged terrorists; mil-
lion-little-piece dope addicts in detox; hookers with hearts of gold;
abused, special needs, or wizard kids; Scout leader sociopaths;
scumbag executives; off-the-wagon AA loose cannons; washed-up
artists or athletes.

Plot-wise, the dead horses best not saddled up: anything about your
screwed-up childhood; a slum-dog millionaire fantasy; an Armageddon
vehicle; a fatal-attraction thriller—unless they involve under-represented
Fourth World characters (Inuits, Djiboutis, Bushmen, Zulu).

To avoid such clichés, the National Novel Writing Month Organization (NaNoWriMo) recommends that authors take the seventy-five-question "Fantasy Novelist's Exam."[1] A few samples:

PLOT/ACTION

- Does your story revolve around an ancient prophesy about "The One" who will save the world and everybody and all the forces of good?

SETTING

- Did you draw a map for your novel that includes places named things like "The Blasted Lands" or "The Forest of Fear" or "The Desert of Desolation" or absolutely anything "of Doom"?

- Do inns in your book exist solely so your main characters can have brawls?

CHARACTER

- Is your main character a young farmhand with mysterious parentage?

- Do any of your female characters exist solely to be captured and rescued?

- Does your novel contain a character that is really a god in disguise?

Again, though the newcomer should steer clear of such canned goods, Franchise writers can continue to indulge since they are the ones who put these goods on the shelf.

---

1 David J. Parker, "Fantasy Novelist's Exam." www.rinkworks.com/fnovel

CHAPTER 43

PUSHING THE
S.A.S. ENVELOPE

> "Young writers make the mistake of enclosing a stamped,
> self-addressed envelope, big enough for the manuscript to come
> back in. This is too much of a temptation for the editor."
> —Ring Lardner

After completing a manuscript suited for today's demanding literary marketplace, the second half of the Ms. Impossible is getting it published. Traditionally. This begins with the pitch.

Let's look at a sample agent e-query for a *Moby-Dick* FanFiction sequel by a resurrected Herman Melville. A seasoned professional, the legendary author includes the query essentials discussed earlier: his credentials and platform, his recommendations, and his plot log line.

MOBY-DICK REDUX

To: Binky Urban/ICM (bc: Mort Janklow/Janklow&Nesbit; Al Zuckerman/Writers House)

Dear Ms. Urban:

My friend, Nathaniel Hawthorne (*The Scarlet Letter*), assures me that my just-completed whaling sequel (again, dedicated to him) might merit your coveted attention. My colleagues, Emerson and Thoreau, also send their fond regards.

When Moby Dick is kidnapped from Sea World, his trainer, Ahab (whose leg he has eaten), stows away on a Greenpeace boat and tries to rescue his beloved pet from Japanese whalers and the U.S. Navy, which has fitted the Cetacean with nuclear missiles for North Korea.

My previous bestseller from Macmillan, *Typee*, recounts my shipwreck and subsequent life with Caribbean cannibals and the chief's daughter. I am a high school dropout but am now working on my GED while living with my mother in upstate New York.

I trust you will find this *Free Willy*-meets-*Namu* action/adventure a timely and heartening update of the original. I also cut the slow parts (300,000 words) about God, Evil, and seafaring trivia.

Your humble servant,
Herman Melville

Melville's pitch to Binky Urban would be spam filtered because she doesn't accept unsolicited material, as the novelist would have known had he done his homework. His copy to Janklow would result in a boilerplate "Not right for us at this time" because the celebrity agent doesn't rep whale fiction, as only a cursory review of the agency's backlist shows; moreover, a whaling vehicle would only be viable in Japan or Norway, in translation. His copy to Writers House might merit a reply from Zuckerman's assistant, reminding him that his original made only a few hundred dollars for Harpers—in short, that he is a SUMP whose only hope is print on demand (POD). She might add that all his characters again seem like unsympathetic guys, including Moby Dick, in spite of some interesting homoerotic overtones.

After a deeper agent Web research (Agentquery.com, Publishers Marketplace, Preditors & Editors, etc.), Melville could move ahead with a well-targeted second submission round that might include two other top-flight reps: Bonnie Nadell of Hill Nadell and Andrew Wylie of the Wylie Agency. Ms. Nadell represented David Foster Wallace and so is sympathetic to suicidal metaphysical novelists with substance-abuse problems, but a *Moby-Dick* query to her would likely go unanswered since the novel's potential domestic audience—the English major—is a dying breed,[1] compelling her to now concentrate on more marketable titles such as *Dangerous Girls, Virgin Soul, Devoured,* and *How to Buy Real Estate Overseas.* Finally, Andrew Wiley would seem to be a promising last resort since his agency has 700 clients, Amis, Eggers, Roth, and Rushdie among them. But the superagent won't open unsolicited material either and, reputedly, prefers to pirate Prestige clients rather than discover them. However, Wylie, known to his rivals as "the Jackal," actively pursues literary estates (Bellow's, Mailer's, Updike's, etc.), so Melville might have a chance here after he dies penniless a second time.

A rejected query comes back as either:

    A Ricochet.

    A Boomerang.

    A Blowback.

Melville's queries to Urban and Wylie would be Ricochets; those to Janklow and Nadell would be boilerplate Boomerangs; the one to Zuckerman, meriting a brief personal reply, would be a Blowback.

So that today's emerging writer might avoid a similar fate, let's look at the most common causes of each type of rejection.

RICOCHET

This is a sudden death shut-out where an agent or editor dismisses a query before even getting past the greeting or introductory sentence. The Ricochet usually happens when:

- **Guidelines are not followed.** The author e-mails though snail mail and SASE are required. His query runs ten pages. It is formatted incorrectly. He states that it is a multiple submission in spite

1   See "The Decline and Fall of the English Major," Verlyn Klinkenborg, http://www.nytimes.com/2013/06/23/opinion/sunday/the-decline-and-fall-of-the-english-major.html?_r=1&

of an in-house policy against this.

- **Ms. sample is a potentially viral attachment,** not pasted into the body of the email as specified.

- **The greeting is wrong.** The author begins "Dear Agent." He misspells the agent's name. He calls a Ms. a Mr., or a Mr. a Ms. Using a form query, he mistakenly pastes in the name of some-body from a rival agency. Or he queries a rep who has left the agency or is dead.

- **The genre is wrong.** The author queries a romance specialist about a horror title, a YA specialist about spy thriller, a nonfiction specialist about a sword and sorcery novel, and so on.

- **The return address** on the snail mailer is from a federal prison or mental hospital.

BOOMERANG

This is delayed-action rejection where an agent or editor reads most or even the entire query before tossing it. The Boomerang usually happens when:

- **English seems to be a second language** for the author, though he claims to be an Iowa Workshop MFA.

- **The agent has a good memory.** She has no recollection of meeting the author at Yaddo, the Algonquin, or a Lorin Stein *Paris Review* mixer, as the author claims.

- **Bad timing:** Her client, the author's alleged "mentor," has just left the agency or is suing it.

- **The ms. has a similar plot** to a novel that she's already sending out.

- **She's heard it one too many times.** The author claims that his novel is based on the actual diaries of his uncle—Ted Bundy, John Wayne Gacy, or Jeffrey Dahmer.

- **The author admits to writing poetry.**

BLOWBACK

This is slow-mo rejection—slightly less dispiriting but often more painful due to the suspense—where a senior agent or editor not only gets all
the way through the query, but checks out the ms., then actually writes
back to the author within a few days, weeks, or months. The Boomerang
usually happens when:

- **The author's credentials are his biggest fiction,** revealed as
  such by an agent Google or BookScan search.

- **The author pushes the billionaire bondage and discipline
  romance envelope too far.** He proposes a *Fifty Shades of Grey*
  FanFiction involving household pets, zombies, or Rupert Murdoch.

- **The author plagiarizes his writing sample.**

- **The agent discovers that the author is a Cracker or a SUMP.**

After serial Richochets, Boomerangs, and Blowbacks, today's emerging MI writer, though still convinced he has the next Kentucky-Fried
Bestseller, begins to feel like Sisyphus. But is he really condemned for
eternity to roll his manuscript to the top of a hill only to have it roll back
down to the bottom of the slush pile just before reaching an agent or
editor's desk?

"I'm fed up with having to go around with my hat out, begging for
money," Stieg Larsson wrote a friend. "Nobody cares. I need a one-
time solution." The solution was his *Girl with the Dragon Tattoo*, which
sold 48 million copies internationally. The only problem was that
Larsson was dead by that time.

Langston Hughes shared this diehard attitude. After countless
rejections, the poet, busing tables in a Washington, D.C., restaurant,
slipped a volume of his verse under the dinner plate of Vachel Lindsay
himself. He delayed the master's entrée and slipped him an extra drink.
So Lindsay took a peek. Soon, Hughes landed a deal with Lindsay's
publisher and was being hailed as "the busboy poet."

The moral of the story: Nothing ventured, nothing gained. When you got nothing, you got nothing to lose.

Author Charles J. Shields also exercised pluck to win luck and become Kurt Vonnegut's biographer. The *Slaughterhouse-Five* creator had endured his own publishing purgatory. "Novelists drag themselves around like gut-shot bears," he said. Finally, he sucked it up, broke in, and became an institution. Then it was his turn to play hard to get. Shields wrote him a letter out of the blue, calling him a genius. Parenthetically, he also mentioned he would be available to write his biography. Vonnegut declined, sending Shields a sketch of himself.

Upping the ante, the wannabe biographer wrote back, "I have important affinities with you: The Midwestern link, my experiences as the son of a World War II vet who wrote short stories while working for a big corporation; my values as a humanist; my admiration for your work."[2]

Vonnegut responded with the same self-portrait postcard, bearing one word: "OK."

Again: tenacity. Stick-to-itiveness. Guts.

Granted, practically speaking, it's hard to muster pluck in a world where lesser talents seem to have the lion's share of luck and suck. But the first thing the purpose-driven writer must learn is to abandon the childish idea that publishing, no less than life, is fair.

No one is more annoying than the person who refuses to take no for an answer, but this is the person who tends to succeed.

Now, let's meet two members of the Impossible Manuscript Force (IMF) A-team who, with ingenuity, disguises, and fierce determination, dodged Ricochets, Boomerangs, and Blowbacks to infiltrate the Bastille and make millions.

---

2 *MediaBistro/GalleyCat,* February 23, 2011.

CHAPTER 44

MS. IMPOSSIBLE

The A-Team

James Frey refused to take no for an answer on his first title, *A Million Little Pieces*. When in 1998 he began the "fictional memoir," as it is now called, he was a struggling L.A. screenwriter with a single credit to his name: the romantic comedy *Kissing a Fool*, which Roger Ebert called "pea-brained." So he decided to write literature like his idols, Hemingway, Mailer, Henry Miller, Kerouac, and Bukowski—something new that would "break a lot of rules … people place on writing and art, which I wholly reject," he later told *Vanity Fair*.[1] But an MFA friend who read the first draft of the detox nightmare told him, "This is unpublishable. This would get destroyed in my workshop."

Soldiering on, Frey signed with Kassie Evashevski of Brillstein-Grey. All eighteen publishers to whom the agent sent the novel rejected it. Then, as now, victim titles—horrific but redemptive memoirs—were cash cows (*Angela's Ashes, Running with Scissors, A Child Called 'It'*, etc.) So Evashevski resubmitted *Pieces* as autobiographical nonfiction. The manuscript was immediately accepted by Random House, one of its original rejecters, and turned over to legendary editor Nan Talese.

---

1 Evgenia Peretz, "James Frey's Morning After," *Vanity Fair*, June, 2008.

Released in 2003, Frey's "colorful mixture of spit, snot, urine, vomit and blood" was showered with accolades. Talese's best-selling novelist Pat Conroy called the title "the *War and Peace* of addiction." Even nonlogrollers found the 420-page root canal "unflinchingly honest," "mesmerizing," "electrifying," "turbo-charged, "incredible." Frey had indeed upped the memoir ante: He portrayed himself as a loose cannon junkie outlaw who decked cops and priests, underwent Marathon Man dentistry without Novocain, and invited chicks to snort coke lines off his penis.

A few quibblers were put off by Frey's masturbatory stream of consciousness, contempt for punctuation, and affection for random caps. In his "Million Little Pieces of Shit" review, critic John Dolan called the book a bad Hemingway knockoff. "This self-aggrandizing, simple-minded, poorly observed, repetitious, maudlin drivel passes for avant-garde literature in America?" he wondered.[2]

Yes, replied Oprah Winfrey. The matron of American letters picked the title for her book club and turned it into a bestseller. But soon The Smoking Gun published "A Million Little Lies," exposing Frey's tabloid nonfiction as fiction.

"The truth is what matters," Frey stubbornly insisted in the book. "It is what I should be remembered by, if I'm remembered at all." Then, after being busted, he told *Esquire* magazine with equal moral indignation, "What's truth and what's not doesn't even matter."[3]

In any case, Oprah had Frey's back, at least in the beginning. When he appeared on *Larry King Live* to answer The Smoking Gun charges, Oprah phoned in to announce, "The underlying message of redemption in James Frey's memoir still resonates with me, and I know it resonates with millions of people. ... To me, it seems to be much ado about nothing."

When other critics picked up the pitchforks and torches, the Queen of Empathy, allowing that objections might be much ado about *something*, invited the author and his editor to her "Truth in America" special broadcast.

---

2 *The eXile,* Issue #167. May 2005.

3 John H. Richardson, "'There Is No Truth,' He Said," *Esquire,* October 13, 2011.

"Then anybody can just walk in off the street with whatever story they have and say this is *my* story," challenged America's bestseller maker.

"Absolutely true," replied Talese.

"That needs to change," snapped Oprah.

"No, you cannot stop people from making up stories," objected Talese. Later, according to *Time* magazine, the editor demanded an apology for her host's "fiercely bad manners" and "ambush."

Random House offered a refund to readers who felt duped. One thousand seven hundred and twenty-nine filed, costing the publisher $27,348, a fraction of their millions in profits for *A Million Little Pieces*. The publisher froze Frey's royalties anyway but soon unfroze them when he threatened to sue based on his prepub "Author's Questionnaire." In it, he had described his title as more "a work of literature" than "a memoir or autobiography."

Avoiding collateral damage, Kassie Evashevski dropped him and Riverhead cancelled the contract for his next two books.[4] "Literally, pretty much everybody I knew in publishing, with the exception of, I think, two people, cut contact off," Frey told *Vanity Fair.*

He was now in nonfiction retreat, reversing his initial bullish advance. During prepublication interviews he had flashed reporters his "ftbsitttd" wrist tattoo—a "Fuck the Bullshit, It's Time to Throw Down" acronym. He was following the advice of the allegedly real-life hero of his *Pieces* sequel, *My Friend Leonard*, a Mafia hit man father figure.

"Every time you meet someone, make a fucking impression," the mob Confucius had supposedly told the novelist in detox. "Make them think you're the hottest shit in the world."[5]

And so he had, after the fashion of his role models, Hemingway and Mailer. He trashed his competitors, including David Foster Wallace and Dave Eggers. Then he went on to predict that he would be recognized as the best writer of his generation.

---

4 Riverhead was burned again in 2008 when Margaret B. Jones' *Love and Consequences*, a memoir of her life as a poor Native American foster child in L.A., was revealed to be the creation of Margaret Seltzer, a wealthy white woman. "I thought it was my opportunity to put a voice to people who people don't listen to," Seltzer said. Riverhead pulled the memoir shortly after publication.

5 James Frey, *My Friend Leonard* (New York: Riverhead, 2005).

Frey was bummed about being a "pariah" of publishing until he had the good fortune of meeting Norman Mailer. "If you would have called me, I would have explained to you how to get through all this mess!" the eighty-three-year-old legend told him. Like a boxer, every rebel artist takes a beating, he explained. Just as the Philistines had for forty Biblical years "stomped on me," the author of *The White Negro* went on, "now you have the privilege of being stomped on for the next forty years."

Redeemed by the master, Frey self-exiled to France and there began his resurrection gospel, *Bright Shiny Morning*. Eric Simonoff of Janklow & Nesbit agreed to represent the title and soon secured a $1.5 million advance from HarperCollins. Still gun shy from the *Million Little Piece* IED, Frey said that before publication this time, "I was expecting to get killed everywhere." So he hired Hell's Angel bodyguards for the *Shiny Morning* book tour, inspired perhaps by how well they'd worked out for the Stones at Altamont.

Blessedly, the bikers' services were not needed with readers or critics, and there was no "Sympathy for the Devil" curtain call with pool cues. Though the *L.A. Times* called the novel "a train wreck" and the *New York Daily News* "schlock," *The New York Times'* Janet Maslin described Frey as a "furiously good storyteller... [who] hit one out of the park." *The Guardian* went further, calling *Shiny Morning* "the literary comeback of the decade. ... If his story tells us anything," it concluded, "it's that being a deluded fantasist and pathological liar may be a disadvantage for a biographer, but it's a decided asset for a novelist."[6]

Publisher's Weekly called this groundbreaking memoir "a startling achievement in his accelerating mastery of the literary form." In the book's afterword, Mister Rogers himself called it, "A virtuous, unflinching, and unsentimental account of one boy's courage amid some of the world's worst cruelties."

Six years after its publication, the *San Francisco Chronicle* called the novel "the greatest literary hoax in a generation."

》》》

6 Irvine Welsh, "Saved by the City of Angels," *The Guardian*, August 1, 2008.

Sarah, by JT LeRoy, was published by Bloomsbury in 1999. JT was Jeremiah Terminator who was Cherry Vanilla who was Sam who was Sarah. JT-Cherry Vanilla-Sam-Sarah was a twelve-year-old boy-girl transvestite runaway and HIV-infected "lot lizard" who pulled tricks at a West Virginia truck stop. JT was a kind of postmodern, Less Than Zero, LGBT Holden Caulfield/Victor Victoria.

In 2005, novelist Stephen Beachy outted the lot lizard.[7] His suspicions were originally aroused when noting an uncanny resemblance between *Sarah* and Armistead Maupin's *The Night Listener,* which itself turned out to be a retread of Anthony Godby Johnson's 1993 Crown title, *A Rock and a Hard Place: One Boy's Triumphant Story*—the "autobiography" of an HIV-infected fourteen-year-old beaten and raped by his parents. Anthony had turned out to be a Union City, New Jersey woman by the name of Vicki Fraginals.

As for JT, after much digging, Beachy discovered that his/her real name was Laura Victoria Albert. Laura had started off as a social worker named Emily Frasier. She then morphed into a Renaissance wo/man by the name of Speedie. She wrote, acted, and sang for a San Francisco punk band called Daddy Don't Go and moonlighted as a phone sex operator.

Like Frey, in spite of her extracurricular activities, Albert was committed above all to literature. "S/he spoke about metaphorical truth, about purity of intent, and of a commitment to writing," reported Beachy. Instead of Frey's "Fuck the Bullshit" lit tattoo, she often wore a typewriter pendant inscribed, "Write Hard, Die Free."

Though he may have written hard, he didn't dwell on mechanics. "He couldn't punctuate to save his life..." wrote one of his many volunteer editors, David Wiegand.[8] "The only reason his spelling isn't worse than it is is because some of the errors are flagged by Microsoft Word." But Weigand does credit the author for both his self-promotion and editorial manipulation skills: "LeRoy works editors much as Louis B. Mayer

---

7 Stephen Beachy, "Who is the Real JT LeRoy?" *New York Magazine,* October 10, 2005. Beachy's most recent novels include *Distortion* (Queer Mojo Publishers, 2010) and *Boneyard* (Verse Chorus Press, 2011).

8 David Wiegand, "First Person, LeRoy and the Art of Getting Editors to Work for Free," *San Francisco Chronicle,* January 10, 2006. Weigand has edited Ann Beattie, among others.

worked writers back in MGM's heyday."

Indeed, LeRoy-Laura-Emily-Speedie proved herself the Luck, Suck, & Pluck Queen. In six years she worked herself from the bottom to the top of the publishing food chain. In 1994, her analyst, Dr. Terrence Owen, passed her first JT story to his neighbor, editor Eric Wilinski. Then she contacted gay novelist Dennis Cooper through his agent, Ira Silverberg, which in turn put her in touch with sympathetic authors Sharon Olds, Mary Karr, and Mary Gaitskill. Meanwhile she placed short stories with Coppola's *Zoetrope* and McSweeney's *Quarterly Concern*. She wrote screenplays for Gus Van Sant, hung with Madonna and Courtney Love, and, finally, scored a Crown contract for *Sarah* through agent Henry Dunow.

Dunow flew to San Francisco to meet his elusive AC/DC golden goose but, as usual, she was a no-show. Surrendering to increased pressure for public readings at last, she showed up in a wig and sunglasses but often hid under tables. She alternated between an English accent, a Brooklyn accent, and—for NPR's *Terry Gross Show*—a West Virginia drawl.

At last this public JT was revealed to be not Laura-Emily-Speedie at all, but Savannah Knoop. In 2008, Ms. Knoop, not to miss the bandwagon, published *Girl Boy Girl: How I Became JT LeRoy*, a memoir about the six years she spent as an HIV-positive teen lot lizard stand-in.

The year before, Antidote International Films sued Laura Albert for putting her JT Hancock on a *Sarah* movie deal. According to *The New York Times*, the author was ordered to pay the production company $116,500 in damages and $350,000 in attorney's fees. Presumably the sum would come out of her royalties for *Sarah* as well as its film-optioned prequel, *The Heart Is Deceitful Above All Things*, plus her "I Am the Real JT LeRoy" T-shirt sales.

As for her publisher, Bloomsbury, unlike Random House in the Frey case, it offered no refunds to readers, nor were any demanded even by bona fide AIDS victims.

Before the LeRoy fraud was exposed, but while it was suspected,

Stephen Beachy asked Laura Albert's last agent, Ira Silverberg,[9] how he funneled royalties to his client. "None of your business," Silverberg told him. Beachy later discovered that checks went to Underdog, Inc., a Nevada enterprise run by Albert's mother, Carolyn, a theater critic. When Beachy went on to ask the agent about the fraud rumors, Silverberg told him, "If it is all a big hustle, it's a great hustle, and I applaud it. … If it's true, it's as Warholian as it gets."

Later the Sterling Lord rep, a judge for the Gregory Kolovako Award for AIDS writing, reconsidered. "To present yourself as a person who is dying of AIDS in a culture which has lost so many writers and voices of great meaning, to take advantage of that sympathy and empathy, is the most unfortunate part of all of this," he told *The New York Times*.[10]

In her first major interview after being outted, the author of *Sarah* told *The Paris Review*, "It's amazing to me for the first time in my life to be out in the world as Laura Albert, the successful writer." As for her charade, she explained, "I never saw it as a hoax. I always felt like JT was a mutation, a shared lung. JT was protection. He was a veil upon a veil—a filter."[11]

As for the professional character of her young alter ego hero, Stephen Beachy concluded, "LeRoy has written about the way prostitutes fulfill other people's fantasies and about the way the literary world can seem like simply a different form of prostitution."

---

9 Silverberg left Sterling Lord Literistic Agency in late 2011 to become Literature Director for the National Endowment for the Arts. Prior to becoming an agent, he was the Grove/Atlantic editor-in-chief.

10 Warren St. John, "The Unmasking of JT Leroy: In Public, He's a She." (*The New York Times*, January 9, 2006)

11 Nathaniel Rich, "Being JT Leroy," *The Paris Review,* Fall 2006.

CHAPTER 45

THE MAD SCIENTIST OF "MS. IMPOSSIBLE" PUBLISHING

"I have high hopes of smashing my name into history so violently that it will take a legendary form."

—L. Ron Hubbard, 1938 letter to his literary agent, Forrest J. Ackerman

The most published author in history, according to *The Guinness Book of World Records*, is the godfather of Tom Cruise, the "Mission Impossible" star himself: L. Ron Hubbard. In his lifetime, he released 1,084 books, twenty-nine of which were novels.

The Scientology founder also holds the record for the most popular self-published book: *Dianetics: The Modern Science of Mental Health*. Bridge Publications, its current printer, states that the title has sold 83 million copies to date. The unfaithful estimate 20 million. The heretical Nielsen BookScan reported 52,000 sold between 2001 and 2005.

In 1938, Macaulay Publishers paid Hubbard $2,500 for his first novel, *Buckskin Brigades*, a Western based on explorers Lewis and Clark's experiences with the Blackfoot Indians. Establishing his platform, the college dropout claimed to have become, at age six, a blood brother to a medicine man of the tribe, although the Blackfoot never practiced the tradition. With his advance, Hubbard bought *The Magician*, a boat. On a trip to Asia as a teen he claimed to have trained with Buddhist lamas and the last in the line of Kublai Khan's wizards.

While sailing the seven seas, Hubbard continued to write novels, stopping in Hollywood to write scripts such as *The Great Adventures of Wild Bill Hickok* (1938) and *The Spider Returns* (1941), though his name never appeared in the Columbia credits.

The cloud-parting of his literary career occurred at about the time he was working on *Wild Bill*. While under the influence of nitrous oxide during a dental extraction, he said he died for eight minutes, during which time "the basic principles of human existence" were revealed to him. Returning to life, he jotted them down and called the work *Excalibur* after Arthurian legend.

Hubbard phoned Arthur J. Burks, President of the American Fiction Guild, informing him he'd just finished 'THE Book," just as Edgar Allan Poe had declared about his *Eureka* and, later, Faulkner about his *Flags in the Dust*. Hubbard upped their ante: He described *Excalibur* as "Somewhat more important ... than the Bible." Burke brushed him off since he was busy working on his own apocalyptic revelation, *Who Do You Think You Are?*

Undiscouraged, Hubbard telegrammed New York publishers, telling them to meet him at Penn Station to review THE Book and make offers.

Nobody showed.

Pressing on, he wrote *Typewriter in the Sky*. This novel concerned a struggling musician who discovers he is a time-traveling pawn in his friend's buccaneer pulp novel, the plot turns of which are preceded by the ding of a celestial typewriter.

The most published author in history then joined the Navy. He allegedly won twenty-one medals, but according to his biographer, Russell Miller,[1] military records only account for four. He was rushed to a military hospital wounded, crippled, and blinded, although documents only mention ulcers and conjunctivitis. And he was pronounced dead twice despite no evidence of claim.

---

1   Russell Miller, *Bare-faced Messiah: The True Story of L. Ron Hubbard* (New York: Henry Holt & Co., 1988).

Postwar, Hubbard wrote that he was "abandoned by family and friends as a supposedly hopeless cripple."[2] In a petition to the Veterans Administration for a pension increase, he complained of "moroseness and suicidal inclinations." But, out of "pride," he admitted to refusing the psychiatric treatment his physician had recommended.

Instead, Hubbard was deputized by the LAPD to study criminals. In his spare time, he cured neurotics from Hollywood to Georgia, he wrote more science fiction thrillers, and he dabbled in black magic.

His wizard mentor was Jack Whitside Parsons, the Jet Propulsion Laboratory founder. Parsons ran the California chapter for the international sorcery temple of The Great Beast, Aleister Crowley, known as "the wickedest man in the world." The scientist wrote the warlock that his new recruit was "in direct touch with some higher intelligence, possibly his Guardian Angel ... a beautiful winged woman with red hair whom he calls the Empress and who has guided him through his life and saved him many times."[3]

The Beast smelled a rat. Crowley prophesied that Hubbard would make off with Parson's own "angel," a twenty-one-year-old Empress by the name of Sara.

And so Hubbard did.

Hubbard's scheme might have succeeded had Parsons not magically conjured a typhoon to intercept his yacht. The pirate and Sara were forced to shore and into the custody of the Florida Coast Guard. Soon Parsons, nearly bankrupt, was blown up in a laboratory explosion.

Hubbard himself survived with a slap on the wrist and a new lease on life. "I became used to being told it was all impossible, that there was no way, no hope. Yet I came to see again and walk again, and I built an entirely new life," he wrote in *My Philosophy*.

At this point he might have at last penned *the* Ms. Impossible novel, which would have made Frey's *Million Little Pieces* and LeRoy's *Sarah* memoirs seem like child's play. He'd been crippled, he'd been blinded, he'd died multiple times. He'd studied with Kublai Khan's sorcerer, he was a Blackfoot medicine man blood brother, and he had nearly

---

2 "My Philosophy," *Church of Scientology International*, 1965.

3 John Symonds, *The Great Beast: The Life and Magick of Aleister Crowley* (MacDonald and Co., 1971).

fathered a "moonchild" Rosemary's baby during "Babalon Working" sessions with his Empress, Sara, whom Crowley called a "vampire."

But, instead of writing such a nonfiction novel synergizing all popular genres—Romance, Mystery, Horror, Fantasy, Action-Adventure, Sci-Fi, and Victim Lit—he set to work on *Dianetics*. Having built an entirely new life for himself, he wished to share his existential secrets with other lost souls.

Hubbard claimed to have completed his 400-page *Modern Science of Mental Health* in three weeks[4] in a trailer (like Stephen King's for *Carrie*) on a long scroll (like Kerouac's for *On the Road*). With customary modesty, he called it "a milestone for man comparable to his discovery of fire and superior to his invention of the wheel."

Neither the *American Medical Association Journal* nor *The American Journal of Psychiatry* agreed. Both summarily rejected the *Dianetics* paper.

When Hubbard submitted the full manuscript to a New York publisher, he told his agent, Forrest J. Ackerman, that the reader threw himself out of a skyscraper window. He went on to warn Ackerman that "whoever read it either went insane or committed suicide."[5]

In order to avoid further publisher casualties, Hubbard formed his own pub company, Hubbard Dianetic Research Foundation. In the spring of 1950, the HDRF released signed, gold-bound copies of his opus, priced at $1,500 apiece ($29,000 now). This premiere special edition warned readers that "four of the first fifteen people who read it went insane." So buyers were required to issue a sworn statement not to lend the book out.

Despite generally poor reviews, *Dianetics* became a blockbuster. Hubbard's ten-book sci-fi novel series, *Mission Earth*—which involves invading ETs pitted against lesbians, nymphomaniacs, and drug dealers—rode its coattails to become a bestseller, too.

The visionary author, according to his followers, dropped his "meat body" in 1986 to continue with his writing and research in other galaxies.

---

4 On other occasions, he said six weeks. Sara, married to Hubbard in 1946 and divorced in 1951, told biographer Bent Corydon that it took eighteen months. Bent Corydon, *L. Ron Hubbard, Messiah or Madman?* (Barricade Books, 1996)

5 "Secret Lives: L. Ron Hubbard," Channel 4 Television, November 19, 1997. Ackerman, a sci-fi writer himself who also did monster movie cameos (his last for Michael Jackson's "Thriller") called himself an "illiterary agent."

He left an unprecedented literary legacy: In outdoing all other modern nonfiction fiction specialists—Capote, Mailer, Frey, Albert—Hubbard not only created a blockbuster but became the messiah protagonist of his own work. In 1948, while writing *Dianetics*, history's most ambitious Ms. Impossible author told a writers convention, "You don't get rich writing science fiction. If you want to get rich, you start a religion."

PART XI

TAKING IT
IN THE SHORTS

CHAPTER 46

BACKSTORY
TO THE BIG BREAKS

"Selling to *The New Yorker* made the whole business of being a short-story writer valid in a way, because I still had these recurring fits of I must give this up and write a novel."

—Alice Munro, most published current fiction writer at *The New Yorker*[1]

If a Bastille break-in still eludes the writer who has aggressively pushed the S.A.S. Envelope and attempted a Frey or LeRoy Nonfiction Fiction coup—he mustn't despair. Many masters have reached this valley and scaled the mountain in the end even so.

How?

They retreated, regrouped, and returned to the front with fast and furious fiction.

Story writing was once considered the nursery for the novel. Then Poe, Maupassant, and Gogol changed all that. And their successors—Chekhov, O'Henry, O'Connor, Carver, Welty, Munro, etc.—further

---

1 Frank Kovarik, "*New Yorker* Fiction by the Numbers," *The Millions,* January 4, 2011. http://www.themillions.com/2011/01/new-yorker-fiction-by-the-numbers-2.html

elevated the medium. The stories of some were like bonsai—no less magnificent than their counterparts.

Many novelists were born in short fiction. At age twenty-nine, Mark Twain established himself with his "Celebrated Jumping Frog of Calaveras County." The name "Dickens" first appeared in London's *Monthly Magazine* with "A Dinner at Poplar Walk." Jack London got his foot in the door with "To Build a Fire," then with *Call of the Wild*, which *The Saturday Evening Post* bought for $750 and serialized.

Poe's career was launched by his "MS. Found in a Bottle" which won $50 in the *Baltimore Saturday Visitor* contest. He submitted a poem as well but lost to one Henry Wilton who turned out to be John Hewitt, the magazine's editor, which resulted in a street brawl between the two.

At age seventeen, John Cheever won the *Boston Herald* fiction contest. Seven years later, *The New Yorker's* Katherine White paid him $45 for "Buffalo."

Mailer and Capote, too, broke into the business as teen competition winners. At age eighteen, the future *American Dream* novelist claimed *Story Magazine's* First Place. At age ten, the future *Breakfast at Tiffany's* author won the *Mobile Press Register* literary contest and, a decade later, the O'Henry Award.

One of the greatest launchpads for talent was *The Paris Review's* Aga Kahn Prize. Winners who went on to become household names include Philip Roth, T.C. Boyle, Jeffrey Eugenides, Charles D'Ambrosio, Rick Moody, David Foster Wallace, and Will Self. The prize debuted in 1956, shortly after *The Paris Review* was founded by George Plimpton and National Book Award laureate Peter Matthiessen.[2]

Story Magazine was another incubator for future heavyweights. William Saroyan debuted there with his 1934 "The Daring Young Man on the Flying Trapeze." Five years later, Whit Burnett, the magazine's editor, took a chance on "The Young Folks" by a student in his Columbia night class, a twenty-year-old college dropout named J.D. Salinger.

---

2 In the Underground Alliance Special Report, "The Fiction of the State," Richard Cummings asserts that both writers were CIA ops using *The Paris Review* as a cover. The CIA allegedly funneled funds to the magazine through the foundation of its publisher, Prince Sadruddin Aga Khan, the Harvard-educated imam of letters.

Besides *Story*, the greatest outlets for American short fiction at this time were *The Saturday Evening Post, Redbook, Harpers*, and *The Atlantic*.[3] The first was a gold mine and at the top of every author's submission list. Fitzgerald wrote Hemingway, "The *Post* now pays the old whore $4,000 a screw. But now it's because she's mastered the 40 positions—in her youth one was enough."[4] At the time, 1929, just before the Crash, the sum amounted to $80,000 in today's economy.

Both the *Post* and *Redbook* had rejected Hemingway's own early stories. At last Boni & Liveright published them in the *In Our Time* collection. Papa had concentrated on short fiction at the outset of his career because he believed that the novel was obsolete, an opinion he abruptly changed after finishing *The Sun Also Rises*.

Hemingway's original marketing assistant, Sherwood Anderson, had also gotten his start with his *Winesburg, Ohio* collection, considered by many critics his best work. Scribner published Fitzgerald's *Flappers and Philosophers* collection the same year as *This Side of Paradise*, but the stories predated his debut novel and had earned him the rejection slips with which he had wallpapered his room.

The glory days of the old *Post* and its competitors are now long gone, especially dollar-wise. Today, top pay for short fiction by an established name comes from *The New Yorker, The Atlantic*, and *Harper's*, but rarely exceeds $10,000—about 12 percent (adjusted for currency devaluation) of what the *Post* paid in its heyday. *Esquire, Playboy, GQ, McCall's, Ms., Elle, Seventeen, Redbook, Good Housekeeping, Glamour*, and others no longer run fiction regularly, or at all. Among the prime paying markets that remain active today are *Glimmer Train* ($700 per story), *ThreePenny Review* ($700), *The Sun* ($300–$1,500), *Narrative* ($150–$1,000), and

---

3 Examples of the diverse short fiction and serialized novels that debuted in these magazines:

Saturday Evening Post: "The Black Cat," "Babylon Revisited," *The Mouse that Roared, Murder on the Orient Express, True Grit*

Redbook: Tarzan the Untamed, The Third Man, "Uncle Fred Flits By" (Wodehouse)

Harper's: "Barn Burning," *Jude the Obscure*, "The Promise" (Steinbeck)

The Atlantic: Portrait of a Lady, The Europeans, The Autobiography of Alice B. Toklas

McClure's magazine, *Collier's Weekly*, and the *American Mercury* were also important story outlets.

4 Matthew J. Bruccoli, ed., *F. Scott Fitzgerald: A Life in Letters* (New York: Scribner/Touchstone, 1995).

The Virginia Quarterly Review (25¢ per word). Academic and independent reviews that pay between $10 and $50 per page include *The Iowa Review, The Southern, Massachusetts, Missouri, Gettysburg, Georgia, Indiana,* and *New England.* Equally prestigious publications that elect not to disclose their payment scale include *Granta, TriQuarterly, Tin House, Zyzzyva, Prairie Schooner, Sewanee, Kenyon Review, Black Warrior, Boston Review, Mississippi Review.* The overwhelming majority of literary magazines, however, offer contributor copies in lieu of payment.[5]

The other manner in which the short story market has evolved is in, like the novel, the number of writers trying to crack it. Former *Virginia Quarterly Review* editor Ted Galloways estimated that in the 1930s major literary journals such as his own and the *Yale Review* received about 500 submissions annually; in 2010 *VQR* received over 15,000.[6] To be sure, more little magazines—both print and digital—exist now and pick up some of the slack, but it's hardly enough to compensate for the submission tsunami. Moreover, as Galloways points out, the average print review releases fewer than 1,500 copies and "no one is reading all this newly produced literature—not even the writers themselves." As a result, the magazine literary story, "like a dying star, seems on the verge of implosion," he argues.

---

5 Before submitting to such journals, the writer is well advised to not only consult the website of the publication for their guidelines but to review an actual copy or two. Other good sources of lit mag information include:

Poets & Writers (www.pw.org/literary_magazines)

Duotrope (https://duotrope.com)

CLMP/Council of Literary Magazines & Presses (http://www.clmp.org/directory)

LitList (http://litlist.net/literary_journals)

6 Ted Genboways, "The Death of Fiction?" *Mother Jones,* Jan-Feb 2010. www.motherjones.com/media/2010/01/death-of-literary-fiction-magazines-journals

CHAPTER 47

THE GREATEST STORY NEVER SOLD

"The Castle hill was hidden, veiled in mist and darkness, nor was there even a glimmer of light to show that a castle was there. ... K. stood for a long time gazing into the illusory emptiness."
—**Franz Kafka,** *The Castle*

Castle dwellers refer to their publication housed in Si Newhouse's Condé Nast Tower in Times Square as "The Magazine." The forty-eight-story high-rise that inspired the architecture of *Battlestar Galactica* boasts a state-of-the-art air filtration system and a labyrinth of high-tech ms.-fed recycling chutes. Below The Magazine reside *Architectural Digest, Bon Appétit, Gourmet, Golf World, GQ, Mademoiselle, Vanity Fair,* and *Webmonkey.*

The New Yorker's founder, Harold Ross, a high school dropout from Aspen, Colorado, had defected from editing the satirical *Judge* magazine, The Onion of the day. He envisioned a publication not geared to "the old lady in Dubuque" but to a more urbane, discriminating audience. Ross won Algonquin Vicious Circle members on the idea, plus his poker partner, Raoul Fleishmann. The yeast heir provided $25,000 seed capital followed by another $400,000 before the enterprise broke even.

The debut issue of *The New Yorker* was published on February 21,
1925, a year before the publication of *The Castle* and two years after
Kafka's death.[1] Its contributing editors included Dorothy Parker, Robert
Benchley, and other Algonquin regulars.

Their captain, Ross, a literary autodidact and punctuation stickler,
was a workaholic. He left the Castle, then went on West 43rd, only to
play cards with the yeast baron around the corner at the Algonquin's
Inside Straight Club. Described as "a passionate, reckless gambler,"
by his editor Brendan Gill,[2] he once lost $20,000 to Fleishmann at back-
gammon in a single night. In the habit of doubling down when losing his
shirt, Ross would exclaim, "I'm cursed! Something I did to God!"

Gill described his boss as "an aggressively ignorant man" who
loved pranks. More than once he had been the target of Ross's sugar
cube wrapper spitballs blown across the dining room. A mischievous
pyromaniac, he also amused himself by throwing lit matches and
once ignited a woman on the dance floor. When firing an employee,
however, the venerable editor-in-chief was more circumspect.
According to Gill, he would first confiscate "a writer's typewriter,
then his pencils and paper, and then his desk and chair, reducing
him by stages to a condition of journalistic paralysis." For Ross, the
worst offense in his administration was not incompetence, sloth, or
stupidity, but disloyalty. For him, wrote Gill, loyalty was "a form of
consenting serfdom."

Despite the intellectual exertions of Ross' team, *The New Yorker*
was regarded as "middle-brow," overshadowed by the older and more
venerable *Harper's* and *The Atlantic*. Ross' assistant, Katherine Angell
White, the Eleanor of Aquitaine of the operation, changed that with the
1940 *Short Stories from The New Yorker*. The anthology helped popu-
larize Thurber's "Secret Life of Walter Mitty," Cheever's "Enormous
Radio," as well as Jackson's "The Lottery," and it went on to become an
eagerly anticipated publication.

Katherine was the wife of the magazine's editor, E.B. White, future
co-author of *The Elements of Style*. White's friend, James Thurber,

---

1 1,500 copies were printed; few sold.

2 Brendan Gill, *Here at the New Yorker* (New York: Random House, 1975).

called her "the fountain and shrine of *The New Yorker.*" Ross had started her at $25 a week but, finding her indispensable immediately, he doubled it to $50 her second week. Among other things, she had a unique talent for dealing with difficult and/or drunk talent, such as John O'Hara.

The New Yorker, however, neglected many other American icons. Brendan Gill considered it a "scandal" that it had not published Hemingway, Faulkner, or Capote, and only one story by Fitzgerald. Still, during the Ross/White dynasty, *The New Yorker* graduated to become the, if not *The*, premiere highbrow weekly, boasting regular contributions by many of America's other great short fiction artists. But not a few were denied immediate admission to the Castle.

It rejected all of Salinger's submissions, 1941 through 1945. These included fifteen poems and seven short stories—"Lunch for Three," "Monologue for a Watery Highball," and "I Went to School with Adolf Hitler" among them. According to his biographer, Salinger became "increasingly bitter" toward *The New Yorker*, claiming that it was open only to its clique of "Little Hemingways."[3] Its editors had tentatively accepted "Slight Rebellion off Madison" just before the war but scrapped it after the Pearl Harbor attack a month later since the story—"too ingenious and ingrown"—focused on "the pre-war" jitters of a kid called Holden Caulfield, the future cultural icon and hero of *The Catcher in the Rye*.[4] At last, in 1948, Salinger stormed the Bastille with his day-at-the-beach suicide story, "A Perfect Day for Bananafish." Subsequently, the magazine ran twelve more of his pieces, but he was still not spared the ax. Truman Capote, a former reader for Ross, reported that in Salinger's post-*Franny and Zooey* reclusive period he had submitted five or six novellas, all of which were turned down.[5]

In spite of being an editor, James Thurber had to pay his dues, too. The humorist was rejected twenty times before he broke in with an allegorical vignette about a man caught in a revolving door. His cartoons had been accepted earlier after E.B. fished them from a trashcan.

---

3 Kenneth Slawenski, *J.D. Salinger: A Life* (New York: Random House, 2010).

4 They finally published the story in December 1946.

5 John Bear, *The Number One New York Times Bestseller* (Ten Speed Press, 1992).

During his own sixty-year tenure, Brendan Gill had submitted sixty pieces and half had been turned down. "The painfulness of being rejected never grows less," he wrote. "In our hearts, we are all six years old."

The New Yorker contributor John O'Hara holds the record for most stories published: 225.[6] Nevertheless, he too suffered occasional rejection. The notoriously thin-skinned author of *Butterfield 8* kept a stiff upper lip until Brendan Gill panned his otherwise well-reviewed novel, *A Rage to Live*. O'Hara informed Shawn he would not write a single word more for the magazine until Gill's head was delivered to him in a basket. Shawn, though he carried a hatchet in his briefcase in case of an elevator breakdown, declined to do so. So The National Book Award winner wrote nothing for the next five years except—with more than his usual dose of spit and vinegar—*Farmer's Hotel* (1957).

Euphemism abandoned the diplomatic Brendan Gill when profiling the publication's stalwarts in his title *Here at The New Yorker*. He called O'Hara—whose work supposedly became the paradigm for "*The New Yorker* story"—a "difficult" megalomaniac. He said Thurber was "malicious" because "other people's miseries made his happiest times." And he made mention of Katherine White's "indomitable competitiveness." Though Gill emphasized that she was Ross' "intellectual conscience" and "beautiful" besides, her son, Roger Angell, told him that his book had made her cry bitterly for two days.

In retaliation for his criticism about her competitiveness, Ms. White waged a "strenuous campaign of falsehoods" against him, said Brendan. She and his other targets clearly hadn't expected such betrayal from a Yale man (one of the many at the magazine), much less a Skull & Bones member. Outside the Castle, the unwashed seemed to have no problem with this. *Here at The New Yorker* spent four months on the *The New York Times* bestseller list in 1975.

The Ross/White Dynasty gave way to the golden Shawn era, followed by the Gottlieb, then the Brown, bringing us to the current Remnick

---

6 Cheever is #2 at 119, Updike #3 at 104.

administration. The magazine has become politicized and *au courant*, but in some respects remains the same.

So, after eighty years, fiction writers at the Castle doors with the next "Enormous Radio" or "Lottery" still ask themselves:

What the dickens *is* a "*New Yorker* story"?

Katherine White is credited for developing the signature phenomenon. To this day, no one knows quite what she had in mind, except that it involves rarified language, quirky character, and a casual, mildly depressing plot. But not always.

In-house editors have graciously tried to tackle this question, including the matriarch's son, Roger Angell, the baseball Balzac, now a nonagenarian.

In his 1994 revelation "Storyville," Angell illustrated *The New Yorker* sensibility with a seven-word V.S. Pritchet line: "A soft owl flew over the lane." Noting that this "short adjective, instead of the expected adverb, is art itself," he declared: "We want that owl." For those who didn't appreciate ornithology or modifier surprise, the fiction editor explained that he and his colleagues looked for stories "exactly like the ones by Borges and Brodkey and Edna O'Brien and John O'Hara and Susan Minot and Eudora Welty and Niccolo Tucci and Isaac Singer ... except with more Keillor and Nabokov."

In short, the dauphin and his court invoke the Popeye/Yahweh I-yam-what-I-yam argument: a *New Yorker* piece is what's *in The New Yorker*.

Indeed, many pieces—whether fiction, humor, investigative journalism, criticism—have the uncanny quality of having been composed by the same owl.

"They've got layers upon layers of editors over there, and they're always second-guessing one another," a regular contributor told *Salon* on the condition of anonymity. "Even the shortest pieces I write go through about seven editors, and at the end of all that I can often barely recognize my voice in the article."[7]

Since only a Zen answer is possible for "What *is* a *New Yorker* piece?" here are two more practical questions: What does it take to get

---

7 www1.salon.com/june97/tina2970625.html

into The New Yorker, and what are the odds?

First, the odds. Twenty years ago, fiction editor Chip McGrath said the magazine received about four hundred short stories per week and published one or two from the slush pile annually. At this time, they were publishing two stories (occasionally three) per weekly issue, or about 112 per year. So, calculating at 1.5 acceptances for 22,400 yearly submissions, the outsider had a .0000669 percent chance of entering the Castle.

The New Yorker's current fiction editor, Deborah Treisman, has not revealed current body count. Outside source estimates vary from two to four thousand per month.[8] So let's say three thousand. Since the Tina Brown reign, only one story is run per issue, not two. So, calculating at 1.5 acceptances for 36,000 yearly submissions, the outsider now might have a .0000416 percent chance of breaking into America's last premiere short fiction venue. Except Brown's fiction editor, Bill Buford, admitted to taking nothing from the slush: So, during his tenure in the '80s and '90s, chances were practically zero percent.

Who are the other 99.9999+ percent? At the top of the heap are the Nobel or Booker recipients, some deceased. Next, come the Franchises: Munro, Trevor, Boyle, Erdrich, Saunders, Proulx, etc.[9] Then there are the MFA wunderkinds and up-and-comers from Knopf and FSG. Below them are the Ivy League staffers and fact-checkers for the magazine itself. And holding anchor are the annual 48,000 Shirley Jackson's Lottery players.

New Yorker paper rejections, now nearly extinct, came in several varieties. For bad stories: an unsigned card with the monocled dandy inspecting the butterfly. For not bad: same form, signed *Sorry*. For marginal: *Sorry, thanks*. For good: *Sorry, thanks, try us again*. For excellent: *Sorry, thanks, but my story beat yours*.

For e-submissions, now the rule, no *Sorrys, LOLs*, or *Thx anyways*. No reply at all. The materialist author prefers the old pink slip with

---

8 2,000: *Crain's New York Business* (http://mycrains.crainsnewyork.com/40under40/profiles/2003/deborah-treisman).

4,000: *The Morning News* (http://www.themorningnews.org/article/among-the-unsavvy)

9 Of the 514 stories published in the last decade, 215 (42%) were written by twenty-eight writers. (*The Millions*, January 4, 2011)

postmark proving that his story was sent and actually existed as dark matter in the space/time continuum. But even during the Bill Buford nineties, Sterling Lord Literistic president Philippa Brophy complained, "Sending stuff to him was like sending stuff to outer space."[10]

Awhile ago, when a piece was accepted, this is what happened according to former editor Renata Adler: "When we did buy material from young or unknown writers, then delayed publication for months, even years, the morale and then the work of those writers declined. ... It is often said that no matter how adverse the circumstances, real writers write. It is not always true. ... The magazine ... was beginning actually to destroy young writers by raising their hopes."[11]

The magazine is said to have amassed an archive of unpublished stories that would take ten years to exhaust. Still, Ms. Treisman—the 2012 Maxwell E. Perkins Award winner—recently assured a *Wall Street Journal* interviewer that her staff continues the noble enterprise of reviewing unsolicited material in order not to discourage the next Munro or Carver.

In 2003, *Book Magazine* asked if she had actually rescued anything from the slush. "Someone who's submitting themselves directly to the fiction editor probably isn't all that savvy about publishing," she replied. Five years later, when asked on *The New Yorker's* own interactive site[12] if the magazine had ever published an unsolicited, unagented fiction writer during her tenure, Ms. Treisman mentioned four: Gina Ochsner, Rebecca Curtis, Uwem Akpan, and David Hoon Kim. Oshsner, published by the magazine in 2004, had won the Flannery O'Connor Award for her 2002 story collection from the University of Georgia. Curtis, published in the same year, was a Syracuse MFA grad. Nigerian Jesuit priest Uwem Akpan, published in 2007, was working on his MFA at University of Michigan. Kim, also in 2007, was an Iowa Workshop MFA (and currently a Wallace Stegner

---

10 "The Gatekeeper For Literature Is Changing At New Yorker." David Carr & David D. Kirkpatrick. *The New York Times.* October 21, 2002. www.nytimes.com/2002/10/21/business/the-gatekeeper-for-literature-is-changing-at-new-yorker

11 *Gone. The Last Days of the New Yorker* (New York: Simon & Schuster, 1999).

12 "Questions for Deborah Treisman," *The New Yorker* online, December 15, 2008. www.newyorker.com/online/blogs/ask/2008/12/questions-for-treisman.html

Fellow at Stanford).

Featuring younger talent, *The New Yorker* released the modestly titled *Future of American Writing* collection in 1999 and, in 2010, *20 Under 40: Stories from The New Yorker*. In her introduction to the last, Ms. Treisman said the twenty writers chosen were those "we felt were, or soon would be, standouts in the diverse and expansive panorama of contemporary fiction."

What does this mean specifically?

The editors identified some of the characteristics they found in the short fiction or novel excerpts chosen:[13]

- A freshness of perspective, observation, humor, or feeling
- A stealthier buildup of thought and linguistic innovation
- A mastery of language and of storytelling
- A palpable sense of ambition

In choosing the hundred and fifty young writers to be reviewed, Ms. Treisman said she and her staff not only consulted with established authors and academics but with "the street." Indeed, the twenty chosen were a mixed bag. International diversity was worthy of the UN: In addition to Americans, there was a Nigerian, a Peruvian, a Latvian, a Chinese, an Ethiopian, a Yugoslavian, and a Russian. Professional experience was also richly varied. There was a film director, an immunology premed, an oncology premed, a derivatives trader, two Harvard Divinity students, and a bricklayer.

Academic background also varied: There were MacArthurs, Guggenheims, and MacDowell Fellows as well as PEN/Faulkner finalists, and many MFAs. Treisman told the *Stanford Arts Review*[14] that she never asks for academic credentials but "sometimes I know someone has been in a workshop because he's been referred by a professor."[15]

---

13 *Talk of the Town* Comment, June, 14, 2010.

14 *SAR* Interview with Deborah Treisman. June 8, 2012. http://artsreview.stanford.edu/?p=8479

15 Competing with Treisman for the Publishing Pinocchio Award, *The Paris Review* editor Lorin Stein says he shares her connection-blind kumbaya attitude: "Names don't matter, CVs don't matter, previous publications don't matter at all." Instead, he insisted that his magazine's fiction criteria related above all to "voice," "urgency," and "actually having a story to tell." http://therumpus.net/2012/10/the-rumpus-interview-with-lorin-stein/

The *20 Under 40* compilation was criticized for being narrowly focused on insiders already on the fast-track for coronation. Lee Siegel called the list a "junior pantheon" and "an artistic affront," proving that "fiction has become culturally irrelevant."[16] Of Siegel, *The New Yorker*'s own David Rieff wrote, "To read him is to be reminded of what criticism used to aspire to in terms of range, learning, high standards, and good writing and—dare one say it?—values."

Since the most common charge against both the compilation and the weekly magazine itself is that it is inbred, if not hermaphroditic, *The Wall Street Journal* asked Ms. Treisman for an example of a truly unknown fiction writer she had recently published. The name was on the tip of her tongue: Jim Gavin. His story, "Costello," had appeared in the December 6, 2010 issue. She pointed out that Gavin was a plumbing salesman with no agent. But his plumbing experience was vast: He was a Stanford Stegner fellow who transferred to the Boston University MFA program and became a lecturer there.

But the autobiographical "Costello" was indeed about his earlier incarnation as a Renaissance L.A. plumbing parts salesman. The week before the story ran, Treisman interviewed her discovery for the magazine's online *Book Bench.* Calling himself a toilet salesman "dilettante," Gavin said he'd been hired by his father, "a plumbing lifer," but had lasted in the business for only two years.

"Relying on nepotism seemed shameful at first," he went on. "... But one thing you find out pretty fast about the plumbing world is that everybody is related to everybody else. Because of this, and the fact that your livelihood depends, literally, on shit, a certain kind of humility and humor presides over the industry."

Luckily, publishing, even at the Castle, is like the plumbing business, too.

In 2002, Dana Goodyear published more poems in *The New Yorker* than anyone else. She was editor-in-chief David Remnick's twenty-five-year-old assistant.

The year prior, "Lucky Girls" appeared in its 2001 Debut Fiction edition. It was written by Goodyear's fellow assistant,

---

16 Lee Siegel, "Where Have All the Mailers Gone?" *New York Observer,* June 22, 2010.

twenty-six-year-old Nell Freudenberger. As already noted, she went on to receive a six-figure offer from HarperCollins for a short story collection she had not yet written.

Today, editors have made breaking into *The New Yorker* easier. The writer can submit a cartoon caption. The contest, which preempts cronyism by excluding employees, draws thousands of entries per week. If yours is the winning caption, you may not find your fiction in the magazine's annual anthology, but you will have at last entered the Castle with a signed copy of the cartoon.

So, at least where humor is concerned, *The New Yorker* has become far more open armed. While attending college in the '40s, Flannery O'Connor submitted many cartoons. All were rejected.[17] Or, by his own admission, thrown in the garbage by Truman Capote, the overworked joke archivist at the time.

---

17 Christina Gombar, *Great Women Writers, 1900–1950* (Facts on File, 1996)

PART XII

VANITY OF VANITIES?
The POD and E-Revolution

CHAPTER 48

DEMAND FOR "PRINT ON DEMAND"

If none of the Schmoozes, Shortcuts, or Pen plans pan out, the writer may have no other option than to join the ranks of his other diehard predecessors—Dumas, Poe, Proust, Carroll, Nin, Woolf, Twain, Crane, Stein, Joyce, et al.—and self-publish.

Scores of commercial titles were vanity printed as well. John Grisham self-published his first novel, *A Time to Kill*, in 1988. After selling out his first run from his mobile Barnes & Noble—the trunk of his car—the attorney turned author scored a 5,000-copy print from Wynwood Press which led to juggernaut sales from Doubleday/Dell. Self-actualized guru Wayne Dyer used the same car delivery MO with his *Your Erroneous Zones*, which later sold 35 million copies, as did Peter McWilliams' *TM Book*.

Following the Grisham-Dyer-McWilliams example, James Redfield unloaded 100,000 copies of *The Celestine Prophecy* from his Honda trunk before signing the thriller over in 1993 to Warner Books which, to date, has sold 20 million units internationally.

Richard Paul Evans' 1994 *The Christmas Box* is the biggest self-Publishing Clearing House winner of all time. Perhaps the original inspiration for the advertising executive's venture was Charles Dickens himself, who printed the best-selling *A Christmas Carol* on his own dime because his preceding title, *Martin Chuzzlewit*, had tanked (though he considered it his best novel). Evans published *The Christmas Box* for his kids. It flew off the shelves in Utah bookstores, sparking a conglomerate bidding war won by Simon & Schuster, which cut him a check for $4.125 million. The holiday title went on to sell 7 million copies. And Evans went on to retire from the ad business and write twenty more popular novels for Simon & Schuster. The latest, *Michael Vey: The Prisoner of Cell 25*, concerns a teenager with Tourette syndrome (like Evans himself) who uses his Taser-like magic hands against school bullies.

In 2008, for the first time in history, more books were self-published than traditionally published. By the following year, 76 percent were self-published. By 2010, of the 3,082,740 titles produced, 316,480 were from established publishers and 2,766,260 were digital or print-on-demand (POD), representing a 169 percent increase from the previous year. Nevertheless, literature titles (47,392) in all forms were down 29 percent.[1] *Poets & Writers* reported that of the 150 titles on the 2011 *USA Today* bestseller list, fifteen were self-published.

In her *New York Times* article, "Self-Publishers Flourish as Writers Pay the Tab," industry expert Motoko Rich predicted that people who write books may soon outnumber those who read them.[2] Unlike conventional publishers, she wrote, POD operations prosper by "capitalizing on the dream of would-be authors to see their work between covers."

In 2007, Author Solutions, Inc., the monopoly Super PAC of self-publishing, took over the three largest print-on-demand companies: iUniverse, AuthorHouse, and Xlibris.[3] ASI CEO Kevin Weiss told Rich,

---

1 "Book Production by the Numbers," *Publishers Weekly* May 23, 2011, Vol. 258, Issue 21.

2 According to its 2011 website report, e-publisher WordPress *10 Day Book Club* states: "A poll of 2,700 U.S. Internet users, representing about 100 million U.S. Internet users, indicates that about 8 million unpublished novels and 17 million unpublished how-to books have been written by the Internet-using population alone."

3 Until 2012, ASI itself was owned by Bertram Capital Management. According to *Bloomberg Businessweek*, Bertram "specializes in management buyouts, shareholder liquidity events, acquisition financings, add-on acquisitions, and growth or expansion financings."

"Even if you're sitting at a dinner party, if you ask how many people want to write a book, everyone will say, 'I've got a book or two in me.'"

"We have helped more than 100,000 authors publish more than 170,000 titles and reach their publishing goals," ASI claims on its website. "We currently have more than 70,000 titles available for all e-book readers, and by mid-2012, we will have 150,000 e-books in distribution. ... We have also helped them [authors] get their work into the hands of Hollywood entertainment executives."

Interjecting reality, Weiss told Rich that each of his company's titles average sales of 150 copies. In 2008, ASI published 13,000 titles, a 12 percent increase from the previous year, dwarfing the output of Random House, the world's largest conventional publisher. In 2008, Susan Driscoll, the vice-president of ASI subsidiary iUniverse, confirmed that the majority of its authors sold fewer than two hundred books. Even ASI's small competitors thrive. The CEO of *Blurb*, Eileen Gittins, told the *Times* that in its founding year (2006) revenues were $1 million and two years later were $30 million.

Before the ASI takeover, the iUniverse CEO revealed that 40 percent of its titles were sold to the authors themselves. Robert Young, Lulu Enterprises CEO, confirmed that most of its own POD books interest only the author, family, and friends. With regard to quality control, he confided to the *Times*, "We have easily published the largest collection of bad poetry in the history of mankind."

Seeing that almost as much money can be made from writers as readers, the Super PAC publishers have jumped the POD bandwagon with enthusiasm. In 2012, Penguin (Pearson PLC) took over POD juggernaut Author Solutions, then Random House (Bertelsmann) took over Penguin. Less than a year after the buyout, however, authors filed a $5 million punitive action suit against ASI for "failing to maintain even the most rudimentary standards of book publishing, profiting not for its authors but from them."

Before the ASI buyout, Penguin partnered with Amazon to launch the ABNA—the Amazon Breakthrough Novel Award, the richest lit lotto of its kind. About ten thousand enter the Las Vegas-based competition. The Grand Prize winner in each of the five categories—general fiction, young adult fiction, mystery/thriller, science fiction/fantasy/

horror, and romance—receives a $50,000 (originally $25,000) contract from Penguin. Amazon offers the 9,998 losers a generous 20 percent discount on some of its CreateSpace and BookSurge self-publishing services. One of the contest's original judges, National Book Critics Circle member Darryl Lorenzo Wellington, wrote that the ABNA was "intended for writers at the bottom of the literary food chain and cynically directed" at those "most susceptible to the culture of hype." He told *Publisher's Weekly* that, though he was "all for a more egalitarian process ... this is a sham way of making this contest look like that, while you just reap people's money."[4]

Another judge, Penguin's editor-in-chief, Eamon Dolan, asserted that the selection process was fundamentally no different than the traditional publication vetting because it works "really well." In defending the process, he invoked the ever-popular Bull of Pamplona: "I do think the cream rises to the top in this business."

To date, Penguin has signed eight winners. Bill Loehfelm was the first. According to Nielsen BookScan, his 2008 winning novel, *Fresh Kills*, sold 5,000 copies.

Had he self-published the title instead, Loehfelm would have needed to sell considerably more to attract the interest of the traditional publishers who keep a close eye on the POD dairy. According to literary agent and POD expert Janet Reid, self-published authors need to sell more than 20,000 copies to interest an established house.[5]

---

4 "And The Winner Is... (Amazon Breakthrough Novel Award)," *Publisher's Weekly,* February 22, 2010, Issue 8.

5 Jason Boog, "What Self-Publishing Can Not Accomplish," *GalleyCat,* October 25, 2012. www.media bistro.com/galleycat/what-self-publishing-can-not-accomplish_b59622

CHAPTER 49

THE E-GOLD RUSH

"One hundred grand. That's how much I've made on Amazon in the last three weeks ... from my self-pubbed books. The one's the Big 6 rejected. I am sooo glad I had so many books rejected. ... This [Kindle] has become the best way in the history of mankind for a writer to earn money."

—Joe Konrath, techno-thriller author[1]

Digital publication now dwarfs POD in popularity. An e-book is less expensive to produce, and it can reach many more markets overnight. True, some still cling to the physical book, but these romantics will soon go the way of the dinosaur.

According to *BookStats*, 2011 electronic book sales reached nearly $2 billion. The previous year, e-books grew by 400 percent in Europe. PricewaterhouseCoopers projects sales in excess of $10 billion by 2016.[2] Currently the 200,000 ePlatinum Club has thirty-seven members— authors who have sold between two million and 200,000 self-published

---

1 *A Newbie's Guide to Publishing.* http://jakonrath.blogspot.com/2012/01/100000.html

2 Jim Lichtenberg, "Building The New Business Model," *Publisher's Weekly,* October 29, 2012.

titles—and the list is rapidly growing.[3]

From the writer's point of view, digital publication may be preferable to traditional in five important ways.

- **Speed to market:** Your title is on the World Wide Web within hours—not after a year or two.

- **Larger share of the profits:** You can earn up to 90 percent—not the traditional 7 to 12 percent.

- **More potential sales:** Because you're earning more, you can charge as little as 99¢ per copy. (However, pricing can affect percentage. Amazon can take a 30 percent cut on books priced between $2.99–$9.99, and 65 percent for books below or above that amount.)

- **No editor interference:** You write exactly what you want, how you want, and you can even include your own artwork inside or on the cover.

- **Longevity:** Your digital title will never be remaindered or pulped.

On the other hand, the comparative merits of traditional publication cannot be underestimated.

- **You get editorial input, proofing, and fact-checking.**

- **Your book is widely distributed to brick-and-mortar stores** and will remain on the shelves for at least six weeks (unless the retailer goes bankrupt before then).

- **Your book may get reviewed in a major publication** if: a) it's hardback, and b) you're a Super PAC Franchise, Bread & Butter, or Prestige.

- If b), **you may get marketing and PR help.**

- **You benefit from traditional respectability,** i.e., readers will not assume your book has already been rejected by everybody.

This is, in fact, what happened to Mark Coker, author of *The Secrets to*

---

3 For names and scores, see: http://selfpublishingsuccessstories.blogspot.com

Ebook Publishing Success. His novel, *Boob Tube*, about TV soap operas, was roundly rejected. So, in 2008, he founded Smashwords and published 140 e-titles. Four years later, he released 200,000. The "superhero of electronic books," as he is now called, has become one of the largest international e-book producers. Smashword authors control their own rights, are distributed free to multiple platforms (Kindle, Kobo, Nook, Sony, Apple) and collect up to 85 percent of sales receipts. By contrast, "Vanity publishing services will gladly empty your pocket of thousands of dollars for services of nebulous value," Coker argues.[4]

New literature titles, both traditional and non, were 29 percent down in 2011 and continue to slide.[5] Even so, according to former HarperCollins head Jane Friedman, e-publication could help save serious fiction. After pledging, "I'm not done by a long shot," at her traditional postmortem party in 2008, the editor founded Open Road Integrated Media the next year. Electronic publication will become "the center of the universe," she told *The New York Times.*[6] In partnership with Grove Atlantic, Friedman's Open Road digitally resurrects classic novelists[7] as well as today's masters.[8]

Publishing maven Tina Brown founded her own e-imprint, Beast Books, in 2009. The operation, in partnership with Perseus Books, speedily releases 40,000-word-and-under political and cultural pieces by the pundits of *Newsweek* (which, due to the high cost but declining revenue of print, went all digital in 2013). The former editor of *Vanity Fair* and *The New Yorker* told *The New York Times* that in today's fast-paced world too many print titles are fatally dated by the time they

---

4 David Henry Sterry, "Mark Coker, Founder of Smashwords, on How to Get People to Read Your Book," *Huffington Post,* February 24, 2012. www.huffingtonpost.com/david-henry-sterry/mark-coker_b_2594203.html

5 "Book Production By the Numbers," *Publishers Weekly,* May 23, 2011, Vol. 258, Issue 21.

6 Motoko Rich, "New E-Book Company to Focus on Older Titles," *New York Times,* October 13, 2009.

7 Pearl Buck, Erskine Caldwell, Howard Fast, Lawrence Durrell, James Jones, Malcolm Lowry, Edna O'Brien, Bud Schulberg, Terry Southern, William Styron, Rebecca West, Jean Paul Sartre, Joseph Heller, Ellery Queen, etc.

8 Michael Chabon, Nicola Barker, Pat Conroy, James Salter, Alice Walker, Susan Minot, Joyce Maynard, etc.

reach the shelves.[9] "One of the big criticisms that one hears about print books is that by the time they get out it's too late and who cares," agrees publishing consultant Constance Sayre of Market Partners International. "The only thing I worry about is that everybody's writing and nobody's reading."

Stephen King was an e-revolution pioneer. In 2000, he released the world's first mass-market e-book, *Riding the Bullet,* about a hitchhiker picked up by a dead, decapitated guy whose head has been sewn back on. The author said he decided to offer the novella as an e-book "to see ... whether or not this is the future." Four hundred thousand copies were downloaded the first day, jamming Simon & Schuster's Softlock server. Seeing that this was indeed the future, many other best-selling authors followed in King's footsteps. With Amazon's introduction of Kindle in 2007, nearly everybody was onboard.

Twitter had been introduced the year before. As soon as the 140-character social networking microblog proved itself more revolutionary than ridiculous, the Twitter story was born. Pulitzer Prize winner and *New Yorker* "Writer for the 21st Century" Rick Moody was among the first to give it a try in 2009. A haiku fan, the novelist was attracted to what he called "the merciless brevity" of the T-Story, no less than to the "Wild West environment" of electronic publication. Most importantly, "I hope that it will lead people back to books."[10] *Electric Literature* ran his 153-Tweet online dating flash fiction, "Some Contemporary Characters," in hourly increments for three days. *EL* founder Andy Hunter, a Brooklyn College MFA, gained ten thousand site followers from the piece, proving Twitter an exciting new literary tool. "That," he said, "is what literature is all about." *The L Magazine* went further, declaring that *Electric Literature* itself was "the best sign that perhaps the end of the publishing industry as we know it won't be the utter disaster we're all dreading."

---

9 Motoko Rich, "Daily Beast Seeks to Publish Faster," *New York Times,* September 28, 2009. www.nytimes.com/2009/09/29/books/29beas.html?_r=2&scp=1&sq=The%20Daily%20Beast&st=cse&

10 Alexandra Alter, "Are Tweets Literature? Rick Moody Thinks They Can Be," *Wall Street Journal,* November 30, 2009. http://blogs.wsj.com/speakeasy/2009/11/30/are-tweets-literature-rick-moody-thinks-they-can-be/

Soon two more Pulitzers gave Twitfic a shot. Salman Rushdie retweeted his Tumblr tale, "A Globe of Heaven." *The New Yorker* magazine posted Jennifer Egan's "Black Box" on its Twitter account for nine days in the spring of 2012. That fall, AllTwitter kicked off its Flash Fiction Contest; the UK, its five-day Twitter Fiction Festival; and seventy-one Joyce fans tweeted *Ulysses* in twenty-four hours. Meanwhile, *The Guardian* ran Twitfics from twenty-one heavyweights including Jeffrey Archer, Geoff Dyer, and Ian Rankin.

"Blaise Pascal didn't tweet and neither did Mark Twain," began the story by the UK MIllennium Poet and Iowa Workshop prof Simon Armitage. "When it came to writing something short and sweet, neither Blaise nor Mark had the time."

Hemingway, however, allegedly did have the time. Legend has it that Hemingway won a bar bet by composing the first Twitfic on an Algonquin bar napkin: "Classified: Baby Goods. For sale, baby shoes, never worn."

The king of brevity already knew what the *Memory & Cognition Journal* discovered in 2013: To the average reader, not just those with ADD, a bite-size literary chunk such as a Tweet is more memorable and "mind-ready" than *Remembrance of Things Past.*

CHAPTER 50

DIGITAL CINDERELLAS
FanFic, Erotic Lit,
and Fairy-Tale Success

"I thank the gods that I came of age before barbaric electrons ate
the printing press."
> —**Tom Robbins, author of**
> ***Even Cowgirls Get the Blues***

FanFiction, the new literary karaoke, has become the most popular
vehicle for e-books. The top three mother titles on Fanfiction.net, the
Internet's largest FanFiction site, are the Harry Potter series (630,000
offspring), the Twilight series (200,000), and *The Lord of the Rings*
(48,000). Eighteen hundred other titles are listed. Many literary masterpieces have gone childless, spawning no fans. So the aspiring FF
scribe might best go for virgin territory such as *Anna Karenina* or
Madame Bovary rather than for another Harry or Twilight retread.

Not all original authors have been enthusiastic about having their
characters commandeered. In 2001, Margaret Mitchell's estate tried
to block the publication of Alice Randall's *The Wind Done Gone*, written from the slave's perspective. In 2009, J.D. Salinger's estate sued
a Swede for turning Holden Caulfield into a geriatric. Though Kurt
Vonnegut gave Phillip Jose Farmer permission to write *Venus on the*

Half-Shell as Kilgore Trout, he came to regret it when the FanFiction became a hit: "The whole adventure muddied my reputation and depressed me," he complained. However, the American icon, a good sport, added, "I congratulate him [Farmer] on writing a bestseller in only six weeks. It takes me years and years."

Proving that there is no stopping the e-FF Oklahoma Land Run even posthumously, the Fanfiction.net archive currently posts 764 *Gone with the Wind*s, 166 *Catcher in the Rye*s, and three *Slaughterhouse-Five*s.

Romances dominate FanFiction. And women dominate romance. The alpha e-dominatrix is British TV executive and mother of two E.L. James, aka Snowqueen's Icedragon. Ms. James' *Twilight* spin-off, *Fifty Shades of Grey*, became history's fastest-selling paperback, selling 65 million copies worldwide in three steps: She posted it on FanFiction websites, then on her own website; The Writer's Coffee Shop, a small Australian e-publisher, released the title; finally, after it went viral on the Internet, Vintage released the paperback in April 2012. The digital presentation of the novel was critical to its success: Women who might have been too embarrassed to carry a copy in public consumed the virtual S&M love story in cyberspace. Might the Marquis de Sade's *120 Days of Sodom* (written 1785, published 1905), broken all publishing sales records had it first been released electronically? Or Anne Rice's sex slave trilogy, *Sleeping Beauty*, published under the penname A.N. Roquelaure in the early '80s and recently rereleased in all formats by Plume?

Like James Patterson, E.L. James concedes that her forte is not in writing but in storytelling. Of the more than seventeen thousand *Shades* reviews on Amazon, there is little gray area: seventy-four hundred are five-stars, five thousand are one-star. The first group loves the story and characters (the virginal Anastasia Steele and the brooding twenty-seven-year-old billionaire Adonis, Christian Grey); the second group hates the story, the characters, and especially the writing:

> "He's my very own Christian Grey-flavored popsicle," Anna rhapsodizes. "I suck harder and harder ... Hmm ... My inner goddess is doing the merengue with some salsa moves."

> "He kneels up and pulls a condom onto his considerable length. Oh no ... Will it? How?"

Might such prose have driven de Sade to weep for mercy, put a stake through the heart of Strunk, and driven Plath to the oven earlier?

In learning her craft, the teenage Joan Didion copied Hemingway word for word. Others have done the same with their own favorite authors. James, like many of her FanFiction colleagues, read and assimilated thousands of romances. No doubt, many a genre novelist will now be studying James as a paradigm much as Didion did Hemingway. What new usage and recurring descriptors can readers look forward to in future BDSM FanFictions based on history's fastest-selling book?

Ana is racked with serial "body-shattering," "turbulent," "agonizing" orgasms. She and her "master of the universe" "gasp" forty-six times and share eighteen "breath hitches."

Yet the twenty-two-year-old "blushes" or "flushes" 125 times (including thirteen "scarlets" and six "crimsons"). In pre- or post-cuffing, whipping, and ravaging, the lovers "murmur" 199 times, "whisper" 195, but keep their "mutters" down to a less-is-more forty-nine. When the billionaire hits the ingenue's "inner goddess" G-spot fifty-eight times, she cries, "Oh my," seventy-two times, "Jeez," eighty-one, and "Oh, crap!" ninety-two.

On the merits of the erotic tour de force, Random House's profits increased 64 percent, and CEO Markus Dohle handed out $5,000 Christmas bonuses to all his employees, editors, and warehouse workers alike. Universal bought the film rights for $5 million, Bret Easton Ellis lobbied to write the screenplay (but lost), and Angelina Jolie has reportedly expressed interest in directing the movie. *Publisher's Weekly* named James, who was making $1 million a week in Kindle sales alone, Publishing Person of the Year for "shaping and transforming the publishing industry." And the *New York Daily News*, not known for its bookishness, broke news of the PW honor with the headline "CIVILIZATION ENDS."

"E.L. James has opened up these genres to a whole new subset of readers who might not have previously been familiar with them," declared

Paul Bogaards, vice president of Knopf, parent of Vintage, her publisher.[1]
Since James' "Mommy Porn" mother lode, he and his colleagues have
been on the lookout for clones to satisfy this formerly underserved subset
of 65 million. Erotica pioneer Anne Rice calls them "one-handed reads."
    The first and most popular was Bared to You by Sylvia Day, presi-
dent of Romance Writers of America and co-founder of Passionate Ink.
The self-published e-title sold 100,000 copies in the spring of 2012,
was quickly snapped up by Penguin/Berkley Books (now merged
with James' publisher Random House/Vintage) and, with its sequel,
Reflected in You, moved 5 million copies. The heroine, twenty-four-
year-old ingénue Eva, and hero, Gideon, a young lone wolf billionaire—
both childhood abuse survivors—heal their wounds by engaging in
therapeutic enslavement, flogging, and explosive sex. The Bared cover
features cufflinks on a gray background with the tag "He possessed
me and obsessed me." Day, who lost her maidenhead with her 2006
Boys Ahoy! defends the originality of her latest, insisting that, unlike
Shades, it's not "a Cinderella story." But she does concede that James'
success contributed to her own and, in her Acknowledgments, writes,
"To E.L. James, who wrote a story that captivated readers and created a
hunger for more." The hunger has fed renewed interest in her earlier
e-romances, from the Carnal Thirst Trilogy to Black Lace Quickies.
    Shades' long petticoat tails have also resurrected the mother of S&M
erotica, Pauline Réage's The Story of O. James' and Day's alma mater,
Random House, rereleased the controversial 1954 title as an e-book
in the spring of 2012. The paperback, released in March 2013, comes
with an introduction by Ms. Day herself. The master of O's universe is
not a Twixter tycoon but the implacable Sir Stephen who pierces her
labia with his monogrammed rings like luggage. The Story of O gar-
nered little attention even from the French until the novel won the 1955
Prix des Deux Magots and went on to become a cult classic. Réage
waited forty years before outing herself as Anne Desclos, the homely
but highly regarded French journalist and translator of Virginia Woolf,
Evelyn Waugh, and F. Scott Fitzgerald. In deference to these masters,

---

1   Lizzie Crocker, "Publishing Looks for S&M," Daily Beast, July16, 2012. http://www.thedailybeast.com/
newsweek/2012/07/15/publishing-looks-for-s-m.html

and lest Sir Stephen give her a tracheotomy, Réage's O refrains from "Jeez's," "Oh my's," or "Oh, crap's!" while being possessed, disciplined, and humiliated.

Spiking profits further, Random House has added four more e-heavyweights to their romance roster. The publisher has fronted Texas mom and poker player Maya Banks seven figures for her Breathless Trilogy. Another *Shades* fan, Sophie Morgan, British journalist and self-described submissive feminist, recently released *The Diary of a Submissive: A Modern True Tale of Sexual Awakening*, which her publisher calls "a memoir by a real-life Anastasia." Fans left wanting have flocked to prepay for Tara Sue Me's The Submissive Trilogy, cover-tagged "The Worldwide Phenomenon." Sylvian Reynard, the last golden goose in Penguin's front list sorority, collected a million-dollar advance for *Gabriel's Inferno* and *Gabriel's Rapture*, "a sinful exploration of sex, love, and redemption," both novels released in a 500,000-copy first run.

The four other Super PAC publishers are trying their best to compete with Bertelsmann's Magnificent 7 BDSM stable[2] but are falling far short. Romance heavy Atria (Simon & Schuster/CBS) gives their frontrunner, Zane, her own imprint, Strebor Books, on the merit of her previous blockbusters *Addicted, Afterburn*, and *Dear G-Spot. Addicted*, about an African-American mother-of-three nymphomaniac, is scheduled to be released as a major motion picture. *Zane's Sex Chronicles* is a Cinemax TV series. Atria hopes their star will overtake James with her upcoming *Z-Rated*, billed as "No shades of grey, just red hot."

Meanwhile, St. Martin's (MacMillan/Holtzbrinck) is putting its money on Sara Fawkes' *Anything He Wants* (Dominated by the Billionaire series). Originally e-published during the spring 2012 romance explosion, Fawkes "ignited readers' imaginations with her unique combination of adrenaline-soaked action and torrid eroticism set in a world of glittering luxury," St. Martin's advertised before their mass-market five-volume paperback release. When BookBinge asked the author to account for the popularity of romance serials, she said it came down to the simple and age-old phenomenon: "Readers connecting with the

---

2 E.L. James, Sylvia Day, Ann Rice, Maya Banks, Sophie Morgan, Tara Sue Me, Sylvian Reynard.

characters" and an insatiable appetite for further developments. "I love
to read and love alpha males and sassy heroines," she concluded, "so
when I find a story like that I'm a happy duck!"[3]

>>>

In her introduction to *Fifty Writers on Fifty Shades* (2012), Lori Perkins
writes, "Until I became an editor of erotic literature, I quickly learned
that the fantasy of complete surrender to an alpha male is the leading daydream of the majority of American women." Ms. Perkins co-
founded Ravenous and Riverdale Avenue e-books. A veteran agent
besides, she is the author of *The Insider's Guide to Getting an Agent.*
Though she considers James' *Fifty Shades* "smut for women," she
expresses admiration for it, as do most of the other fifty contributors to
her collection, including Sylvia Day.

Another best-selling contributor, M.J. Rose, compares James favor-
ably to her literary predecessors, Anaïs Nin, Pauline Réage, and Erica
Jong (though Jong called *Fifty Shades* "dull and poorly written"). A
romance pioneer, Ms. Rose preceded the e-BDSM juggernaut by nearly
two decades. In 1996, the young creative director for a major advertising firm completed her debut novel, *Lip Service.* All editors to whom her
agent sent the manuscript offered what she called "rave rejections" of
the story about a Manhattan psychiatrist's wife whose writing research
leads to a phone sex operator job. "Editors were intrigued, but marketing departments were terrified," she told *Forbes* magazine.[4] Her
agent warned her not to try self-publishing the title because she would
never "live down the stigma." Risking it anyway, Rose e-published the
novel under her own imprint, Lady Chatterley's Library, in 2000. The
marketing expert sent out *Lip Service* teasers to two thousand e-mail
addresses purchased from Postmasterdirect.com. She sold 500 ms.
photocopies at $20 apiece, 150 downloads at $10 and, due to password
piracy, was ripped off for 1,000. Encouraged, she printed 3,000 paperbacks. But when she took them to book stores, "I basically got laughed
at," she said.

---

3 http://www.thebookbinge.com/2013/01/author-interview-lauren-jameson.html

4 Michael Maiello, "Loose Lips," *Forbes* magazine, November 29, 1999.

Though Luck wasn't with Rose, her Pluck paid off. She signed on to Amazon's Author Advantage Program and relentlessly queried online editors for reviews until Doubleday Literary Guild advanced her $2,000 for her novel. *Newsweek, Entertainment Weekly,* and *New York Magazine* picked up the story that in turn led to a deal from Pocket. Rose has gone on to publish eleven novels as well as two nonfiction titles on marketing, *Buzz Your Book* and *Buzz Your Online Auction,* based on her publishing blog, Buzz, Balls, & Hype.

In 2005, Rose founded Authorbuzz, which she calls "the first ad agency for authors." The outfit is tailor-made for writers who know little about e-marketing or for those who would prefer to spend more time writing and less time e-marketing.

One last e-publishing sensation is just such a writer: Amanda Hocking. In 2011, the twenty-seven-year-old landed a four-book, $2-million deal from St. Martin's after a bidding war. Blogging about her defection from digital to traditional, Hocking explained, "I want to be a writer. I do not want to spend 40 hours a week handling e-mails, formatting covers, finding editors, etc. Right now, being me is a full-time corporation."[5] Before hitting the slots, Hocking was an $18,000 assisted living nurse with seventeen rejected YA vampire and zombie romances in her closet. Hoping to raise $300 to attend a Chicago Muppets convention, she e-published and unloaded 150,000 copies of *My Blood Approves* and her other latest titles for $20,000, thereby activating the alarms at the Big Six. St. Martin's has enjoyed a substantial return on Hocking's work that *The New York Times* called "literature as candy, a mash-up of creativity and commerce."[6]

St. Martin's/Macmillan editors say that the Hocking deal disproves the notion that traditional publishing is being marginalized by nontraditional. Both can work hand in glove, insists editor Matthew Shear. "It's always been the same since the days when people self-published from the back of their car," he says, "The cream will rise to the top."[7]

In fact, a digital market testing ground is a wet dream for the Super

---

5 Julie Bosman, "Self-Publisher Signs Four-Book Deal with St. Martin's," *New York Times,* March 24, 2011.

6 Strawberry Saroyan, "Storyteller," *New York Times Magazine,* June 17, 2011.

7 Ed Pilkington, "Amanda Hocking, the writer who made Millions by self-publishing online," *The Guardian,* Jan. 12, 2012. www.guardian.co.uk/books/2012/jan/12/amanda-hocking-self-publishing

PACs. Breakout e-books help solve the original $64,000 question Frank Doubleday and the Harper Brothers asked themselves years ago: Why don't we just sell bestsellers? Today, publishing houses no longer have to consult their crystal balls. Eliminating risk, they capitalize on an e-sensation such as *Fifty Shades*. The trick is to snap up the title before it crests and to get readers to pay three to four times the original self-publishing price, which is sometimes as little as 99¢.

From the successful e-author's side of this, the symbiosis cannot be denied. When *BookPage* asked Sylvia Day about the greatest advantages of selling out to Penguin, the novelist identified three things: print run, distribution, and PR.

"There's no way I would've come anywhere near 500,000 print copies, nor would *Bared to You* have ever been found in Walmart, Target, Costco, BJs, Kroger, etc., as a self-published book," she said. "Penguin brought to the table a dedicated, enthusiastic team of individuals with a broad network of connections, which far outweigh what I was capable of doing at home alone."[8]

---

8 Eliza Borne, "The Latest Romance Sensation is Hot, Hot, Hot," *BookPage*. http://bookpage.com/interview/the-latest-romance-sensation-is-hot-hot-hot

CHAPTER 51

LUCK, SUCK,
& PLUCK 2.O

Like traditional authors, the e-romance sorority sisters and other non-traditionalists concede that no small amount of Luck was involved in their success. However, if they'd had it out of the gate, they wouldn't have had to self-publish.

As for Suck, Submission and Domination writers seem to know more about this than, say, horror specialists. On the other hand, no goddesses have put on a thong and dog collar for even Rupert Murdoch, Jeff Bezos, or any other billionaire masters of the publishing universe.

Which brings us to: Pluck. The silver bullet of success.

The first and most important part of Pluck, especially for a self-publisher, is to stand out from a million competitors[1] by hitting a homer; i.e., writing a good book. By Booker or Pulitzer standards it might be a bad book—but it has to be a *good* bad book. This is hard work, though the writer may make it seem easy—the mark of a pro in any field, from baseball to brain surgery.

---

[1] E-publishing blogger Steve Bichard reports that more than 1.1 million writers have uploaded over 1.4 million books onto Amazon, or around 5,000 a day with 1,000 new writers joining per day. http://steve bichard.com/2012/05/19/can-you-make-money-from-publishing-on-amazon/

The second half of Pluck is marketing the product of your hard work. 24/7. By yourself. Or with the help of a marketing operation such as Authorbuzz. As founder M.J. Rose says: "Nothing sells books like word of mouth." But how do you get the first three hundred or five hundred or two thousand?

Smashword founder Mark Coker provides some answers for free.

- Price your title as low as possible. If it's your first, consider offering it for free.

- Get the word out through all social networks (Facebook, MySpace, Twitter, LinkedIn, etc.)

- Cast a wide distribution net using discovery algorithms, viral catalysts, and Tag Clouds for search engine optimization.

- Create an eye-catching cover.

A five-star customer review on Amazon, Barnes & Noble, or Goodreads can also be helpful. In his digital title, *How I Sold 1 Million eBooks in 5 Months*, e-vangelist John Locke confirms the importance of such reviews while providing e-testimonials as impressive as a new miracle diet program. Later, the former door-to-door insurance salesman told *The New York Times* he paid for three hundred reviews because "it's a lot easier to buy them than cultivating an audience."[2] Locke purchased his kudos from GetBookReviews.com, founded in 2010 by Todd Jason Rutherford. The entrepreneur offered a cheaper-by-the-dozen rate scale: $99 for 1 review, $499 for twenty, $999 for fifty. Rutherford went on to commission 4,531 reviews while earning up to $28,000 per month. His hopes for a multimillion dollar enterprise were dashed by a yelping e-author, a Google ad suspension, and a partial review purge by Amazon.[3] Rutherford turned to RV sales in Oklahoma City and, in 2012, released

---

2 David Streitfeld, "The Best Reviews Money Can Buy," *The New York Times*, August 25, 2012. http://www.nytimes.com/2012/08/26/business/book-reviewers-for-hire-meet-a-demand-for-online-raves.html?pagewanted=all&_r=0

3 As a result of the Rutherford case and others, Amazon launched their Sock Puppet Detection Program, which eliminated all "suspect" reviews from the site, many of them bona fide, angering more than a few innocent authors. www.techdirt.com/articles/20121101/20074920913/amazon-freaks-out-about-sock-puppet-reviews-deletes-bunch-real-reviews.shtml

The Publishing Guru on Writing, a self-helper for e-authors. As for John Locke, thanks to his marketing savvy and Rutherford's raves, he became the first self-published author to join the fourteen-member Kindle Million Club.[4]

Other pay-per-review services are now available on the Net. Booktweetingservice offers them along with Tweets. Their website claims, "We tweet your book, blog or author website to 60,000+ readers, editors, publishers and writers ... for maximum exposure." Their entry-level, one-day Tweet program starts at $29. The self-publisher might also consider investing in Facebook ads, currently at 33¢ per click and up to $650 for over 50,000.

But a 2012 Reuters study reports that four out of five Facebook visitors have never bought a product or service advertised or commented upon and that 34 percent are spending less time on the site. Moreover, Pegemodo, Facebook's marketing company, reports that only 25 percent of parties polled enjoyed measurable sales increases.[5]

To help launch his debut "genre-busting" sci-fi novel, *Ready Player One* (2011), Ernest Cline embedded clues in the text, leading readers to a video game, the winner of which would get a 1981 Delorean, his book tour car.[6] The coupe came with a flux capacitor and oscillation overthruster that he said equipped it to "travel through time AND solid matter!" Earlier, Ernest self-published his chapbook, *The Importance of Being Ernest*, and wrote a sequel to *Buckaroo Banzai,* which he posted on the Net.

San Francisco surfer journalist Jaimal Yogis went green for his 2013 San Francisco book launch. He podcasted his evening swim through the Bay's hypothermic, shark-infested waters to his Book Passage signing of *The Fear Project: What Our Most Primal Emotion Taught Me About Survival, Success, Surfing ... and Love.*

Weeks later, Sam Pink tried sexting instead of swimming for

---

4 Members, in order of admission (2010–2011): Stieg Larsson, James Patterson, Nora Roberts, Charlaine Harris, Lee Child, Suzanne Collins, Michael Connelly, John Locke, Kathryn Stockett, Janet Evanovich, George R.R. Martin, Amanda Hocking, Stephenie Meyer.

5 Ewan Morrison, "Why Social Media Isn't The Magic Bullet For Self-Published Authors," *The Guardian,* July 30, 2012. www.guardian.co.uk/books/2012/jul/30/tweet-about-cats-just-write

6 www.mediabistro.com/galleycat/ernest-cline-to-give-away-a-delorean_b52630

Electric Literature's Valentine's Day release of his novel *Rontel*.[7] Customers who preordered the $4.99 e-book received, in lieu of a signed copy, a sext from the author and the number of his Electric Lit iPhone. *Rontel's* hero can't relate to others or himself.

Struggling novelist Mark Davis, formerly an ad man, upped the ante on outside-the-social-networking-box marketing schemes. A failed novelist, he wrote a book about a failed novelist. He called it *Rejection*. Adopting the name of *Rejection's* hero, Davis posted publishing industry rants in every writer chat room, driving traffic to his website, thelastrejection.com. Posted there were the first chapters of *Rejection* wherein his hero kidnaps the daughter of a celebrity agent and gives the rep ninety days to land a deal for his novel. The novelist then sent a podcast of a staged kidnapping to countless real agents with an e-mail which began, "By the time you receive this, I will have already kidnapped your child."[8]

Kidnapping, sexting, swimming, Lone Starring, and even Delorean drawings have not as yet helped anyone join the Kindle Platinum Club or score a multimillion-dollar Super PAC deal. But marketing schemes such as these show just how keen the competition for attention is in the e-world of a million authors.

---

7 www.mediabistro.com/galleycat/pre-order-a-novel-get-a-valentines-day-sext-from-the-author_b64953

8 Darrell Laurant, "Lynchburg Writer Fakes Kidnapping to Promote New Book," *News & Advance,* Lynchburg, VA, June 2011. www2.newsadvance.com/lifestyles/2011/jun/27/lynchburg-writer-fakes-kidnapping-promote-new-book-ar-1136854/

CHAPTER 52

E-ROMANCE

The Next Chapter

Genre will likely continue to dominate e-fiction, with romance leading fantasy, horror, and thriller. Romance writers tend to be frighteningly prolific, some producing a novel every trimester. Is the market—especially for erotica—reaching a saturation point? Penguin/Random House surely hopes not, but its editors know better than anyone how the pendulum swings and populace cycles play out.

The extraordinary thing about *Fifty Shades of Grey* is that a good percentage of its 65 million readers were not regular readers. The wave of E.L. James "Mommy Porn" made readers out of nonreaders—formerly a publisher's pipe dream. More astounding still, 30 percent were men—otherwise the largest nonreader demographic. *Fifty Shades* weaned many off ESPN, if only briefly, to find out what their wives or lovers were orgasming over. True, some women gave their lesser half a dog-eared copy for Valentine's or an anniversary. James received piles of fan mail from wives thanking her for "saving" their marriages. "I get so many people telling me, 'My God, this book has empowered me, and I can really explore my sexuality now,'" she told Marlo Thomas in a *Huffington Post* interview.

So, as the pendulum swings to another fiction or FanFiction

groundswell, publishers hope that a new James will pop out of cyber-space to draw men. If the new title is romance, the envelope must be pushed. Smashword recently released former women's magazine editor A.J. Hamilton's erotica Billionaire Series with *Breed Me ... While My Husband Watches Us*, and her Monster Breeding Series, *Forced to Breed with the Dungeon Beasts*.

A few years ago, most publishers would have laughed at a prediction that BDSM erotica would become an industry lifeline. Who would have dreamed that billionaire-on-bobby-sox bondage and sadomasochism would electrify self-identified feminists?

The successful e-novels of the future are likely to be romance/fantasy/YA/ horror hybrids, and many, even those released by tradional publishers, could be free. Random House is now developing movies from their popular titles. Like TV shows, they could be paid for by means of between-chapter pop-ups or podcasts for products the novel's characters themselves use. Romances could be sponsored by Cialis, AndroGel, or ChristianMingle. Horror by Prilosec or Lunestra. Literature could be underwritten by NoDoz, antidepressants, or Phillips Colon Health probiotics for gas and bloating. Each ad e-novel posted on a publisher site might be linked to the author's own website which, like a TV station itself, would broadcast 24/7 teasers and trailers for her other work.

The future of *e* may be IF—Interactive Fiction. IF turns the novel into a computer game. By following hyperlinks embedded in the text, the reader can manipulate the characters and plot. Penguin, Simon & Schuster, and Scholastic have recently introduced books with video so the reader can also play with images.

In 1997, John Updike announced his decision to partner with Amazon and "stick my head into the mouth of the electronic lion." But, lest things go south on him, Rabbit's creator, like Siegfried and Roy, charged for his services. According to his publisher Knopf's PR director, Paul Bogaards, Amazon paid him a five-figure sum to write the first and last paragraphs of its *Greatest Story Ever Told* IF murder mystery. Michael Chabon, Christopher Buckley, and thirty-seven other authors filled in the middle over the course of forty-four days. Expressing a common reaction to the experiment, Deborah Treisman (then fiction editor for *Grand Street*, now *The New Yorker*), said that, while the story showed promise in the first three paragraphs, it "descended into a kind of schizophrenic bedlam."[1] The criticism of course pertained to the collaborative nature of the project, not the digital format. Moreover, it wasn't hypertext or video driven. Still, Updike himself was underwhelmed. "Books haven't really been totally ousted yet," he told *Time* magazine with no small relief.[2]

The IF Mayflower had set sail two decades earlier with *The Adventures of You* gamebook for children. Author Edward Packard used the second person to make the reader the hero who could choose his role and plot developments from an option menu. After being rejected by nine publishers, the Vermont Crossroads Press released the title and quickly sold 8,000 copies. Pocket Books then took it on and sold far more. Finally, Bantam moved in, retitled it *Choose Your Own Adventure,* and unloaded more than 250 million copies between 1979 and 1998.

In 1996, Robert Arellano, a founder of the Literary Advisory Board of the Electronic Literature Organization, introduced to the Internet the first hypertext IF, *Sunshine '69.* Navigable maps, scene calendars, and a multiple point-of-view selector "suitcase" were among the novel's digital bells and whistles.

When Underland Press introduced the Web novel, or "Wovel," in 2008, one thousand readers immediately signed on. Author Kealan Patrick Burke wrote an episode of *The Living,* waited for readers to vote on how they wanted the plot to develop, then wrote another along these guidelines. The novel is ongoing and renews every Monday.

Meanwhile, HarperCollins had released Heather McElhatton's second-person "Do-Over" novel, *Pretty Little Mistakes,* in paperback. The reader can choose between 150 endings such as becoming a Denny's waitress, a feminist jeweler, or an African relief worker blown up by a pipe bomb. Before then, one is given countless other fateful options such as becoming a meth head, a monkey molester, or the mother of a motel manager's baby. The IF title is in its fifteenth printing. A Warren

---

1 Matthew Mirapaul, "*The Greatest Tale Ever Told,* A Column Becomes a Collaboration," *The New York Times,* August 28, 1997. http://theater.nytimes.com/library/cyber/mirapaul/082897mirapaul.html

2 Linton Weeks, "Cyberprose and Cons," *Washington Post,* October 12, 1998.

Wilson College MFA, Ms. McElhatton is a Pushcart Nominee for a story in the *Ontario Review. A Million Little Mistakes,* her 2010 sequel to *Pretty Little Mistakes,* gives the reader a $22 million lottery jackpot and many decisions about what to do with it—half of them leading to a happi-ly-ever-after, the other half to disaster.

A digital, Web-based Wovel such as *The Living* offers readers far greater interactive capability than paperbacks like *Pretty Little Mistakes.* Nearly limitless prefab character types, plots, and settings are available. Profiling apps such as O.P.R.A.H.—Online Passive Reader's Algorithmic Helpers—can also lead a reader to specific titles in any given genre most likely to appeal to his or her unique taste. Type in your Desert Island Top 10 books, and Amazon will soon be able to recommend your future favorite title with remarkable accuracy.

Pioneers in digital literature such as Jane Friedman have yet to introduce interactive versions of classics for literary FanFiction fans, but they are surely soon to come. How many of us have longed to see Laertes run Hamlet through in Act 1 before another intolerable solilo-quy? Or for Vronsky to break his back in the steeplechase instead of his mare, Frou Frou? Or for Holden Caulfield to beat up Maurice the pimp and run off with Sunny, the nuns, or Mr. Antolini?

»»

Philip M. Parker calls himself "the most published author in the history of the planet." Professor of International Strategy and Economics at the University of California (and, formerly, Harvard, MIT, and Stanford), Parker does not exaggerate. To date, he has authored over 200,000 titles, and his company, ICON Group International, nearly 800,000. Ninety-five percent are digital; the rest are POD. With his patented computer algorithm, the professor can complete a one-hundred-page book on a tech or business-related subject in twenty minutes.[3]

Having made his mark in digital nonfiction, Parker has set his sights on fiction, romance in particular. If IBM's Watson can beat *Jeopardy's* greatest contestants, Ken and Brad, with two terabytes tied behind its

---

3 Victor Wishna, "Why Computers Can't Write Novels.... Yet," *BookRiot,* February 4, 2013. http://bookriot.com/2013/02/04/why-computers-cant-write-novels-yet/#!/exjun_

back, why can't his own machine, with fifty shades of silicone, take on the E.L. James sorority? wonders Parker. "I have already set it [the romance algorithm] up," he told *The New York Times*. "There are only so many body parts."[4]

Romance fans cried foul over the remark. They insisted that a hot Harlequin Temptation or Kensington Aphrodesia is far more than sex, which the most published author in history would know had he read a single one. The professor has apparently realized this since his computer-generated robo romance has yet to be released by Penguin or even Smashword. Though he may already have his binary big bangs in Hal's ram, he has yet to put his digital ducks in a row on character quirks, nuanced dialogue, and plot MacGuffins. Elements such as these come naturally to carbon-based creatures, but to silicones they are still puzzles. So Parker won't be trying to tackle horror, fantasy, sci-fi, or any other more challenging genres anytime soon with his machine already equipped with NewNovelist, WritersBlock, and WhiteSmoke software. Still, in the end, Edison, Alexander Graham Bell, and the Wright Brothers prevailed after many setbacks and seemingly insurmountable obstacles.

Is anyone willing to bet that by 2050, even without Steve Jobs, we won't have a SuperMac that can mass-produce IF Pattersons, Jameses, and Danielle Steels tailor-made to each reader's taste? After all, on the Net nobody knows if you're human. And what modern man would care anyway?

---

4 Noam Cohen, "He Wrote 200,000 Books (But Computers Did Some of the Work)," *The New York Times*, April 14, 2010. www.nytimes.com/2008/04/14/business/media/14link.html?pagewanted=all&_r=0

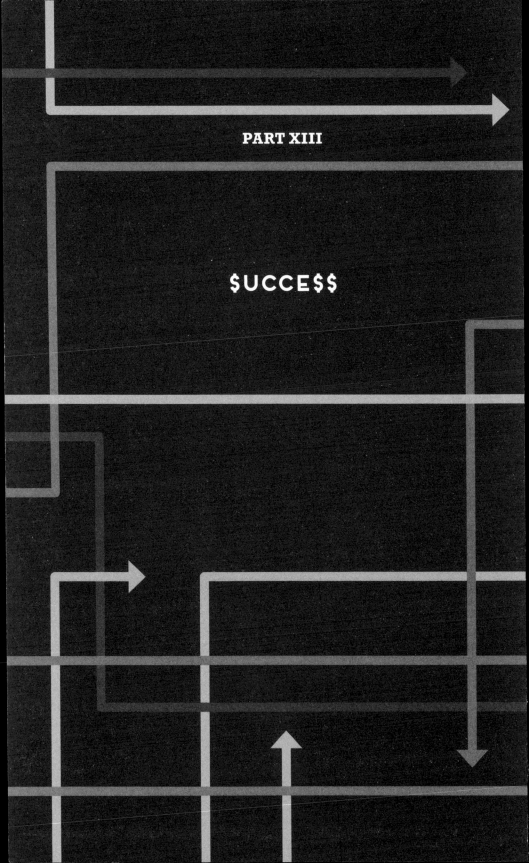

PART XIII

$UCCE$$

CHAPTER 53

DANTE'S HONEYMOON

> "I am no longer 'beat,' I have money, a career. I am
> more alone than when I lurked on Times Square at 4 a.m.
> or hitchhiked penniless."
> —**Jack Kerouac**

The saying about being careful what you wish for might have been coined by Fitzgerald, Salinger, Vonnegut, Lowry, Wallace and many of their colleagues. As we have seen, many scribes are not cheery people, and, in the end, publication has made some less so.

When Henry Miller finally broke into print after twenty years, he complained to *The Paris Review*, "It's unreal to me, the whole thing. ... In fact, I rather dislike it. ... All I see is more disruption in my life, more intrusions, more nonsense."

To escape the nonsense, Steinbeck distanced himself from his famous work: "The rows of my books on the shelf are to me like very well embalmed corpses," he told *The Paris Review*. "They are neither alive nor mine. ... I have forgotten them."

So, before becoming famous, the writer should remind himself of the disruption and disillusionment he is being spared in the meantime.

Publication can be a short honeymoon followed by a long purgatory. As Baudelaire observed long ago, "On the day the young writer
corrects his first proof sheet he is as proud as a schoolboy who has just
gotten his first dose of the pox."

After the full manuscript is delivered, editors go to work on the
language, fact-checkers on the facts, and the lawyers on anything that
might be libelous or lifted. After a Palestinian negotiation that can blow
up over a semicolon, a tort, or even the title itself, the ms. goes to print.
The author now may become a galley slave for a ship that he soon may
not recognize as his own anymore.

Knowing that a book is judged by its cover, publishers often forbid
the author to have any say about its design since of course he has no
aesthetic or commercial sense. Should he hate the cover, he must grin
and bear it for fear of souring the honeymoon before it's started.

Some can console themselves with the fact that they're getting
a hardcover, another decision the professionals reserve for themselves. But usually the print run will be paper, and few paperbacks get
reviewed. The publisher insists that even without the reviews more
$15.95 copies will sell than $32.95s. Still, the author—arithmetic and
common-sense challenged, too—cannot shake his hardcover envy.
Wishing to be a team player, though, he soldiers on.

A year or two after the contract is signed, with luck, the book
reaches the shelves. "This is the time when most writers go into some
kind of free fall," reports Betsy Lerner.[1]

When his first novel, *This Side of Paradise*, was released by Scribner
in 1920, F. Scott Fitzgerald wept uncontrollably in a New York taxi.[2] Not
only had the twenty-four-year-old realized his dream of early publication, his dream girl, Zelda, the flamboyant southern belle, had agreed
to marry him because of it. He spent the rest of his life drunkenly
chasing that first high—jumping into fountains, driving his editor, Max
Perkins, into a pond, and spitting one-hundred franc notes from his

---

1 Betsy Lerner, *The Forest for the Trees: An Editor's Advice to Writers* (Riverhead, 2001).

2 Allen Churchill, *The Literary Decade: A Panorama of the Writers, Publishers, and Litterateurs of the
1920's* (New York: Prentice Hall, 1971).

mouth along the Montparnasse—only to break down again because he could never catch it.

When Harry Scherman chose Margaret Mitchell's novel, *Gone with the Wind*, to become a Book of the Month Club selection, she wrote him, "When I heard that you all had selected it, it was too much to be borne and I went to bed and was ill, with an ice pack and large quantities of aspirin."[3]

John Cheever dealt with his own postpartum more proactively. "To diminish shock," he told *The Paris Review*, "I throw high dice, get sauced, go to Egypt, scythe a field, screw, dive into a cold pool."

Elation and dread often electrify the publishing honeymoon. For many, the fun is just getting started.

By the time a novel reaches stores, it's ancient history to the writer, who is usually well into another project by then. But he must look enthusiastic as he abandons this and goes on a book tour for his Warhol fifteen minutes to fifteen weeks. This is a POW march from Barnes & Noble, to PBS radio affiliates, to predawn TV talk shows watched by local insomniacs and speed freaks.

At the signings, the scrivener is provided with a desk, a stack of his screed, a Bic, and an Evian. He looks like a mannequin in a writer's petting zoo. The only thing worse than drawing a crowd is drawing nobody at all. Then the author, avoiding the pitiful glances of the clerks, resists the impulse to perform seppuku with his pen. At last, compassion gets the best of a customer and, for 30 percent off $15.95, she expects the author to jot *Ode to a Grecian Urn* on the title page, dedicated to her daughter who is at work on a novel herself and would appreciate agent recommendations.

During the tour, the star is regularly asked how many copies he's sold. This is a source of insatiable curiosity to bookstore clerks, radio interviewers, not to mention family and "friends." The writer may or may not have some idea about his early numbers, depending on

---

3 Al Silverman, *The Time of Their Lives, The Golden Age of Great American Publishers, Their Editors, and Authors* (New York: St. Martins, 2008).

whether he can still get his agent on the phone or whether his publisher is covering his per diem for Greyhound, Motel 6, and Denny's.

Returning home, the weary Bartleby resumes his follow-up book. Though healthy before his departure, he may now find the ms. nearly flatlined. CPR may or may not help. Either way, he starts medicating himself, if he hasn't already. Meantime, family and friends have given up asking how many copies of the book have sold; they now need to know if the agent will be bothering with a 1099.

At last the title is probably remaindered. The author may have an opportunity to see his creation at one of the traveling liquidators who rent mall space around the holidays. Then it goes to the incinerators. Finally, if he has managed to deliver a sequel, his publisher may exercise its contractual right of First Refusal.

Like Miller and others, it took Céline many years to break into print. When he finally did and *Death on the Installment Plan* became an underground hit, this is all the former physician had to say: "What I'm interested in is being completely ignored."[4]

---

4 Jacques Darribehaude and Jean Geunot, *The Paris Review* interview with Louis-Ferdinand Céline. The Art of Fiction No. 33, 1956.

CHAPTER 54

THE SEVENTH CIRCLE OF SALES

"What of writers today? ... We have to tramp like trained dogs through the wasteland of Midwestern malls on our book tours, begging the consumer—our fellow citizens!—to admire us, to buy us. But we are like Kafka's Hunger Artist, performing astonishing feats for a nonexistent audience."

—**T.C. Boyle,** *The Paris Review* **interview, 2000**

An average advance for a fiction debut, literary or genre, is $2,500 to $10,000. Publishers Marketplace calls this "a nice deal." Every professional tries for the "very nice deal" ($50,000–$99,000), the "good" ($100,000–$250,000), the significant ($251,000–$499,000), but, mostly, the "major deal" ($500,000 and up).

Better than 90 percent of the working literary force winds up with "nice." Beggars can't be choosers.

Authors aren't greedy, per se. The more a traditional publisher advances, the larger the book's first print run. Meaning the more it has to lose. Meaning the more likely it is to help with marketing. Meaning the author may not have put a kidney on Craigslist to cover his own campaign.

The advance determines the print run. At 7.5 percent royalty, the $10K writer earns about $1 per paperback, so 10K are printed. Since nine out of ten debut titles never go to a second printing, most authors never earn more than their advance. One reason for this is the lack of publisher marketing support.

If you are an unsupported author, you must become your own sales and PR person. If frugal, you fly solo; if a financial kamikaze you hire a New York PR agent. A basic campaign starts at $10,000. This buys fifty to one hundred hours of pro PR time. The investment breaks even if her efforts sell ten thousand extra books and the moon is blue.

Another arrangement is to pay the agent for performance, not time. Say, ten grand for getting you on *Oprah*, five for *Charlie Rose*, one for a Maslin review. After all, you've hired her not for her rocket science sales know-how or even a Harvard MBA, but for her connections. Her mojo. Her suck. If she doesn't have that, why pay her one hundred times your own pay grade?

Though this may seem a reasonable argument to a writer, the marketing maven will dismiss it as delusional, if not psychotic. She will patiently explain the ABCs of book sales to you, then lay out her three-prong strategy: a signing tour, a viral dispatch to late-night radio talk shows, and a Titanic title launch party. So you flush your advance for her to drop a dime on graveyard deejays, lick envelopes, and buy Sangria and party hats.

Post-Waterloo, you get a courtesy campaign wrap-up call from your professional, telling you how well she thought everything went "in today's extremely challenging marketplace." If you are impolite enough to express your regret that she failed to get you on NPR, she may impolitely remind you that you are not Joyce Carol Oates or Snooki.

At this point you are at the mezzanine of the marketing money pit, headed for the Mariana Trench. Currently, you are ten grand down, plus travel expenses to the signings, talk shows, and your gala.

Working solo again, you must send out complimentary copies of your book to everybody. The freebie mailing involves another catch-22: The most likely people to buy your book are friends, but friends expect a free copy; so you send one to all, and nobody is left to buy your book. Too often the only part of the text a friend is interested in is your dedication and acknowledgments. If you forget to mention them, they may not reach page 1; if you do, they may break down and buy a few discount copies for their own friends.

As for online marketing, as we have seen, today no sane author works without a Net. To build an audience, you must blog, Tweet, text, YouTube, podcast, chat, forum, RSS feed, Facebook, and MySpace. If you're a nonfiction specialist, in order to establish expertise in your field, you should invest another few thousand for a webpage. Fill this with excerpts, teasers, Q&As, blurbs, and blogs. Then link, bait, meme, aggregate, social bookmark, and search engine optimize. Since a million other writers are doing the same, consider spending a few dollars extra for Authorbuzz, Google ads, banner ads, floaters, pop-ups, and interstitial and/or superstitial ads.

By this time, the debut author is hemorrhaging fifteen to twenty Gs in red ink, but the cost should be kept in perspective—it's five times less than an MFA.

Still, one wonders: If Hemingway had had to endure today's Seventh Circle of Sales, would he have cut his losses and remaindered himself after *The Sun Also Rises*?

CHAPTER 55

THE GOD ALMIGHTY DOLLAR

In his preface to *A Heartbreaking Work of Staggering Genius (2000)*, Dave Eggers broke the author code of silence. He revealed that he earned $100,000 for the manuscript. After expenses, this left him $39,567.68. Had he spent a year of forty-hour weeks to complete the Pulitzer finalist title (though presumably it was many times that), he earned $17.66 per hour. In short: less than a third of what a plumber makes, a tenth of what the average lawyer makes, a hundredth of what an NFL benchwarmer makes.

The following year, 2001, novelist Walter Kirn received a low-six-figure advance for his *Up In the Air*, which George Clooney soon picked up. This "allowed me to work at less than minimum wage for three years," he told *The New York Times*.[1]

Earnings figures from popular genre fiction can be no less sobering. Onyx/New American Library advanced Lynn Viehl (aka Rebecca Kelly) $50,000 for her vampire romance *Twilight Fall*, which debuted on the 2009 *Times* bestseller list at #19. In her "Reality of a *Times*

---

1 Michael Meyer, "About That Book Advance," *New York Times*, April 10, 2009. www.nytimes. com/2009/04/12/books/review/Meyer-t.html?_r=1

Bestseller," Viehl revealed that she netted $26,000 after paying her agent $7,500, the IRS $15,000, and defraying office expenses. "…Which is, believe it or not, very good," she pointed out, because "most authors are lucky if they can make 10 percent profit on any book." She concluded, "This should also shut up everyone who says all best-selling authors make millions."[2]

Eggers and Kirn went on to become Publisher Clearing House winners. Ninety-nine percent of their colleagues are not so fortunate.

Yesterday, the average literary pay scale was no more princely.

Milton was paid £5 for *Paradise Lost,* which failed to cover his optometry bill after going blind on the project. For *The Canterbury Tales,* King Edward III allotted Chaucer a gallon of wine a day for the rest of his life. Joseph Conrad, abandoning hope of getting any advance, finally settled for "a fountain pen of good repute."

For people who are supposed to be smart, where did writers get the idea that the profession promised subsistence, much less riches?

Not surprisingly, those most determined to make a fortune grew up poor but with a rich fantasy life. The first to hit the mother lode, Dickens and Twain, made no secret that they wrote, above all, for money. But, being poor financial managers, both later had to book "bankruptcy" lecture tours.

"Sir, no man but a blockhead ever wrote except for money," proclaimed Samuel Johnson, another opponent of the art-for-art's-sake school.

"I am physically incapable of writing anything I don't think will be paid for," seconded Truman Capote, burdened with mortgages in Sag Harbor, Palm Springs, and Switzerland, not to mention a $16,000 Plaza masked ball bill.

In a supposedly nonmaterialist profession devoted to the higher sensibilities, money was and is, as we've seen, the *sine qua non* of success. Geniuses who died poor—Melville, Poe, and Fitzgerald, to name a few—considered themselves failures.

After Fitzgerald's career went south and Hemingway's in the opposite direction, Fitzgerald wrote, "I could talk with the authority of failure—Ernest, with the authority of success. We could never sit across

---

2 Lynn Viehl, "The Reality of a Times Bestseller," *Genreality,* April 17, 2009. www.genreality.net/the-reality-of-a-times-bestseller

the table again."[3] While Fitzgerald was "whoring" for Hollywood, as
he called it, and struggling with *The Last Tycoon*, his friend sent him a
copy of his just-released *For Whom the Bell Tolls*, inscribed "To Scott,
w/affection and esteem."

The novel sold a half million copies and became a Book of the
Month Club selection, and Paramount bought the rights for $100,000.[4]

Fitzgerald, who had been fired from his $1,250 weekly job with
MGM, wrote back, "Congratulations on your new book's great success.
I envy you like hell and there is no irony in this." He died months later.
A few years earlier, he had tried to OD on morphine and afterward had
told a friend that he had proved to be a failure even at suicide.

So, according to the money litmus test perpetrated by the writers
themselves, the paradigms were established: Fitzgerald the failure,
Hemingway the success.

In the end came the great leveler: Failures and successes alike were
immortalized on coins and stamps. Poe graced the $65 silver *Nevermore*
memorial metal (twice what he made on the poem), Steinbeck and Frost
a half-ounce gold, Shakespeare the pound sterling. Suitable for SASEs,
Steinbeck became a 15¢ stamp, Melville 20¢, Faulkner 22¢, Fitzgerald
23¢, Hemingway 25¢. Masters are now licked, affixed, or flipped in the
air, heads over tails, to win or lose bets.

Hemingway would be pleased to have bested his rivals on postage,
just as he had in royalties. Pound blamed him for selling out, but not to
his face.

Following his *For Whom the Bell Tolls* windfall, his third wife, Martha,
also a writer, told her husband, "I wish we could stop it all now, the prestige, the possessions, the position, the knowledge."[5] Under the weight of
it all, their marriage was smothered. But Hemingway felt self-righteously
incorruptible to the end, scorning his friends as the sellouts.

"Have you ever seen the possession of money corrupt a man as it
has Dos [Passos]?" he wrote Edmund Wilson.

---

3 Jeffrey Meyers, *Scott Fitzgerald: A Biography* (New York: HarperCollins, 2004).

4 The 1943 movie, starring Gary Cooper and Ingrid Bergman, was nominated for nine Academy
Awards, including Best Picture. It lost to *Casablanca*.

5 James R. Mellow, *Hemingway: A Life Without Consequence* (New York: Houghton Mifflin, 1992).

Dos Passos wrote *The Big Money*, about a disillusioned communist. In his *Moveable Feast* chapter "The Pilot Fish and the Rich," Hemingway identified his old friend as a pilot fish. The parasite, he wrote, "has the latent and long denied love of money. He ends up rich himself, having moved one dollar's width to the right with every dollar that he made." Papa went on to romanticize his early days in Paris, living off his first wife, Hadley's, trust fund "when we were very poor and very happy."

Steinbeck knew poor. In 1934, he reported making $870 for his last seven years of writing. While living in a one-room shack, which he called "The Sphincter," he'd survived on odd jobs, plus $25 monthly from his nearly bankrupt father. When he finally broke through with *Tortilla Flat*, he wrote, "For the moment the financial burdens have been removed. But it is not permanent. I was not made for success."[6]

Five years later, *The Grapes of Wrath* sold a half million copies. Like Martha Hemingway, Carol Steinbeck discovered that money costs too much. When a Hollywood studio head called and offered her husband $5,000 a week to write scripts, she screamed into the phone, "What the hell would we do with $5,000 a week? Don't bother us!"

Knowing that money and the muse can be oil and water, Sherwood Anderson didn't want to be bothered either. His New York publisher Horace Liveright of Boni & Liveright, hadn't been sending him weekly $75 checks for long before the novelist rushed into his office, begging, "Horace, Horace, please stop these checks. Give me back my poverty!"[7]

FICTION FREAKONOMICS: HOW MUCH THE MASTERS MADE

William Shakespeare (1564–1616)
- £20 – average annual salary
- 20 shillings – original price of Shakespeare's *First Folio* collection of comedies, histories, and tragedies (1623)

---

6 Jay Parini, *John Steinbeck: A Biography* (New York: Henry Holt, 1995).

7 Al Silverman, *The Time of Their Lives, The Golden Age of Great American Publishers, Their Editors, and Authors* (New York: St. Martins, 2008).

- $5.2 million – amount paid for *First Folio* (750 copies now in existence) at Sotheby's 2006 auction

Jane Austen (1775-1817)
- £10 – amount paid for rights to her first novel, *Northanger Abbey* (1818)
- $1.6 million – amount Oxford University's Bodleian Library paid at auction for sixty-eight handwritten pages of Austen's unfinished novel, *The Watsons*

Edgar Allan Poe (1809-1849)
- $14 – book advance for *Eureka* (partially refunded for lack of sales)
- $50 – amount Poe asked for copyright of his entire short story collection (1846)
- $9 – amount *New York Evening Mirror* paid for "The Raven" (1845)
- $662,5000 – 2009 Christie's auction price for original copy (of twelve remaining)

Harriet Beecher Stowe (1811-1896)
- $300 – advance for *Uncle Tom's Cabin* (1852), serialized in forty installments in antislavery periodical *The National Era*

Jack London (1876-1916)
- $5 – payment for his first published story, "To the Man on the Trail" (1898)
- $52.50 – amount London paid Sinclair Lewis for twenty-three story plots
- $2,500 – 1900 earnings (approx. $75,000 today)

Franz Kafka (1883-1924)
- $0 – advance received by author's estate for posthumous publication of *The Trial*
- 3.5 million marks – amount paid at 1988 Sotheby's for original *Trial* manuscript

F. Scott Fitzgerald (1896-1940)
- $879 – 1919 earnings
- $3,939 – 1921 Scribner advance for *The Great Gatsby*
- $113,000 – total earnings from novel royalties, magazine stories, movie sales, 1920–24
- $32 – 1929 royalties

Henry Miller (1891-1980)
- $500 – advance for *Air-Conditioned Nightmare* from Doubleday (1940), which he spent on a 1932 Buick
- $6,872 – gross income, 1953 (combined royalties from *Air-Conditioned Nightmare, Crazy Cock, Tropic of Cancer, Tropic of Capricorn, Black Sparing, Colossus of Maroussi, The Rosy Crucifixion* trilogy)
- $75,000 – sum of his loans to others by 1966 (which he said had not been repaid). He complained, "Everybody has been bleeding me since I came into money."

William Faulkner (1897-1962)
- $200 – Boni & Liveright advance for *Soldiers Pay*
- 60¢ – amount he told his editor, Bennett Cerf, he had left in 1941
- $100 – sum borrowed from his agent, Harold Ober, to prevent electric shutoff

Jack Kerouac (1922-1969)
- $1,000 – Viking advance for *On the Road* (1957)
- $89 – amount Kerouac owed the IRS in 1950 (which he couldn't pay)
- $2.43 million – amount paid by Indianapolis Colts owner, Jim Irsay, for original 120-foot typed scroll of the *On the Road* manuscript

Norman Mailer (1923-2007)
- $200,000 – minimum amount he told his agent, Scott Meredith, he needed for annual living expenses
- $50 – amount Mailer charged each couple for his 1973 Four Season's vanity party (five thousand invitations sent; five hundred attend)
- $4 Million – 1983 advance from Random House for his next four novels (*Tough Guys Don't Dance, Harlot's Ghost, The Gospel According to the Son, The Castle in the Forest*)

Stephen King (1947-)
- $1.60 – his hourly wage at motel laundry job, early 1970s
- $6,400 – annual salary as English teacher
- $2,500 – advance for first novel, *Carrie* (1974)
- $1,500 – amount King paid for minivan that almost killed him in 1999
- $34 million – 2009 earnings

E.L. James (1963–):
- $1.3 million – *Forbes'* estimate of her weekly earnings for *Fifty Shades of Grey* (2011)

J.K. Rowling (1965–)
- $8 million – Little Brown advance for *The Casual Vacancy* (2012)

James Patterson (1947–)
- $94 million – book earnings in 2012

CHAPTER 56

THE NOBEL JAR

"All I do is give interviews and spend time being photographed...
It's been a bloody disaster."
—**Doris Lessing, after receiving
the 2007 Nobel Prize**

When Faulkner won the Holy Grail in 1950, Hemingway sent a note of congratulations but received no reply. He then wrote his confidante Harvey Breit, "As long as I am alive he has to drink to feel good about having the Nobel Prize." He added that, in spite of having "no respect for the institution," he was "truly happy" when his rival got it. But more so four years later when he himself did, calling to fourth wife, Mary, "My Kitten, I've got that thing!"

Convalescing from another bush plane crash, Hemingway had Swedish ambassador John Cabot deliver his acceptance and collect his check. He'd told art scholar Bernard Berenson, "Publicity, admiration, adulation, or simply being fashionable are all worthless and are extremely harmful if one is susceptible to them."

When Faulkner spoke about his Nobel in an interview, John Steinbeck, with eighteen titles under his belt, wrote, "When those old writing boys get to talking about The Artist, meaning themselves, I want to leave the profession. I don't know whether the Nobel Prize does it or not, but if it does, thank God I have not been so honored."

Reacting to the acclaim for *Of Mice and Men*, he'd complained to his agent, "This ballyhoo is driving me nuts." He took a sabbatical to Sweden, insisting he needed to "get away from being John Steinbeck." But later, *The Grapes of Wrath* ballyhoo became what he called a "nightmare." "I'm afraid of myself ... the creature that has been built up," he wrote his friend, Dook Sheffield.

His 1961 title, *The Winter of Our Discontent* "brought an end to his career as a novelist," writes his biographer, Jay Parini. The book excited no ballyhoo and few good reviews. Steinbeck won the Nobel the next year. Like his celebrated colleagues, he'd been battling the bottle throughout his career, but he told his wife, Elaine, he was determined to be the first American since Pearl Buck (in 1938) to go to Stockholm sober. And so he did. On arrival, asked by the press if he thought he deserved the coveted award, he replied, "Frankly, no."

Returning stateside with literature's highest award, the novelist wrote his editor, Pat Covici, "I consider the body of my work and do not find it good ... I'm not the young writer of promise anymore. I'm a worked-over claim." Many critics agreed. They said he hadn't done anything noteworthy since *The Grapes of Wrath*. (Hemingway was charged with the same after *For Whom the Bell Tolls*, Faulkner after *As I Lay Dying*, Fitzgerald after *Gatsby*.)

In saying he didn't deserve the Nobel, Steinbeck may have been thinking of his predecessors who had been overlooked by the Royal Academy.[1] Among them was his friend John O'Hara. After Hemingway was honored, O'Hara believed his turn was next. He wrote his daughter that he wanted the Nobel "so bad I can taste it." According to his biographer, Frank MacShane, he was told by T.S. Eliot that he had been nominated twice. When Steinbeck won instead of him, he wired his colleague: "Congratulations, I can think of only one other author I'd rather see get it."

---

1 Proust, Joyce, Kafka, Chekhov, Ibsen, Anderson, Fitzgerald, Dreiser, Woolf, Conrad, Maugham, Orwell.

Kurt Vonnegut was more philosophical about being neglected by the Nobel Committee. "My failure as a [Saab] dealer so long ago explains what would otherwise remain a deep mystery: Why the Swedes have never given me a Nobel Prize for Literature. Old Norwegian proverb: 'Swedes have short dicks but long memories.'"[2]

The most puzzling oversight by the Nordic judges was Tolstoy, generally considered the greatest novelist in history. But had Tolstoy won the prize in the last nine years of his life,[3] he likely would have refused it, as did Sartre, Saroyan, and Pasternak later on. Becoming a Christian ascetic, the Count called his books an "embarrassment." Even as a young man he had been ambivalent about a literary career. "To write novels that are charming and entertaining to read, at 31 years of age—I gasp at the thought!"[4] At age forty-nine, he recoiled at the public "delirium" his *Anna Karenina* caused, much as Steinbeck had with the ballyhoo over his own work.

"What's so difficult about describing how an officer gets entangled with a woman?" the novelist wrote to his son. "It serves no worthwhile purpose."

Plunged into a deep depression, he worked alongside his peasants on his estate, wishing to become "as stupid as a horse." And in the end, he proclaimed with relief, "I'm not much use as a writer any more."

Tolstoy and Faulkner are the favorite authors of Toni Morrison.[5] She won the Nobel in 1993. In 2011, she was paid $30,000 to deliver the commencement address at Rutgers University, where she once taught. Several months before, the university paid Snooki, twenty-four-year-old TV reality star (*Jersey Shore*) and novelist (*Shore Thing*), $2,000 more to deliver advice to the student body such as "Study hard, party harder!"

Upon winning literature's top award, Ms. Morrison told *Time*

---

2 Kurt Vonnegut "Have I Got a Car for You!" *In These Times*, November 24, 2004.

3 Since its 1901 founding and Tolstoy's death nine years later, the Nobel Committee awarded the following writers instead: Paul Johann Ludwig Heyse (1910), Selma Ottilia Lovisa Lagerlöf (1909), Rudolf Christoph Eucken (1908), Rudyard Kipling (1907), Giosuè Carducci (1906), Henryk Sienkiewicz (1905),Frédéric Mistral, José Echegaray y Eizaguirre (1904), Bjørnstjerne Martinus Bjørnson (1903), Christian Matthias Theodor Mommsen (1902), Sully Prudhomme (1901).

4 Neil Heims, *Tortured Noble: The Story of Leo Tolstoy* (Morgan Reynolds Publishing, 2007).

5 Her 1955 Cornell Masters' thesis was a study of suicides in the work of Faulkner and Virginia Woolf.

magazine, "The Nobel Prize is the best thing that can happen to a writer in terms of how it affects your contracts. ... And if you let it, it will intimidate you about future projects."

Faulkner was intimidated long before receiving the prize. His last major novel, *Absalom, Absalom!,* was completed fourteen years before he went to Stockholm. Three years before the trip, in 1947, he admitted as much to his University of Mississippi students, saying, "I feel I'm written out."

CHAPTER 57

THIS SIDE OF PUBLISHING PARADISE

"I began to bawl because I had everything I wanted and knew I
would never be so happy again."
        —**F. Scott Fitzgerald, on the day his first novel
        was published**

At age eighty-seven, Wallace Stegner told *The Paris Review* he knew of
no American novelist of "advanced age" who was "still writing well,"
though he himself had finished his highly acclaimed *Crossing to Safety*
at age seventy-eight.

The problem, according to some of his colleagues—William
Styron, Susan Sontag, among others—is that writing, unlike other
professions, seems to get harder with practice, not easier. This may in
part be because an author's greatness is often proportional to his or
her ambition, and the ambitious are forever setting the bar higher for
themselves, sometimes impossibly high. Which makes the process
less than fun for some.

Especially those facing the artist's worst fear—that his best work
is behind him—a fear arising from ruthless self-examination, critical
blowback, and/or plummeting sales.

After Kerouac's last novel, *Vanity of Duluoz*, bombed critically and commercially, he was generally dismissed as written out and unpublishable. He raved that the "Jewish Mafia" and "rich homosexual literati of New York" had blacklisted him. Yet he conceded to crushing "self-inadequacy." Moreover, he feared he had been brain damaged in two near-fatal street assaults. Though desperate for recognition from the start, after *On the Road* he complained of all the fan letters "insanely demanding something." He wrote to his fellow dharma bum, poet Gary Snyder, about "what a crock of shit it is to have to satisfy every Tom Dick and Harry stranger in the world." He fantasized about "getting away in the mountains forever" where he could "get back into my mind." And while money made him feel like a sellout, too, he bitched about never having enough. He told his friend Ellis Amburn he wanted to make as much as John le Carré had on the 1963 blockbuster *The Spy Who Came in from the Cold.* But when *Desolation Angels* came out in 1965, he told Seymour Krim, who wrote the book's foreword, that he couldn't afford to travel to New York for the publication launch. "Can you explain to me why a guy with a name as 'famous' as mine and fourteen books and translated into fifteen languages around the world has to worry about rent?" he demanded.[1]

Vonnegut's albatross was *Timequake.* Putnam dropped him after the novel tanked in 1997. The American icon had, by his own estimation, been in decline for nearly thirty years, since *Slaughterhouse-Five.* Vonnegut graded his novels in *Palm Sunday: Cat's Cradle* (1967) A-; *Slaughterhouse* (1969) A+; *Breakfast of Champions* (1973) C; *Slapstick* (1976) D. His critics, too, were becoming less and less charitable: After trashing *Palm Sunday,* the *Times'* Anatole Broyard added, "Contrary to public opinion, a literary reputation is the hardest thing in the world to lose." Over lunch one day, Vonnegut told Martin Amis, "The only way I can regain credit for my early work is to die."[2] In the wake of the *Deadeye Dick* debacle, he'd given this a shot with booze and pills in 1984 but failed. After *Timequake* went DOA, Kurt announced his retirement. Eight years later, Seven Stories released his essay collection, *A Man Without a*

---

1 Paul Maher Jr., *Kerouac: The Definitive Biography* (Taylor Trade Publishing, 2004).

2 Charles J. Shields, *And So It Goes: Kurt Vonnegut: A Life* (New York: Henry Holt, 2011).

Country. Kurt, then eighty-three, thanked his publisher for "doing for me what Jesus did for Lazarus."[3]

Salinger's swan song was *Hapworth 16, 1924. The New Yorker* ran the complete novella in 1965, the same year both Vonnegut's *God Bless You, Mr. Rosewater* and Kerouac's *Desolation Angels* were released. Though Salinger later told a publisher that he considered the piece the "high point" of his writing,[4] the *Times'* Michiko Kakutani called *Hapworth* "impenetrable," "narcissistic," and "ridiculous." Janet Maslin wrote that the novel—a camp letter from an impossibly precocious and acerbic seven-year-old Seymour Glass—"seemed to confirm the growing critical consensus that Salinger was going to hell in a handbasket." The author's biographer[5] speculated that, in reaction, he stopped publishing. But, in a rare 1974 interview, Salinger insisted that he hadn't published anything since *Hapworth* because "publishing is a terrible invasion of my privacy."[6]

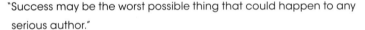

FAILURE: THE SILVER LINING

"Success may be the worst possible thing that could happen to any serious author."

—**Malcolm Lowry, in a letter to his mother-in-law after the success of *Under the Volcano* (1947)**

"Beware success. It will destroy you quicker and more permanently than men, women, or the bottle."

—**Eugene O'Neil to Thornton Wilder**

---

3 Andrew Purcell, "Kurt Vonnegut's Last Interview" *(Sunday Herald,* March 2006). http://www.andrew
purcell.net/?p=50

4 Roger Lathbury, "Betraying Salinger," *New York Magazine,* April 4, 2010. http://nymag.com/arts/
books/features/65210/

5 Warren French, *J. D. Salinger, Revisited* (Boston: Twayne Publishers, 1988).

6 Lacey Fosburgh, "J.D. Salinger Speaks About His Silence" *(The New York Times,* November 3, 1974).
http://www.nytimes.com/books/98/09/13/specials/salinger-speaks.html

"If you have a success you have it for the wrong reasons. If you become popular it is always because of the worst aspects of your work."

—Ernest Hemingway

"Good people are good because they've come to wisdom through failure."

—William Saroyan

"We are all failures—at least the best of us are."

—J.M. Barrie

"Failure is a human condition, not victory over odds. ... I'm drawn to failure. I feel that I'm contending with it constantly in my own life."

—Joyce Carol Oates, Academy of Achievement interview, May 1997

CHAPTER 58

CHICKEN SOUP
FOR THE S.O.L.

There are three kinds of people: Somebodys, Nobodys, and Everybody Else.

Somebodys have escaped being Nobodys.

Nobodys have failed to become Somebodys.

Everybody Else sleeps, wakes up, eats, works, and watches Somebodys on television without worrying about their contribution to civilization.

As we've seen, not a few Somebodys in literature wished to return to being Nobodys again. Failing that, they became success recluses like Salinger or Harper Lee.

For the 99 percent artist, the advantages of being a Nobody are many. For starters, your phone isn't ringing all the time, so you can get some work done. You are at liberty to say and write stupid or meaning-less things with impunity. You don't have to worry about equaling, much less exceeding, your last masterpiece, lest you be labeled a one-hit wonder or a has-been.

As one one-hit wonder, Joseph Heller, said, "Success and failure are both difficult to endure. Along with success come drugs, divorce, for-nication, bullying, travel, meditation, medication, depression, neurosis, and suicide. With failure comes failure." The *Catch-22* icon fleshed all this out in his last, and posthumously published, autobiographical novel, *Portrait of an Artist, as an Old Man.*

Despite its purgatorial history, "success" is still held in high regard by writers who feel they haven't got it. Many are driven toward it negatively—by a fear of failure.

But failophobics defeat themselves by being cautious. No great artist in history has been cautious.

As J.K. Rowling, the welfare mother who became the first billionaire author, said, "It is impossible to live without failing at something, unless you live so cautiously that you might as well not have lived at all—in which case, you fail by default."[1]

Steinbeck wrote in his journal that the real writer "always works at the impossible." He goes out on a limb where no one else has dared and, from here, throws the Hail Mary pass. In a profession of rejection, chances of bombing are great. But it is a vocation that offers only two choices: being a risk taker or being a typist.

Success teaches nothing; it feeds self-satisfaction and complacency. Failure teaches everything; it feeds further exploration. Failure is only failure if you learn nothing from it. In the end, the cliché is true: The only failure is giving up.

As Thomas Edison said while trying to make the light bulb: "I have not failed. I've just found ten thousand ways that won't work."

It comes down to will. The artist can't boast of her talent because she's either born with it or she isn't. She can only take credit for her will, which perfects that talent and tolerates no obstacles.

Writing a follow-up to a "success" requires little character; writing a follow-up to a "failure" requires a great deal. "You write a hit the same way you write a flop," wrote William Saroyon in his play *My Heart's in the Highlands.*

In a profession of catch-22s this is the greatest: When you embrace the creative journey itself, rather than some idealized, often illusory, destination, you may have a chance at real success as an artist.

---

1   http://www.goodreads.com/author/quotes/1077326.J_K_Rowling

SELECTED INDEX

WD WRITER'S DIGEST

Is Your Manuscript Ready?

Trust 2nd Draft Critique Service to prepare your writing to catch the eye of agents and editors. You can expect:

- Expert evaluation from a hand-selected, professional critiquer
- Know-how on reaching your target audience
- Red flags for consistency, mechanics, and grammar
- Tips on revising your work to increase your odds of publication

Visit **WritersDigestShop.com/2nd-draft** for more information.

A 6-MONTH PLAN FOR CRAFTING AN EXCEPTIONAL
NOVEL AND OTHER WORKS OF FICTION
Write and Revise for Publication

JACK SMITH

Your first draft is a work of imagination, but that doesn't mean it's a work of art—not yet. Writing is a complex act, one that calls upon all the powers of our creative resources, and with Jack Smith's technical and inspirational guidance, you can turn your initial draft into a compelling story brimming with memorable characters and a page-turning plot.

Available from WritersDigestShop.com and your favorite book retailers.

To get started join our mailing list: **WritersDigest.com/enews**

FOLLOW US ON:

Find more great tips, networking and advice by following **@writersdigest**

And become a fan of our Facebook page:
facebook.com/writersdigest